NEOLIBERALISM AND CONTEMPORARY

AMERICAN LITERATURE

RE-MAPPING THE TRANSNATIONAL
A Dartmouth Series in American Studies

SERIES EDITOR
Donald E. Pease
Avalon Foundation Chair of Humanities
Founding Director of the Futures of American Studies Institute
Dartmouth College

The emergence of Transnational American Studies in the wake of the Cold War marks the most significant reconfiguration of American Studies since its inception. The shock waves generated by a newly globalized world order demanded an understanding of America's embeddedness within global and local processes rather than scholarly reaffirmations of its splendid isolation. The series Re-Mapping the Transnational seeks to foster the cross-national dialogues needed to sustain the vitality of this emergent field. To advance a truly comparativist understanding of this scholarly endeavor, Dartmouth College Press welcomes monographs from scholars both inside and outside the United States.

For a complete list of books available in this series, see www.upne.com.

Liam Kennedy and Stephen Shapiro, editors, *Neoliberalism and Contemporary American Literature*
Florian Tatschner, *The Other Presences: Reading Literature Other-Wise after the Transnational Turn in American Studies*
Julius Greve, *Shreds of Matter: Cormac McCarthy and the Concept of Nature*
Elisabeth Ceppi, *Invisible Masters: Gender, Race, and the Economy of Service in Early New England*
Yael Ben-zvi, *Native Land Talk: Indigenous and Arrivant Rights Theories and the US Settler State*
Joanne Chassot, *Ghosts of the African Diaspora: Re-Visioning History, Memory, and Identity*
Samuele F. S. Pardini, *In the Name of the Mother: Italian Americans, African Americans, and Modernity from Booker T. Washington to Bruce Springsteen*
Sonja Schillings, *Enemies of All Humankind: Fictions of Legitimate Violence*
Günter H. Lenz, edited by Reinhard Isensee, Klaus J. Milich, Donald E. Pease, John Carlos Rowe, *A Critical History of the New American Studies, 1970–1990*
Helmbrecht Breinig, *Hemispheric Imaginations: North American Fictions of Latin America*
Jimmy Fazzino, *World Beats: Beat Generation Writing and the Worlding of U.S. Literature*

LIAM KENNEDY AND STEPHEN SHAPIRO | EDITORS

NEOLIBERALISM AND CONTEMPORARY AMERICAN LITERATURE

DARTMOUTH COLLEGE PRESS
HANOVER, NEW HAMPSHIRE

Dartmouth College Press
© 2019 Trustees of Dartmouth College
All rights reserved
Manufactured in the United States of America

For permission to reproduce any of the material in this book, contact Permissions, Dartmouth College Press, 6025 Baker-Berry Library, Hanover, NH 03755; or visit university.press.new.england-author@dartmouth.edu

Library of Congress Cataloging-in-Publication Data available upon request

Hardcover ISBN: 978-1-5126-0360-6
Paperback ISBN: 978-1-5126-0361-3
Ebook ISBN: 978-1-5126-0362-0

5 4 3 2 1

For our former teachers,
Bill Lazenbatt and David L. Smith
And for Anne and Milla.

CONTENTS

Acknowledgments xi

1 Introduction 1
LIAM KENNEDY AND STEPHEN SHAPIRO

2 Literature, Theory, and the Temporalities of Neoliberalism 22
ELI JELLY-SCHAPIRO

3 Foucault, Neoliberalism, Algorithmic Governmentality, and the Loss of Liberal Culture 43
STEPHEN SHAPIRO

4 *The Flamethrowers* and the Making of Modern Art 73
MYKA TUCKER-ABRAMSON

5 "On the Very Edge of Fiction": Risk, Representation, and the Subject of Contemporary Fiction in Ben Lerner's *10:04* 92
HAMILTON CARROLL

6 Fictions of Human Capital; Or, Redemption in Neoliberal Times 114
CHRISTIAN P. HAINES

7 The Uncanny Re-Worlding of the Post-9/11 American Novel, Joseph O'Neill's *Netherland*; Or, The Cultural Fantasy Work of Neoliberalism 136
DONALD E. PEASE

8 Desert Stories: Liberal Anxieties and the Neoliberal Novel 151
LIAM KENNEDY

9 Beyond Precarity: Ideologies of Labor in Anti-Trafficking Crime Fiction 168
CAREN IRR

10 "Terminal Insomnia": Sleeplessness, Labor, and Neoliberal Ecology in Karen Russell's *Sleep Donation* and Alex Rivera's *Sleep Dealer* 187
SHARAE DECKARD

11   Postcapitalism in Space: Kim Stanley Robinson's
     Utopian Science Fiction   207
     DAN HASSLER-FOREST

     Contributor Biographies   229
     Index   231

ACKNOWLEDGMENTS

WE WISH TO THANK all of those who helped to organize and participated in the conference on Neoliberalism and American Literature at University College Dublin in 2016, which was a key platform for the inception of this book. In particular, thanks to Catherine Carey of the UCD Clinton Institute for her support with that event. We are grateful to Richard Pult at University Press of New England for his faith in this project and patience with its development.

NEOLIBERALISM AND CONTEMPORARY

AMERICAN LITERATURE

LIAM KENNEDY AND STEPHEN SHAPIRO

INTRODUCTION

NEOLIBERALISM IS A TERM that confuses as much as it illuminates, not least of all because it refers to both material and ideological transformations in relations between capitalism, the State, and the subject. Its usage entails discrete yet interlinked histories of a material transformation in capitalist regimes of accumulation *and* an ideological and discursive shift in the logics of governmentality and modes of social regulation that has intensified capitalist commodification of human relations. The immanence of the neoliberal present—what we will define here as the "contemporary"—is a particular moment in this relationship, which reflects altered relations between capital and culture, and the expansion and dissemination of market values across fields of representation and social experience. The dominance of neoliberal capital is such that it is thought to subsume our capacities to imagine alternatives and render cultural production a site for the reproduction and naturalization of competitive market values.[1] These epistemic changes under conditions of neoliberal hegemony have particular implications for the making and meaning of literature. Does it make sense to speak of an "American" literature in neoliberal times? Can literature function as either an innocent category or a privileged narrative of national imagination at a time of manifold crises for paradigms of the nation-state and of liberal capitalism? In the United States, as elsewhere, the conjunction between the nation-state, liberal capitalism, and literary form has a long history, bespeaking determinate relations between writer and reader within an imagined national community. As this community loses the coherence gained from symbolic efficiency in the age of neoliberal capital, so, too, do the parameters and possibilities of literary production and representation shift. *Neoliberalism and Contemporary American Literature* examines how literature both models and interrogates the neoliberal present.

Neoliberalism and the Contemporary

Discussions of neoliberalism can often tend toward the diffuse due to the multiple objects that the term is often marshalled to cover. Taylor Boas and Jordan Gans-Moore suggest that "Neoliberalism is commonly used in at least five different ways in the study of development: as a set of economic policies, a development model, an ideology, an academic paradigm, and an historical era. Moreover, beyond a shared emphasis on the free market and frequent connotations of radicalism and negativity, it is not immediately clear how these varied uses are interconnected."[2] When the conversation turns to consider the relationship between neoliberalism and cultural production and the social reproduction of civil society, labor and class stratification, and status identities (like those involving and intertwining sex/gender or ethnoracial ones), further confusion often reigns. Such terminological spread (or incoherence) has led many critics and commentators to exasperation, questioning the value of using the term. While acknowledging the broad horizon used in considerations of neoliberalism, and the increasingly variant studies that deploy the term, we endorse its usage here. Our approach, and use of terms like "neoliberalism," "American," and "contemporary (literature)," to chart out social, cultural, and historical transformations can be outlined as follows through four main points.[3]

Firstly, neoliberalism proposes a significantly different configuration of the relations among the State, national and world markets, the enmeshed polity and those excluded from this category, and the management of social reproduction, including cultural communications, than those found within a particular phase of liberalism, sometimes known as Fordism, that is characterized within the United States by the double hinge of the New Deal phase of the 1930s and 1940s and an ensuing military Keynesianism from the late 1940s until the first third of the 1970s. Although aspects of neoliberalism do engage with aspects of liberalism, as understood as emerging within the mid- to late-eighteenth-century arguments—often called classical political economy and exemplified by Adam Smith—the first perspective in discussions of neoliberalism must be one that places it in contrast to processes specific to the twentieth century that arose as responses to the Great Depression and its attendant socio-political emergences, such as the far-right corporate nationalism of the Nazi, Fascist, and Falangist regimes.

Neoliberalism, consequently, should be considered within a world-systems perspective that locates contemporary America within a history of two roughly 40 to 50 years long phases that each have internal patterns of loosely equal economic contraction and expansion, and an ecology of multiple players within the world market, but chiefly these four: the United

States, the USSR, Europe, and "the rest," the nation-states later known as the Third World or, more recently, the Global South.[4] The primacy of this world-systems perspective explains our use of "America," rather than the "United States," in this collection, which largely focuses on primary evidentiary material that has its original provenance from within the United States. We do no not use the term "America" as a form of privileged amnesia about the existence of other nation-states in the western hemisphere. To the contrary, we use "America" precisely as a gesture to indicate that the United States must always be understood constitutively within a world-systems framework. "America" is the term we use as shorthand for the United States within the world-system.

The two phases in this consideration are firstly that between 1929 and the mid-1960s/mid-1970s, involving an inflection period of 1944–1949, as the time between the Bretton Woods Conference and the formation of the North Atlantic Treaty Organization (NATO). The next phase can be considered as existing between the manifest crises of the early 1970s of stagflation and petro-shock and the financial crises of 2008–2011, involving an inflection period around the 1989 fall of the Soviet imperial system and formal end to the Cold War, typified by the reunification of the two Germanys (more on this periodization to follow). Concatenating these longer phases is an overlapping phase from the mid-1960s and mid-1970s, which belongs to both of the other longer sequences. This mini-*Sattelzeit* is likewise analogous in function to the phase from the early 2010s through the composition of this collection. While we decline to be hostage to fortune and make predictions about whether neoliberalism, as we understand the term, is a spent force now, in its last gasps, or is about to be reinstated for a third, longer cycle, we do believe that the 2010s stand as a linking moment between two greater cycles. Hence, we use the term "contemporary," not in the mere sense of the recent, but as a way of isolating the span of years as different from that ranging from the 1970s through the first decade of the twenty-first century. We, thus, inferentially propose a reason for why the mid-1960s–mid-1970s, as a prior bridging time, might be intriguingly comparative to our ongoing experience within another bridging phase.

Secondly, neoliberalism shifts an understanding of the marketplace away from the initial anti-mercantilist and anti-physiocratic predicates established through eighteenth-century Smithian laissez-faire. This early version of liberalism proposed that the marketplace be seen as a realm that deserved to be protected from the (absolutist) States, since while the marketplace was always catalyzed by selfish desires, when these were expanded beyond the sole prerogative of the old regime court, they would, nonetheless, establish a cooperative and civilizing social equilibrium. The slightly later utilitarian respondents to Smith proposed a return to some forms of intervention by the "free trade" projects of the post-Napoleonic State and its imperial expansionism by seeking mathematical calculations of the balance between the individual's grasping desire and social harmony. Partly as a response to the ensuing phase of scientific racism as deployed by far-right collectivism in the early to mid-twentieth century, many of those conveyed as neoliberals proposed an altered relation between the State and the marketplace by elevating the competitive marketplace as (paradoxically) both a natural phenomenon greater than all others and a necessary fabrication of profit accumulation that should inform all aspects of State and civil society processes. One difficulty of ascertaining the historical particularity of neoliberalism is that while it emerges as a response to the conditions of the 1930s, it does so by excavating (and somewhat inventing) the terms of eighteenth-century political economy, precisely to erase an intervening history of different configurations of the economy, the State, civil society, and international relations.

Thirdly, as parcel to what was just outlined, a significant and highly consequential feature of neoliberalism is the radical dissolution of public and private distinctions to form what might be called privatized publicness, involving the erasure of ostensibly protected realms of exclusion from both the State and the marketplace, be these the commons of rural or urban spaces, civil society, or the interiority of Romantic-era subjectivity, intimacy, and creative inter-relationality, one form of which is the *Bildungsroman*. Once the authenticity of an inward "self" or collective (social and "natural") environment is degraded or falsified, a newly conglomerated field made by the fusion of the two sides, a new mass publicness, is then turned over to the competitive market, a new mass private property-ness. The individual that was previously bifurcated into a public role and a private self is placed entirely, on the one hand, into a new field, a social network, but, on the other, this domain is entirely organized by profit-seeking predicates.

In this erasure of the separation between the public and private, Wendy Brown has argued that a fundamental feature of neoliberalism involves its antagonism to the demos and driven efforts to disenfranchise the collective.[5] While agreeing with the point of this claim, we hesitate over its terms, for Brown unproblematically uses the term "democracy" for what is actually meant as postwar liberalism, a system that as Sarah Brouillette, among others, has reminded us was hardly free from structuring multiple kinds of social inequalities and non-democratic forms of governance.[6] Furthermore, it bears remembering that many of the figures initially promulgating neoliberal claims had experienced the horrors of Europe's authoritarian populist regimes during the 1930s and 1940s. If many neoliberals were disinclined to encourage public participation in the allocation of social resources, their traumatic past experiences help provide a context for their hesitations over the public sphere. Similarly, many European neoliberal advocates' concern to prevent corporate monopolies emerged from anxieties about the consequences of the State and its citizenry fusing as tightly as it had in the corporatist (Nazi, Fascist, Falangist) State. The desire for catalyzing competition among individuals may be unquestionably carried to sociopathic extremes within neoliberalism, but may also have been presented initially as an attractive interruption of the centripetal force of far right-wing nationalist racisms.

In this discussion of the collapse of the public-private distinction, many accounts of neoliberalism feel it necessary to fall into two camps of emphasis. One Marxist tendency highlights neoliberal production of economic inequalities and marketizing directives. Another Foucauldian approach highlights neoliberal alteration of governmentality and behavioral conducts. Rather than seek to adjudicate the superiority or appositeness of one strand over another, or even attempt a new synthesis, this collection seeks to show that these perspectives should be read as always conjoined aspects of a many-sided social phenomenon.[7] To overcome this antimony, we recall Michel Aglietta's useful consideration, in his discussion of the crisis of Fordism and the onset of a new regime (which in 1998 he still called "globalization"), of the necessary intertwining between an economic *regime of accumulation* and a sociocultural *mode of regulation*.[8]

Our fourth touchstone insists that the shifts described are simultaneously constituted by and experienced through the entire constellation of social reproduction arenas, involving sex/gender roles, the acts, rituals, and credentializing passages constituted as socializing, nurturing, caring, and marking developmental phases, especially those of nationality and citizenship; the role of educational institutions as supervising personal formation and bureaucratic professionalization; forms of domestic policing and internment; labor identities; non-electoral forms of civic engagement and exclusion; and all modes of cultural communication and transmission, in which those documents consecrated as "literature" stand as a remarkably small category, especially in its nationalist exceptionalist formations. While multiple rearrangements of these factors exist, the one that is especially salient for this collection is the expansion of the personal debt-driven consumer marketplace that is substantially different from the 1930s–mid-1970s period. No simple return to New Deal Keynesianism is possible because these macroeconomic policies were designed for Western polities in which there was a vastly reduced field of consumer choices and access to personal credit. Credit was still largely a matter for States and corporations, and individuals either acquired it only within a highly regulated market for a small set of long duration goods (housing and transportation being the two largest) or an informal market (layaway plans, for instance) for others. The massification of personal credit marks a key transition in the United States towards neoliberalism as it reduced the experience of being "broke" in the mid-twentieth century to being "indebted" in the neoliberal era. While discourses of financialization often attend to the proliferation of fictitious capital at the high end of the marketplace, we also want to draw attention to its granularity on individuals in this time.

Mitchum Huehls and Rachel Greenwald Smith have recently considered neoliberalism and American literature through a four-phase or stage model in which neoliberalism appears and moves sequentially through what they call the economic, the political-ideological, the sociocultural, and the ontological.[9] While admitting the presence of German-language neoliberalism, they see the period before the 1970s as one of "theoretical utopianism," ideas about the economy that were still mainly contained within academic debates.[10] From the 1970s onwards, Huehls and Greenwald Smith see an expansion of neoliberalism into electoral politics leading to the ascension of Ronald Reagan and Margaret Thatcher. From here, neoliberal ideas began, according to them, to be brought into official policies. Once instantiated through State interventions, neoliberalism seeped into the cultural realm, where it spread to now stand as a current ontological horizon. In this scheme, they consider American literature of each moment as exemplifying the state of the neoliberal spread. Yet as initially compelling or commonsensical to anglophones as is their historical narrative, we do not endorse it for three reasons.

Firstly, as we will explain, the notion that neoliberalism was mainly a conceptual formation before becoming political policy during the rule of Reagan and Thatcher profoundly mistakes its actual history, especially with regards Germany, in order to shoehorn it into an otherwise conventional (declension) tale of American exceptionalism. Secondly, the charting of illustrative titles to read off the presence of other primary processes makes cultural production secondary and always belated to other (economic, political, and intellectual) realms in ways that reinstate a base-superstructure or reflection theory model that would otherwise be avoided in contemporary cultural and materialist studies. Thirdly, the categories, and especially that of "ontology," overly homogenize cultural productions, which in actuality always contain a varied mixture of thematic, theoretical, and transformative responses to a spectrum of residual, emergent, and dominant social aspects. The keyword "ontology" seems to function as an unsatisfactory replacement for what Patricia Ventura, in her discussion of neoliberal culture, has named a "structure of feeling," a term that better captures the manner in which hegemonic consent, counter-hegemonic discontent, and class realignments or blocs are constructed.[11] Lastly, the ontological seems to consider the current moment as one of post-history and without exit. Such a capitulation to this final stage notion misreads the host of self-consciously, anti-neoliberal alternatives and social movements emerging recently, as well as other disruptive challenges, not the least of which being the ecological crisis. Rather than approach the discussion about neoliberalism and cultural production through imposed and abstract categories, we instead propose a chronology involving the rhythms of capitalist crisis and altering class relations, as seen through a world-systems perspective.

A Brief Outline of Neoliberalism Phase I:
1929–(1944–1949)–mid-1960s

We do not see the bundle of macroeconomic ideas captured within the term Keynesianism and the ones under the term neoliberalism as sequential, but instead as contemporaneous, and often interdependent, responses to the general economic crisis of the Great Depression and the socio-political catastrophe of the rise of the European (Nazi, Fascist, and Falangist) far-right, alongside the rising military aggression of Hirohito's Japan. Within the vortex of this political and economic crisis, there were complex, often internally contradictory, partial, and provisional responses. One strand that became dominant in the anglophone realms is conventionally clustered under the names of the New Deal in the United States and the Keynesian Welfare State in the United Kingdom. These plans broadly sought to restore and undergird Fordist regimes of capitalist accumulation and their attendant composition of class relations and social reproduction schemes by engaging in massive State interventions to create employment and stimulate a controlled consumer market. Stalinist Russia had its own, not entirely dissimilar, version of command macroeconomics.

In the later years of the Weimar Republic, a set of German-speaking figures including Alexander Rüstow (credited with the first use of the term neoliberalism at the 1938 Colloque Walter Lippmann), Wilhelm Röpke, and Walter Eucken, argued for an "authoritarian-liberal" program that would grant State bureaucracies a much reduced role in economic planning.[12] While this group splintered during the Hitler era, they reconvened after the war, and began shifting away from some of their pre-war positions. These figures are sometimes known as the "Freiburg School," where several taught, but are also called ordoliberals, in reference to their 1948-founded house journal, *Ordo: Jahrbuch für die Ordnung von Wirtschaft und Gesellschaft* (Yearbook for the Arrangement of Economy and Society) where they honed their ideas into a more recognizable and coherent perspective.[13]

Yet these elaborations of the ordoliberals' theories in the 1950s were themselves somewhat belated exercises in relation to enacted State policy through the late 1940s and early 1950s, which gave concrete shape to a cluster of somewhat impressionistically posed pre-war neoliberal claims. Bavarian Ludwig Erhard became the "spokesperson of the creed of the neo-liberals in German and European politics" in his sequential roles as the leader of the Allied Bizone's Special Office for Money and Credit (1947–1948), director of economics for the Bizone Economic Council (1948–1949), Economics Minister under Konrad Adenauer (1949–1963), Vice-Chancellor (1957–1963) and Chancellor (1963–1966).[14] If ordoliberal formulations and axiomatic predicates became cemented throughout the 1950s, this was enabled as a result of watching their claims be enacted as State directives. Here, theory followed practice in many ways. Furthermore, Erhard's imposition of neoliberal perspectives within the slogan of a "social market" was arguably foundational in the cementing of the Cold War. In 1948, he removed "the entire structure of Nazi-era price and wage controls, while slashing taxes on incomes and capital, establishing what has since been celebrated as a deregulatory tabula rasa."[15] The consequences were immediate since "three days later, the Russians established the Berlin blockade, in order to contain the effects of currency reform, triggering the beginning of the Cold War."[16]

This brief review of ordoliberals as neoliberals looks to make three points relevant to this collection. Firstly, it is the significant failure of most anglophone genealogies of neoliberalism to recognize the role of neoliberalism as sanctioned (West) German State policy throughout the *Wirtschaftswunder* (economic miracle) postwar phase. Anglophone accounts typically tell a tale of a small group of European intellectuals huddled together in marginal safe spaces, like the Mont Perelin Society, until some, like Friedrich Hayek, came to the United States where they could mentor Americans, like Milton Friedman, who then, in turn, influenced American (and British) politics. Such a reading is not only rife with Anglocentric prejudices and exceptionalism, but it fundamentally overlooks the ways in which conceptual paradigms and State policy intertwined to variously lead one another long before the 1970s.

Secondly, this amnesia about the actual history of the postwar West has made it hard to see that the military Keynesianism of postwar America was complementary to, and, in fact, existed because of German neoliberalism. Ordoliberal polices and aversion to central bureaucratic oversight, including price controls, can be seen as wholly integral to the 4 Ds policy of the Allies with regards to Germany: decentralization, democratization, denazification, and demilitarization. Hence, American-led "liberalism" after 1946 *depended* on the success of German neoliberalism, as the German abandonment of nationalist protections was the necessary feature on which the postwar American export economy depended.[17] Accounts that present neoliberalism as appearing *after* liberalism or as mutually incompatible are basically untenable with any basic history of the late 1940s onwards.

Thirdly, the interlacing of American (and British) liberalism and German neoliberalism was also made possible by two other key world-systemic features: the Cold War and the onset of decolonization and the Bandung Era (1950–1970s). Erhard's policies created the foundation on which American hegemony through the Cold War was initially built. Additionally, Quinn Slobodian contends that it was the rise of decolonizing nationalist movements after World War II that provided an incitement, challenge, and counterweight to the postwar world-system otherwise formed by the United States, Europe, and the USSR. By following Slobodian, and insisting on the constitutive effect of the Bandung era's decolonization, we seek to revise Naomi Klein's dating of neoliberal intervention in State policy with Augusto Pinochet's 1973 coup in Chile as too late a dating of the role of the so-called Third World in shaping the global ecology for neoliberalism. In reality, all four geographic spheres created pressures and limits, opportunities and incentives, for varying models of the relation of the nation-state to the capitalist world-market shaped by long-spiral economic expansions and contractions.

Even within America, neoliberal influence was already key to shaping the environment far before the 1970s. Business interests that had been contained throughout the New Deal and war years saw the transition towards military Keynesianism as their chance to weaken their enemies, as seen with the so-called textbook controversy. In 1947, Lorie Tarshis, a Canadian-born student of Keynes at Cambridge who then became an American citizen and a Tufts professor, published *The Elements of Economics: An Introduction to the Theory of Price and Employment*, the first textbook to introduce American undergraduates to Keynesian principles. Initially adopted widely, Tarshis's reader-friendly book immediately became the target of a successful red-baiting campaign to remove it from American syllabi. Mindful of how Tarshis's book had been written for a broad audience, Paul A. Samuelson wrote his own textbook, *Economics: An Introductory Analysis* (1948), in far more technical and statistical language, so as to avoid attack from the right. Samuelson's book then became the standard introduction to economics for American undergraduates for generations, with sales in the millions over its numerous editions, and becoming the template for economics textbooks for all ensuing (American) college textbooks.[18] Yet British Keynesians complained that Samuelson had misrepresented their claims, and Catherine Lawson argues that monetarist, neoliberal interventions in the 1970s were successful because Samuelson's canonical version of Keynes did not have responses to the crisis that Tarshis's text could have provided, had it been more widely known and influential. In this way, American advocates for neoliberalism were able to powerfully shape and weaken Keynesian thought, even within the 1940s, by contesting it at the point of cultural influence at the undergraduate level.

Neoliberal thought was also widely circulated to popular audiences in the 1940s. *Reader's Digest* published a condensed version of Hayek's *The Road to Serfdom* (1944) in its April 1945 issue, thus giving it a mass-market dissemination that few other economists had ever had at that point.[19] This abbreviation then sold in the millions through Book of the Month club reprints that cost five cents, and General Motors paid for an illustrated "*The Road to Serfdom* in Cartoons" that was reproduced, in turn, in *Look* magazine in 1945.[20] As a result, when Hayek came to America for his first lecture circuit, he unexpectedly discovered that his speaking venues had been changed to accommodate audiences in the hundreds.[21] As a result of the digest, Midwestern businessman Harold Luhnow, now in charge of the Volker Fund, had the Fund heavily finance links between ordoliberals and Americans. Luhnow paid for all of Hayek's expenses during the 1946 speaking tour.[22] The Volker Fund would then go on to underwrite Hayek's academic position at the University of Chicago and ordoliberal Ludwig von Mises's at New York University, so that Hayek's "entire ten years at Chicago were financed *exclusively* by Luhnow's ample resources."[23] When Luhnow failed to convince Hayek to write a more popular version of *The Road to Serfdom*, he then paid for "the project that would ultimately result in the publication of Milton Friedman's *Capitalism and Freedom*."[24]

This popular dissemination of neoliberal ideas in America, even before their placement within academic economics departments, suggests that the cultural, political, and theoretical movements are not easily isolated from one another or easily separated into a developmental sequence. The sorties between New Deal and military Keynesian positions and neoliberal ones begin to lose their efficacy, however, during the 1960s.

The Hinge (mid-1960s to mid-1970s) and Neoliberalism's Second Phase (mid-1960s to 2008/2010s)

A conventional and usually dominant narrative has the first victories and policy installations of neoliberal thought as occurring during the conjunctural crises of the early 1970s. As a result of a more confident American labor force's pay demands, increasing insistence for the expansion of civil and working rights by social factors, mainly women and racial minorities, and the costs of prolonged military engagement in Vietnam, the US-organized world-system faced a crisis of decreasing profitability.[25] Nixon's 1971 abandonment of the gold standard, as parcel to the dismantling of the Bretton Woods currency system conjoined with the oil embargo of 1973–1974, which set off an Organization of the Petroleum Exporting Countries (OPEC) retaliation for American support for the State of Israel during the Yom Kippur War, suggested that Keynesian macro-economics was bereft of a functioning response to stagflation of rising prices and unemployment. American neoliberals, like Milton Friedman, seized the day as a chance to finally replace long-established Keynesian principles. From this period, neoliberalism was primarily directed to dismantling the working class's economic, social, and political achievements and life security provisions.

The seismic events of the early 1970s seem obvious markers of the first segment of a new cycle's downward, contractive phase. Yet we consider the crisis of the early 1970s as manifestations of pressures, what Alain Lipietz calls a "latent erosion," that were already in formation from the mid-1960s, involving the downturn in profitability.[26] The mid-1960s until the mid-1970s has a dual character as an overlapping period that contains both the last downwards segment of the prior long phase from 1929, while also initiating the next one. On one hand, the world-systemic configuration that had girded the postwar system began to buckle under multiple points of fracture. In the USSR, Brezhnev's 1964 ascension put a coda to the particular Cold War organization that had held throughout Khrushchev's rule. The changed ecology, as a result of a different shape of USSR policy, synchronized with increasing dissatisfaction within Germany over Erhard's neoliberal regime and desire for a new kind of *Ostpolitik*, as advanced by Willy Brandt. Erhard lost the chancellorship in 1966, and while the Sozialdemokratische Partei Deutschlands (SPD's) Brandt did not formally take over until 1969, Germany's neoliberalism began to be replaced by renewed social welfare provisions. Jamie Peck says that, "Ordo histories recount [Erhard's] exit from office, in 1966, coincided with the country's surrender to the evils of bureaucratic intervention, welfarism, overregulation, and 'penal' levels of taxation."[27] Not coincidentally, the Group of 77 was also formed in 1964, amidst civil rights campaigns in the United States.

The catalyst year of 1968 emerges as the manifestation of world-systemic pressures in all its components as signaling the accelerating collapse of US-hegemonic liberalism's dominance, as well as the onset of neoliberalism from being the policy carried out by a European junior partner to insurgent presence within America. We think this mini-periodization of a brief *Sattelzeit*, or transistor period, within the inter-decade years and involving the overlapping of the mid-1960s as the last phase of a long period as well as standing as the prelude and first notes of another one, from the 1970s onwards, helps clarify what has long been a topic of confusion over when to date the onset of postmodern cultural products.

Furthermore, the introduction of the idea of a concatenating phase of combined and uneven development helps clarify our present moment and the purposes of this collection, for we see the 2010s, analogously, as the last phase of a long cycle and the start of either a third neoliberal phase or of something else entirely. For our purposes, though, it is the particularities of this temporal mixture that we seek to indicate by using the keyword "contemporary," which means more than merely *now* in our title. If some today believe that neoliberalism as a term lacks purchase, then this turn away from the phase partially captures a truth, though not necessarily about the absence of neoliberalism, but that we are currently within a time of reformulation, much like the mid-1960s to the mid-1970s.

To return to the moment after this hinge or saddle period between the first and second phases of neoliberalism, we date the first half of the second phase as running between the early and mid-1970s and the mid-1990s. This phase can be essentially characterized as the great unwiring of the advances and conditions that the American working class secured during the New Deal and postwar military Keynesianism. Though this period has its own set of conjunctural moments, the broadest strokes also involve the opening up of nation-statist protections that were characterized at the time as "globalization."[28] This phase's inflection point comes with the 1989 end of the Soviet empire, which removed the last of the Cold War protections against jobs competition that the American and Western European laboring class had, as now East European laborers were available to the West in ways that facilitated downwards wage pressures. If the immediate years after 1989 involve the wrapping up of this contracting segment, the mid-1990s stand as the start of an expansive phase. In this phase, however, the neoliberal practices that were initially directed against the working class now begin to be turned against the middle class, so that the mid-1990s marks the start of the middle class's decline in absolute numbers and influence, stalling social mobility, and the rise of the conditions of inequality that match the pre-1929 period.[29] Characteristic features here are Bill Clinton's concluding blow to the American working class in the Personal Responsibility and Work Opportunity Reconciliation Act of 1996 and opening salvo against the middle class with the dissolution of the 1933 Glass-Steagall protections in the Gramm-Leach-Bailey Act of 1999. In terms of cultural transformations, the Telecommunications Act of 1996 massively deregulated the media environment, kickstarting a new so-called Golden Age of prestige television marked by the screening in 1997 of HBO's *Oz*. Cable television's rise can be taken as the medium par excellence for registering the class decomposition of the middle class, so that the 1990 start of the tale of Tony Soprano resonates with its viewers in ways that the 1983 *Scarface* did not. Similarly, in terms of new cultural modes of production, the mass market digital age can be said to begin with the 1995 introduction of DVDs and America Online's move in late 1996 from charging hourly fees for the internet to a flat monthly fee, a move that accelerated use of the internet, now newly equipped with visual browsers, rather than text hyperlinks, to access and navigate the World Wide Web.

The phase of the mid-1990s leads to its conclusion with the 2008 crash and the few years of instability. We contend that "the contemporary" should be understood as the period roughly from 2011 onwards, as either a bridge to a new phase or a significant turn away from the liberal-neoliberal couplet that has shaped the world-system since the 1930s. Markers of this new phase involve the contained Arab Springs of 2010, Occupy Wall Street 2011, and the return of Vladimir Putin to the Russian presidency in 2012. These years also saw the onset of social media with Twitter's 2011 new implementation leading to a 2013 initial public offering (IPO), in the wake of Facebook's 2012 IPO, and Google's 2011 launch of Google+. From here the start of the so-called gig economy, with the rise of zero-hour jobs. Similarly, concerns over automation and its creation of a jobless future now begin, as a sign of the incipient algorithmic age. It is to this period that our questions about the form and content of American literature today properly belong.

Neoliberalism and Contemporary American Literature

This volume examines relations between American literature and the neoliberal present. It identifies new relations between economic rationalities and literary forms; it considers ways in which literature gives form to barely legible processes of economic activity and illuminates the cultural dream work of neoliberal capitalism, which works to restructure political desires and fantasies and mystify economic inequalities. Has literary realism, for instance, been exhausted as a narrative form capable of being commensurate to the time and space of neoliberalism? Can contemporary literature still imagine either the end of capitalism or an alternative to it? Several of the authors here comment on the limits of representation circumscribed by contemporary "capitalist realism."[30] In doing so, they reflect a broader impetus (by writers and scholars alike) to identify what remains of the critical capacities of literature—to imagine, map, or challenge neoliberal ideology, beyond the consolations of literary form. In some part, this is a concern that the demos, however compromised in American liberal culture, has been all but extinguished as an active public sphere. American declension is a common motif in the literature under analysis, as is middle class precarity, both signifying a peculiarly American sense of crisis about neoliberal culture as an inescapable system of indebtedness.

This collection also considers new formations of subjectivity and relationality, and new regimes of the body in literary representations that follow the vectors of neoliberal accumulation and biopolitical control. These include narratives of self-actualization and self-fashioning, which reflect a cultivation of individuality that equates freedom with consumer choice and lifestyle, but also reflect the severe and growing inequalities enforced by the biopolitical calculus of credit and debt. They also include narratives of geopolitical mobility and encounter in which differential norms—such as humanity and otherness—are reconfigured by neoliberal forces. Much of the literature under analysis connotes the interplay between the subject, the market, and the State as the primal drama of neoliberal hegemony and its composition of ideological norms. As such, it foregrounds the altered relations and ensuing tensions between liberal government and the free market, what Michel Foucault termed the "economic-juridical complex," and extends this to the broader, global frictions between unfettered capital and national territory as core themes of a more "worldly" American literature, one which registers the decline in American global hegemony.

The first two chapters offer critical perspectives on the history of thinking about neoliberalism, viewing it not primarily as a set of economic beliefs, but as a "government style." Eli Jelly-Schapiro parses neoliberal capital in terms of three distinct but overlapping temporalities—primitive accumulation, expanded reproduction, and accumulation by fabrication—that exhibit different forms of governance. He acknowledges the appeal of concepts of the "precariat" and the "multitude" as emergent political sensibilities and collective imaginaries that offer to connect the global spaces and lifeworlds of shared depredations, and considers how these are represented in literary narratives. Stephen Shapiro carefully charts the evolution of Foucault's thinking on neoliberalism, made challenging due to the fragmented publication of key lectures and writings, to underline that it implies a new understanding of power beyond sovereignty and discipline. Most recently, he argues, the advent of data logics and data-behaviorism marks a new phase of neoliberalism in which an algorithmic governmentality functions "without a subject," as there is no need for a disciplinary individuality in the logic of neoliberal competition. The implications for the contemporary novel are bleak on this reading, voided of its cultural purpose of modelling the "liberal subject's developmental interiority."

Jelly-Schapiro concludes his chapter with a commentary on Rachel Kushner's novel *The Flamethrowers* (2013), finding in it a conjunction of the three temporalities of contemporary capitalism that he outlines. Myka Tucker-Abramson provides a lengthier analysis of the novel in her chapter, detailing how it connects disparate times and spaces, from Brazilian rubber plantations in the 1940s to social and artistic movements in New York and Italy in the 1970s to the present day, linking uneven processes of capital investment and disinvestment. The 1970s moment is pivotal, entrenching global neoliberalism, while also recalling the energies of artistic practices that critiqued the dialectics of industrialization and deindustrialization in the United States at that time. As such, Tucker-Abramson argues, the novel offers critical glimpses of the processes of economic globalization that conjoin the times and spaces of neoliberal capital accumulation, though she notes this is a reading that depends on the reader disinvesting from the protagonist's limited comprehension so as to bring into view the background of connected historical struggles. Hamilton Carroll also explores the relation between literary and artistic modes of representation in his chapter, which looks closely at Ben Lerner's novel *10:04* (2014), as it depicts subject formations of precarity and insecurity summoned by millennial conditions of catastrophe and risk. He focuses on how the novel represents a form of "reinvigorated realism" in its attempts to map a new social totality, using ekphrastic representation to explore the capacities and limitations of textual narrative and authorship. In the following chapter, Christian Haines is also interested in how precarity, and more particularly indebtedness, characterizes the subject positions of characters in selected writings. He argues that there is a "moral economy" to neoliberalism's conflation of financial and social obligations, that pressures individuals to self-evaluate as human capital, and is characterized by irredeemable indebtedness. He contrasts novels by Gary Shteyngart and Don DeLillo, both of which represent desires to achieve redemption by financing extensions to biological life. Whereas Shteyngart offers a "consolatory vision" of a belated and vulnerable mortality undervalued by the speculative class, DeLillo foregrounds affinities between aesthetic and financial risk and speculation and makes of redemption itself "a financial instrument."

Donald Pease provides a provocative reading of what has become a canonical text of the "post-9/11" genre, Joseph O'Neill's *Netherland* (2008) As he notes, it has been widely celebrated by scholars and critics, who have valued it for moving beyond the insular, domestic formats common to the genre to confidently de-territorialize narratives of nationhood and assert a cosmopolitan vision that is indicative of a new "worlding" of American literature. This "hypercanonization" represents a very rapid accrual of cultural capital that Pease acutely questions by charging that the novel has serviced a form of fantasy work by reviewers, who projected onto it a cosmopolitan imaginary that is not inscribed in the narrative. More particularly, he argues that reviewers have (mis)identified with the character of Chuck Ramkissoon, imaginatively and emotionally buying into his dream of a post-racial America symbolized by an idealized democracy of the cricket field—a form of fantasy work that is symptomatic of neoliberalism in masking economic inequalities. It is a compelling reading that alerts us (as does Tucker-Abramson) to some tough questions about the values and assumptions shared by a liberal readership. Liam Kennedy also considers claims for the contemporary "worlding" of American literature, with critical attention to two novels, Dave Eggers' *A Hologram for the King* (2012) and Joseph O'Neill's *The Dog* (2014), wherein deep-seated liberal anxieties are narrativized against the backdrops of Middle Eastern settings of rapid urban development that attract international flows of speculative finance. He argues that the novels evince a distinctly American unease about the legitimacy of liberal democracy under global conditions of neoliberal capitalist hegemony. Both writers represent the worlding of the American novel as an apprehensive charting of new relations between the national and the global, wherein learned habits and values are losing their meaning and utility. This is not only an ideological unease, it is also a matter of formal uncertainty about the capacity of literary fiction to express the realities of a post-American world.

Our final three chapters all consider how specific genres have represented globalized or planetary networks of economic interactions that trouble American hegemony. Caren Irr examines how crime fiction depicts narratives of human trafficking, particularly as they represent neoliberal forms of labor exploitation. In the "anti-trafficking discourse" of this literature she detects homologies with "neoliberal discourses of market freedom and US hegemony." In the novels she notes the prevalence of rescue plots, passive victims, prostitution stories, and the fantasy that labor in the laissez-faire market will restore freedom and dignity. Correspondingly, many of the novels signify limitations of agency and insight among State actors in the investigative plots, most notably the police investigators whose belated moral authority contrasts with the troubling depiction of traffickers as neoliberal entrepreneurs. Yet the commonplace depiction of trafficking as a moral panic also justifies State violence, a reassertion of American power/hegemony that does not conceal the tensions between unfettered capital and State agencies. The global interconnectedness of indebted exchanges that Irr identifies in the world of traffickers in crime fiction is echoed in Sharae Deckard's examples of science fiction in Karen Russell's novella *Sleep Donation* (2014) and Alex Rivera's film *Sleep Dealer* (2008). These texts understand sleep as a commodity, reflecting its value under the "insomniac conditions" of neoliberal efforts to maximize labor in "24/7" environments. In *Sleep Donation*, set in an insomnia-plagued America, the sleepless consumers embody the anxious subjectivity of the growing middle-class precariat and more particularly the erosion of healthcare. The sleep crisis induces terrors that are subject to State securitization and also link to a global ecological crisis of exhausted resources and extreme forms of extraction. Where Russell imagines the future effects of insomnia at financialized capital's core, Rivera's cinematic "science fiction from below" imagines intensified extraction at the semi-periphery, as an industry of virtual reality factories on the Mexican border where overworked "cybraceros" labor ceaselessly. *Sleep Dealer* satirizes the "American Dream of virtual outsourcing," foregrounding the violated bodies and psyches of the Mexican workers, and presents a vision of the future that is dystopian, yet not without possibilities of collective political agency. Dan Hassler-Forest also takes up the question of how science fiction can imagine alternative futures, especially as a counterforce to the sense of futurelessness that is entailed by neoliberalism's "ideology of the present" and perpetual indebtedness. He argues that the genre's "utopian imaginary" retains value as speculative fiction that is imaginatively "post-capitalist" and notes in particular its capacity for "world-building," creating evolving systems of socio-economic relations, and that it is not necessarily focused on the individual human psyche. He looks in some detail at the work of Kim Stanley Robinson and in particular his Mars trilogy, which is written in response to the development of global capitalism, and seeks the limit points of capitalism's speculative and exploitative expansion and accumulation in logics of accelerationism and posthumanism. Like Rivera, Robinson grounds techno-futurism in the ecological crises of the present, refuting science fiction's imperialist history, and finds hope as well as despair in neoliberalism's (American) declensions.

Notes

1. Mark Fisher, *Capitalist Realism* (Winchester, UK: Zero Books, 2009).
2. Taylor Boas and Jordan Gans-Morse quoted in Philip Mirowski, "Postface: Defining Neoliberalism" in *The Road from Mont Pèlerin: The Making of the Neoliberal Thought Collective*, ed. Philip Mirowski and Dieter Plehwe (Cambridge, MA: Harvard University Press, 2009), 433–434.
3. Significant studies of neoliberalism include: Jean Comaroff and John L. Comaroff, eds. *Millennial Capitalism and the Culture of Neoliberalism* (Durham, NC: Duke University Press, 2001); David Harvey, *A Brief History of Neoliberalism* (Oxford: Oxford University Press, 2005); Luc Boltanski and Eve Chiapello, *The New Spirit of Capitalism*, trans. Gregory Elliott (London: Verso, 2005); Dieter Plehwe, Bernhard Walpen, and Gisela Neunhöffer, eds. *Neoliberal Hegemony: A Global Critique* (London: Routledge, 2006); Naomi Klein, *The Shock Doctrine: The Rise of Disaster Capitalism* (New York: Metropolitan Books:

2007); Michel Foucault, *The Birth of Biopolitics: Lectures at the College de France, 1978–9*, ed. Michel Senellart. Trans. by Graham Burchell (London: Palgrave MacMillan, 2008); Melinda Cooper, *Life as Surplus: Biotechnology and Capitalism in the Neoliberal Era* (Seattle: University of Washington Press, 2008); Christian Marazzi, *Capital and Language: From the New Economy to the War Economy*, trans. Gregory Conti (New York: Semiotext(e), 2008); Loïc Wacquant, *Punishing the Poor: The Neoliberal Government of Social Insecurity* (Durham, NC: Duke University Press, 2009); Philip Mirowski and Dieter Plehwe, eds. *The Road from Mont Pélerin: The Making of the Neoliberal Thought Collective* (Oxford: Oxford University Press, 2009); Jamie Peck, *Constructions of Neoliberal Reason* (Oxford: Oxford University Press, 2010); Philip Mirowski, *Never Let a Serious Crisis Go to Waste: How Neoliberalism Survived the Financial Meltdown* (London: Verso, 2010); Gérard Duménil and Dominique Lévy, *The Crisis of Neoliberalism* (Cambridge, MA: Harvard University Press, 2011); Yann Moulier Boutang, *Cognitive Capitalism*, trans. Ed Emery (London: Polity, 2011); Angus Burgin, *The Great Persuasion: Reinventing the Free Markets Since the Depression* (Cambridge, MA: Harvard University Press, 2012); Patricia Ventura, *Neoliberal Culture: Living with American Neoliberalism* (Farnham, UK; Ashgate, 2012); Daniel Stedman Jones, *Masters of the Universe: Hayek, Friedman, and the Birth of Neoliberal Politics* (Princeton, NJ: Princeton University Press, 2012); Pierre Dardot and Christian Laval, *The New Way of the World: On Neoliberal Society*, trans. Gregory Elliot (London: Verso, 2013); William Davies, *The Limits of Neoliberalism: Authority, Sovereignty, and the Logic of Competition* (London: Sage, 2014); Wendy Brown, *Undoing the Demos: Neoliberalism's Stealth Revolution* (New York: Zone Books, 2015); David M. Lotz, *The Rise and Fall of Neoliberal Capitalism* (Cambridge, MA: Harvard University Press, 2015); Quinn Slobodian, *Globalists: The End of Empire and the Birth of Neoliberalism* (Cambridge, MA: Harvard University Press, 2018); Adam Kotsko, *Neoliberalism's Demons: On the Political Theology of Late Capital* (Stanford, CA: Stanford University Press, 2018).

Studies that focus on the relation of literature to neoliberalism include: Rachel Greenwald Smith, *Affect and American Literature in the Age of Neoliberalism* (Cambridge, UK: Cambridge University Press, 2015); Emily Johannssen and Alissa G. Karl, eds. *Neoliberalism and the Novel* (London: Routledge, 2016); Mitchum Huehls, *After Critique: Twenty-First Century Literature in a Neoliberal Age* (Oxford: Oxford University Press, 2016); Mitchum Huehls and Rachel Greenwald Smith, eds. *Neoliberalism and Contemporary Literary Culture* (Baltimore: Johns Hopkins Press, 2017); Jane Elliot, *The Microeconomic Mode: Reimagining Political Subjectivity in the 21st Century* (New York: Columbia University Press, 2018); and Jane Elliot and Gillian Harkins, the special issue "Genres of Neoliberalism," *Social Text*, Summer 2013.

4. For overviews of a world-system perspective, see: Immanuel Wallerstein, *The Modern World-System*, Volumes I–IV (Berkeley: University of California Press, 2011); Thomas R. Shannon, *An Introduction to the World-System Perspective* (Boulder, CO: Westview Press, 1989); Christopher K. Chase-Dunn, *Global Formation: Structures of the World Economy* (London: Basil Blackwell, 1991); Immanuel Wallerstein, *World-Systems Analysis: An Introduction* (Durham, NC: Duke University Press, 2004). For prior usages of world-systems perspectives for literary and cultural studies, see, Stephen Shapiro, *The Culture and Commerce of the Early American Novel: Reading the Atlantic World-System* (University Park, PA: Penn State Press, 2008); WReC, *Combined and Uneven Development:*

Introduction [19]

Towards a New Theory of World-Literature (Liverpool: Liverpool University Press, 2015); Stephen Shapiro and Philip Barnard, *Pentecostal Modernism: Lovecraft, Los Angeles, and World-Systems Culture* (London: Bloomsbury, 2017), and Sharae Deckard and Stephen Shapiro, "World-Culture and the Neoliberal World-System: An Introduction" in *World Literature, Neoliberalism, and the Culture of Discontent*, eds. Sharae Deckard and Stephen Shapiro (London: Palgrave, 2019).

5. Brown, *Undoing the Demos*.

6. Sarah Brouillette, "Neoliberalism and the Demise of the Literary" in *Neoliberalism and Contemporary American Literature*, ed. Mitchum Huehls and Rachel Greenwald-Smith (Baltimore: Johns Hopkins University Press, 2017), 277–290.

7. We have previously argued that such an opposition between Marx and Foucault is not sustainable within an attentive reading of Foucault, whose work throughout the 1970s was oriented to elucidating a complementary history of capitalism to Marx's, but one that distanced itself from the Stalinist version sought for by the French Communist Party. Anne Schwan and Stephen Shapiro, *How to Read Foucault's Discipline and Punish* (London: Pluto Press, 2011) and Philip Barnard and Stephen Shapiro, "Introduction," *The Productive Body*, François Guéry and Didier Deleule, (Winchester, UK: Zero Books, 2014). See also Jacques Bidet, *Foucault with Marx*, trans. Steve Corcoran (London: Zed Books, 2016); Antonio Negri, *Marx and Foucault: Essays*, trans. Ed Emery (London: Polity, 2017); and Christian Laval, Luca Paltrinieri, and Ferhat Taylan, eds. *Marx & Foucault: Lectures, Usages, Confrontations* (Paris: La Découverte, 2015).

8. A *regime of accumulation* is the historically specific "form of social transformation that increases relative surplus-value under the stable constraints of the most general norms that define absolute surplus-value," while a *mode of regulation* "is a set of mediations which ensure that the distortions created by the accumulation of capital are kept within limits which are compatible with social cohesion within each nation." Michel Aglietta, *A Theory of Capitalist Regulation: The US Experience*, trans. David Fernbach (London: Verso 2015), 68; Michel Aglietta, "Capitalism at the Turn of the Century: Regulation Theory and the Challenge of Social Change," *New Left Review* 232 (Nov.–Dec. 1998), 44. Aglietta considered the post-Fordist mode of regulation as responding to "the triple challenge of the globalization of capitalism, the disintegration of social identity and the shrinkage of the state . . . these three ills are closely interlinked. The same applies to the encouraging trends, the initiatives and aspirations that might bring forth new mediation mechanisms capable of redefining the regulatory system," i.e. what we might now call neoliberalism. Aglietta, "Capitalism at the Turn of the Century," 44.

9. Huehls and Greenwald-Smith, *Neoliberalism*, 1–20.

10. Huehls and Greenwald-Smith, *Neoliberalism*, 5.

11. Ventura, *Neoliberal Culture*, 1.

12. Gerhard Lembruch, "The Institutional Embedding of Market Economies: The German 'Model' and its Impact on Japan" in *The Origins of Nonliberal Capitalism: Germany and Japan in Comparison*, ed. Wolfgang Streeck and Kozo Yamamura (Ithaca, NY: Cornell University Press, 2005), 80.

13. The effect of the war is crucial for the history of German-speaking ordoliberal thought, as it stands as an important experience for its proponents. During the Hitler era, several left Germany, (Röpke and the Jewish Rüstow went to Turkey), but others remained in the economics section of the Akademie für Deutsches Recht. "Some of its

outstanding members were Walter Eucken, Franz Böhm, Leonhard Miksch, and Alfred Müller-Armack, all of whom were to gain prominence in the Adenauer era," and several taught as members of the "Freiburg School" (Lembruch, "The Institutional Embedding of Market Economies," 78). After the war, though, the ordoliberal concern about pooled power took on a more reflective tone and motive due to the events of the Nazi era. Quinn Slobodian argues that Nazi-era jurist Carl Schmitt's 1950 *Nomos of the Earth in the International Law of Jus Publicum Europaeum* was as significant a touchstone for the postwar German ordoliberals as was Keynes' *General Theory*. Slobodian argues that the German neoliberal economists took Schmitt's defense of nationalist economies in opposition to the global mobility of goods and labor as a conceptual framework to define themselves by a point-by-point rejection of Schmitt's articulation of his theories. (Slobodian, *Globalists*, 9–11).

A similar contrast of emphasis between pre- and postwar ordoliberals can be seen in the response to them by German born, but American naturalized, Carl J. Friedrich, Professor of Government at Harvard. In his 1945 review of Hayek's *The Road to Serfdom*, Friedrich wrote, "As far as one can make out, this 'free society' of Hayek's is the bleak 1840's in England when Manchester exploitation reigned supreme, when the enterpriser was wholly free to practice his 'astuteness for ambushing the community's loose change,' as Veblen once so sardonically expressed it. Although 'freedom' is a key concept in Hayek's thought pattern, it nowhere receives any careful analysis, and the intricate problems of who is to be free for what, which have troubled since men began to think about freedom, are left unattended." Carl J. Friedrich, "The Road to Serfdom" in *The American Political Science Review*, 39:3 (Jun., 1945): 575–579.

Yet by 1955, Friedrich was more comfortable in arguing that the "central concern . . . of the entire neo-liberal group" was a critique of "the totalitarian tendencies of our time," a more favorable summary from a scholar who was considered to be one of the foremost authorities on totalitarianism in his time. Carl J. Friedrich, "The Political Thought of Neo-Liberalism," *The American Political Science Review*, 49:2 (Jun., 1955): 509–525.

Friedrich claimed that Rustow's magnum opus *Ortsbestimmung der Gegenwart* (Determination of the Present Location) (1952–55) is "specifically a critique of German culture" and particularly the persistence and increasing autonomy of State bureaucracies that initially arose to place limits on the monarchy, but then continued to enable German totalitarianism. For Friedrich, Rustow's critique of Germany is also "occasionally interspersed with suggestions that imply all is not well in the Anglo-Saxon world, that imperialism and colonialism, and the treatment of Negroes and Indians, fits into a pattern that is uncomfortably close to the [formerly Nazi] German one" (519–21).

14. Friedrich, "Neo-Liberalism," 510.
15. Peck, *Neoliberal Reason*, 56.
16. Peck, *Neoliberal Reason*, 56.
17. Mark K. Berger, "The Neoliberal Ascendency and East Asia: Geo-politics, Development Theory and the End of the Authoritarian Developmental State in South Korea" in *Neoliberal Hegemony*, 107.
18. Catherine Lawson, "The 'Textbook Controversy': Lessons for Contemporary Economics" *AAUP Journal of Academic Freedom* 6 (2015): 1–14. Accessed June 20, 2018. https://www.aaup.org/sites/default/files/Lawson.pdf; David C. Colander and Harry Landreth, eds. *The Coming of Keynesianism to America: Conversations with the Founders*

of Keynesian Economics (Cheltenham, UK: Edward Elgar, 1996); David C. Colander and Harry Landreth, "Political Influence on the Textbook Keynesian Revolution: God, Man, and Laurie Tarshis at Yale," in Omar F. and Betsey B. Price (eds), *Keynesianism and the Keynesian Revolution in America: A Memorial Volume in Honour of Lorie Tarshis* (Cheltenham: Edward Elgar, 1998), 59–72; and David Colander, "The Evolution of U.S. Economics Textbooks," Middlebury Economics Discussion Paper no 10-37 (October 2010). http://sandcat.middlebury.edu/econ/repec/mdl/ancoec/1037.pdf. Accessed June 2018. See also the discussion of Luhnow's influence in Rob Van Horn and Philip Mirowski, "The Rise of the Chicago School of Economics and the Birth of Neoliberalism" in Philip Mirowski and Dieter Plehwe, eds. *The Road from Mont Pèlerin: The Making of the Neoliberal Thought Collective* (Oxford: Oxford University Press, 2009), 139–178.

19. Alan Ebenstein, *Friedrich Hayek: A Biography* (Chicago: University of Chicago Press, 2001), 135–16; Bruce Caldwell, "Introduction" in *The Collected Works of F.A. Hayek*, Vol. 2 (London: Routledge, 2008), 19.

20. Jennifer Schuessler, "Hayek: The Back Story" *New York Times*, July 9, 2010. Accessed June 2018. https://www.nytimes.com/2010/07/11/books/review/Schuessler-t.html. Both the abbreviated and illustrated versions are reproduced in *The Reader's Digest Condensed Version* of *The Road to Serfdom* (London: The Institute of Economic Affairs, 1999). Online version.

21. Ebenstein, *Friedrich Hayek*, 135–136.

22. Van Horn and Mirowski, "The Rise of the Chicago School of Economics," 150.

23. Lawson, "The 'Textbook Controversy,'" 8.

24. Lawson, "The 'Textbook Controversy,'" 9.

25. Aglietta, *A Theory of Capitalist Regulation*; Alain Lipietz, *Mirages and Miracles: The Crises of Global Fordism*, trans. David Macey (London: Verso, 1987); Giovanni Arrighi, *The Long Twentieth Century: Money, Power, and the Origins of Our Times* (London: Verso, 1994); and Robert Brenner, *The Economics of Global Turbulence* (London: Verso, 2005). See also, Gérard Duménil and Dominique Lévy, *Insurgent Capital: The Roots of the Neoliberal Revolution* (Cambridge, MA: Harvard University Press, 2004).

26. Lipietz, *Mirages and Miracles*, 41.

27. Peck, *Neoliberal Reason*, 57.

28. When raising the question of accumulation by dispossession under neoliberalism in *Brief History of Neoliberalism*, David Harvey draws his readers' attention to an earlier 2000 chapter, "Contemporary Globalization." While the historical aspects remain the same between his 2000 and 2005 discussion, the earlier one highlights "globalization" and only begins to use the term "neoliberalism" late in the essay. David Harvey, *Spaces of Hope* (Edinburgh: Edinburgh University Press, 2000), 53–72. This chapter is largely a reprint of David Harvey, "Globalization in Question," *Rethinking Marxism*, 8:4, (1995): 1–17.

29. For a synoptic summary, see Alissa Quart, *Squeezed: Why Our Families Can't Afford America* (New York: HarperCollins, 2018).

30. Fisher, *Capitalist Realism*.

[2]   ELI JELLY-SCHAPIRO

LITERATURE, THEORY, AND THE TEMPORALITIES OF NEOLIBERALISM

HISTORIANS AND THEORISTS COMMONLY trace the economic and political origins of neoliberalism to the early 1970s, when conjoined crises of energy and accumulation prefaced a constellation of transformations that have reshaped the world in the decades since: the intensification of crude forms of dispossession, the innovation of various mechanisms of "flexible" production and financial speculation, the declension of the welfare state, the clarification of new rationalities of the responsible and entrepreneurial self, and the general expansion and deepening of market logics.[1]

If the term "neoliberalism" implies a distinct periodization, though, the neoliberal present is composed of—its defining features correspond to and derive from—multiple temporalities. In the moment of primitive accumulation, ongoing processes of extraction, trafficking, and enclosure are enabled by forms of state (or extra-state) violence. In the moment of expanded reproduction—wherein "growth," the reinvestment of the surplus, remains a primary objective and outcome of accumulation—the maintenance and perpetuation of capitalist social relations is guaranteed by the "silent compulsion" of the market. And in the moment of what I want to call "accumulation by fabrication," the synthetic creation and subsequent assimilation of an outside to capital—through the devaluation of assets and labor or privatization of public services and resources—contributes to the waning efficacy of ideology and heightened importance of state repression.

One key task of contemporary critique is to simultaneously distinguish between the three temporalities of neoliberal capital—the unique rationalities of governance and accumulation that are paradigmatic to each—and evince the dynamics of their contingent interrelation. In the pages that follow, I delineate each of these temporalities, and the theoretical frameworks to which they correspond, in turn, conforming first of all to the abstraction of their progressive linearity before gesturing toward their concrete synchrony in the present conjuncture. I then move to an examination of how primitive accumulation, expanded reproduction, and accumulation by fabrication are figured in recent works of fiction. The majority of the theoretical and literary works that I address privilege one of these moments above the others—and thus help to elucidate their distinction. There are, though, historical and contemporary texts—notable examples of which I enter into dialogue with—that illuminate instead their structural combination. It is the latter critical current that this essay aspires to join and advance.

Primitive Accumulation

In the final part of *Capital*'s first volume, Karl Marx undertakes a suggestive meditation on the notion of "so-called primitive accumulation": the violent "divorcing of the producer from the means of production," but also "the extirpation, enslavement and entombment in mines of the indigenous population of [America] . . . the conquest and plunder of India, the conversion of Africa into a preserve for the commercial hunting of black skins."[2] As the modifier "so-called" suggests, Marx was keen to highlight the ideological content of the concept of "primitive accumulation," as it was theorized by classical political economy and narrated by the "bourgeois historians." He placed a particular accent on the contradictory emancipation signified by the figure of the "free worker"—the wage-laborer who had been liberated from the feudal relation but also "freed" from "any means of production of their own."[3] The history of this expropriation, Marx wrote, is written "in letters of blood and fire."[4] The enclosure of the commons and other "terroristic laws" worked to "set free" the small farmer—to transform the agricultural population into an industrial proletariat. This process was justified, by the philosophers and legislators of enclosure, via appeal, not simply to its liberatory consequences, but to its ameliorative contributions to the material security of the political community. Marx cited one supporter of enclosure, J. Arbuthnot, who argued that "if, by converting the farmers into a body of men who must work for others, more labor is produced, it is an advantage which the nation should wish for."[5] Enclosure, in other words, is imagined, in this ideological framework, as hastening not the disappearance of society's common stock but its expansionary enrichment. There is an evident continuity here with neoliberal ideology, which extols the emancipatory effects and material benefits of the declension of the social commons.

The "improving" effects of enclosure—the gift of dispossession to the common stock of humanity, including the dispossessed—were also invoked by intellectual arguments for the settler-colonial theft of indigenous lands. The settler who encloses "the wild woods and uncultivated waste of

America," John Locke opined, "and has a greater plenty of the conveniences of life from ten acres than he could have had from a hundred left to nature, may truly be said to give ninety acres to mankind."[6] In Marx's formulation, this and other forms of colonial plunder enabled the advent of industrial capital in the Old World. "The treasures captured outside Europe," Marx wrote, "by undisguised looting, enslavement and murder flowed back to the mother country and were turned into capital there."[7] The capital provided by colonial dispossession and chattel slavery combined with the "free and rightless" proletariat engendered by domestic processes of enclosure. This alchemy of the two primary sites or moments of primitive accumulation, Marx observed, made possible the genesis of industrial capitalism.

Though accenting the terror of capital's birth, Marx shared with classical/liberal political economy an understanding of primitive accumulation as a *specific* moment in the emergence and evolution of the capitalist mode of production. He did not, in other words, devote a great deal of attention to the not simply primordial but perpetual importance of "so-called primitive accumulation" to the reproduction of capital and its attendant social relations. In *Capital*, the foundational terror of primitive accumulation gives way to the "silent compulsion" of the market. This is a protracted process, unfolding over centuries even, but a finite one. "In its embryonic state, in its state of becoming," Marx wrote, "capital cannot yet use the sheer force of economic relations to secure its right to absorb a sufficient quantity of surplus labor, but must be aided by the power of the state." In time, however, "the 'free' worker, owing to the greater development of the capitalist mode of production, makes a voluntary agreement, i.e. is compelled by social conditions to sell the whole of his active life."[8]

Later thinkers, however, did develop empirical and theoretical treatments of the ways in which primitive accumulation remains central to the maintenance, and continuous reinvention, of capitalism. "The original sin of simple robbery," as Hannah Arendt observed, "must be repeated lest the motor of accumulation suddenly die down."[9] Arendt's insight borrowed from Rosa Luxemburg, who highlighted capitalism's dependence on "non-capitalist social strata." In order to survive, Luxemburg argued, capital must constantly find and expropriate spaces outside of its dominion. Luxemburg, along with Marxist theorists of imperialism such as Rudolf Hilferding and V.I. Lenin, was responding to an epoch in the history of capitalism that Marx himself did not live to witness—the late-nineteenth-century highpoint of modern European imperialism, which evinced with a particular clarity the "spatial fix" to conjoined crises of over-production and under-consumption. This moment and the theoretical interventions it provoked, that is, revealed the enduring importance of primitive accumulation and coercive state violence within a mature stage of capitalism that Marx himself imagined as defined by expanded reproduction and the "silent compulsion" of the market.

The connection between this fin de siècle moment and our own neoliberal era is not merely analogic but genealogic. In India, for example, the 1894 Land Acquisition Act governed the dispossession of small holders until 2013. Putting a neoliberal accent on this old colonial law, the Indian government has transformed lands acquired through the Act into Special Economic Zones (SEZs) — spaces of economic exception that oil the machinery of corporate rule and financial speculation. In some cases, these expropriations appear to model the same processes of enclosure and proletarianization described by Marx. In West Bengal, for example, the government has sold forcibly acquired lands — at a price exponentially above the compensation offered to the land's previous owners — to the Tata Motor Company, the factories of which entrap the producer divorced from the means of production.[10] But as Marx himself was careful to emphasize, enclosure always creates not only the wage laborer but the masses of unemployed. The proletariat formed by the "forcible expropriation of the people from the soil," Marx observed, "could not possibly be absorbed by the nascent manufactures as fast as it was thrown upon the world."[11] The uniqueness of neoliberal primitive accumulation is defined in part by the shifting balance between the waged and "wageless" subjects of dispossession.[12] Those displaced by state land grabs — as by free trade agreements and the structural adjustment programs that have reversed progressive land reforms in the global South — move toward the assembly line, but their migration is more likely to terminate in the informal rather than formal sites of economic production. Importantly, though, the "wageless" are still structurally entangled with the factory, as the expansion of the "reserve army" degrades wages and thereby increases the rate of exploitation.

Expanded Reproduction

In the moment of its genesis, Marx argued, capitalist production is enabled by state violence. But once the primitive accumulation of capital has been achieved, the mechanisms of valorization are guaranteed rather by the "natural laws of production." If the production of capital is made possible by crude force, that is, its expanded reproduction is, in Marx's formulation, guaranteed rather by the less visible workings of culture, by "education, tradition, and habit," which ensure the willful participation of the worker in a system that is premised on their exploitation.[13]

Over the course of the past century or so, the vocabulary that guides the theorization of this "silent compulsion" has been various — from Max

Weber's concept of "spirit," to Louis Althusser's critique of "ideology," to Michel Foucault's elaboration of "governmentality." In the current moment, the Foucauldian framework is ascendant—in large part because Foucault was an early and prescient theorist of neoliberal rationality. Foucault's account, which was composed in the late 1970s, locates neoliberalism within the longer history of what he terms the "liberal art of government." Whereas in classical liberalism, Foucault observed, the state conferred legitimacy upon the market, in neoliberal order this relationship is reversed; the market legitimates the state. And whereas in classical liberalism the social and the economic were imagined as separate spheres, each conforming to its own rationality, under neoliberal governance the distinction between the social and the economic, society and the market, is blurred or dissolved completely. Finally, whereas the tradition of eighteenth and nineteenth century liberalism imagined the workings of the market—its mechanisms of competition and exchange—as a given of nature, the original neoliberals—the postwar German ordoliberals especially—disavowed the naturalism of laissez faire as naïve. They understood competition, to borrow Foucault's words, as a "historical objective of governmental art and not as a natural given that must be respected."[14] (As Karl Polanyi put it, "laissez faire was planned.") In this, the ordoliberals shared with Marxist thought an understanding of laissez faire as an ideology imposed upon human social relations rather than a truth deduced from them.

The concept of governmentality describes the "conduct of conduct"—a technology of power that operates not through explicit command but by compelling the individual subject, from a position of invisible remove, to internalize and act in conformity with a particular logic of governance. Foucault's elaboration of "governmentality" helps to define the distinction between the classical liberal tradition and its neoliberal transmutation. In the eighteenth century, Foucault observed, *homo oeconomicus* is "the person who must be left alone ... the subject or object of *laissez-faire*." According to neoliberal rationality, by contrast, *homo oeconomicus* is "someone who is eminently governable ... the correlate of a governmentality which will act on the environment and systematically modify its variables."[15] In the neoliberal context, in other words, the rational behavior of *homo oeconomicus* is not a precondition of government but something that must be produced, or conditioned, by it. And as Wendy Brown, writing in the contemporary moment, has contended, if in classical liberalism *homo oeconomicus* naturally resides in the economic sphere, in the neoliberal moment the boundaries of his habitat encompass all spaces of public and private life. "Neoliberal rationality," she notes, "disseminates the model of the market to all domains and activities ... and configures human beings exhaustively as market actors, always, only, and everywhere." As a result, Brown argues, the demos—the space of democratic imaginaries, forms, and subjectivities—is narrowed to the point of disappearance.[16]

Though Brown acknowledges that neoliberal policy is occasionally imposed through violence, she contends that it is "more often enacted through specific techniques of governance, through best practices and legal tweaks, in short, through 'soft power' drawing on consensus and buy in." Neoliberalization, Brown contends, "is more termitelike than lionlike . . . its mode of reason boring in capillary fashion into the trunks and branches of workplaces, schools, public agencies, social and political discourse, and above all, the subject."[17] The emphasis here is on what Althusser termed the "ideological state apparatuses." And indeed, the most visible contributions to the historiography of neoliberalism—from David Harvey's *Brief History of Neoliberalism* (2005) to Daniel Stedman Jones's *Masters of the Universe* (2014)—highlight precisely this circulation of neoliberal ideas through think tanks, educational institutions, churches, and so on. The substance of this pervasive ideology is distinguished by its particular understanding of freedom. According to neoliberal rationality, the freedom of the individual—the entrepreneurial subject—is conditioned by the freedoms of the market and liberty (qua security) of the private property that is accumulated therein. For Brown, this relocation of freedom from the political to the economic sphere ensures the inequality of the latter; market freedom is not just a diversion from the demos, but an agent of its undoing.[18]

The question of how neoliberal rationality is naturalized has also provoked explicitly Weberian responses. Beyond his particular inquiry into the enabling affinity between Calvinism and boundless accumulation, Weber's more fundamental insight in *The Protestant Ethic and the Spirit of Capitalism* (1905) was that people require ethical and moral reasons for participating in capitalist processes. The "spirit" of capitalism, as the French sociologists Luc Boltanski and Eve Chiapello define it, is simply "the ideology that justifies engagement in capitalism." Bringing this problem to bear on the neoliberal moment, Boltanski and Chiapello's *The New Spirit of Capitalism* (2005) focuses on the central importance of the *cadres*—a sort of managerial proletariat—to the legitimation and reproduction of post-Fordist capitalism in France. The *cadres* occupy a liminal space within the capital–labor binary. Afforded a modest security by capital, they are tasked in exchange with convincing first themselves and then the workers that they manage that "the prescribed way of making profit might be desirable, interesting, exciting, innovative or commendable."[19] Since the 1990s, Boltanski and Chiapello observe, the exigencies of "flexible" accumulation have corresponded to the innovation of a managerial lexicon that emphasizes the ideals of self-organization, creativity, and "intrinsic motivation." In one sense, then, the undoing of the Fordist archetype of the centralized hierarchical firm—and its displacement by the horizontal and spatially diffuse "network"—signals the redundancy of the managerial class to the reproduction of capitalist social relations. If workers are self-governed and self-mobilized, the *cadres* are a drain on the surplus rather than one of its key conditions. But in another sense, the "autonomous teams" of workers that replace the verticality of the firm represent, not the disappearance of the managerial class, but its universalization.[20] On the neoliberal shop floor, all workers are managers.

I am concerned to stress here that the imbricated theorizations of governmentality, ideology, and spirit belong to the temporality of expanded reproduction. They privilege spaces of putative economic or political belonging—the workplace, the marketplace, and the enfranchised public sphere—rather than exclusion. Even if the rabble in the shanty town are structurally necessary to the mechanisms of profit generation, their ideological consent is not required.

Accumulation by Fabrication

That the perpetuation of capital requires non-capitalist strata, Luxemburg contended, is evidence of capitalism's mortality. When there is no longer an "outside" to capital—non-commoditized spaces or non-integrated markets—accumulation will cease.[21] Primitive accumulation is a finite process, in other words, because the planet—its land, resources, and people—is finite. Luxemburg, though, did not anticipate neoliberalism's ingenious solution to this seemingly immutable contradiction: in the absence of an outside, one must simply be created. This fabricated outside, as Harvey has outlined, is achieved via a multiplicity of means: financialization (in particular the speculative claim to a future surplus rather than direct investment in production), the privatization of public assets and services, and the deliberate devaluation of assets and labor (so as to enable their later seizure by currently idle capital).[22] Importantly, the social and economic consequence of these processes is magnified by their imbrication. When the bubbles created by liberated financial capital burst, the resultant crisis justifies the imposition of austerity and further rounds of privatization and devaluation. This regressive redistribution of wealth—which consolidates the power of the capitalist class, but which discourages meaningful economic growth—corresponds to the generalization of social and economic precariousness. The expansion and deepening of insecurity, meanwhile, occasions a breakdown of consent, not simply within the working classes, but, increasingly, the putatively secure middles classes as well. Crises of accumulation, in other words, occasion crises of governmentality. And as the market and its compulsion are denaturalized, the repressive apparatuses of the state reenter the governmental foreground.

Harvey's concept of "accumulation by dispossession" joins original forms of primitive accumulation to latter-day technologies of synthetic depredation. Marx, too, was keen to illuminate the connections between the former and the latter. His treatment of primitive accumulation not only addressed the enclosure of common lands and plunder of bodies and resources; it also highlighted the fundamental contributions of "stock-exchange gambling and the modern bankocracy," as well as the "expropriation of the expropriators" (a phrase that nicely captures the asset-stripping methods of contemporary private equity).[23] I am eager to emulate Harvey's insistence on the genealogical and structural connections between these two moments of accumulation by dispossession. I also want to insist, though, on their distinction—the unique spaces in which they unfold, and the particular subjects that are proper to each. Focusing on the moment of primitive accumulation, we are drawn to agrarian regions—of the global South in particular—and the migratory routes traveled by the dispossessed farmer to the informal spaces of the expanding metropolis. Privileging the moment of accumulation by fabrication, we are directed rather to the unemployment office, or to spaces of newly insecure employment and habitation—the driver's seat of an Uber, occupied by the downsized autoworker; the room of an Extended Stay hotel, occupied by the evicted or foreclosed upon family.

Beyond the work of Harvey and others on mechanisms of privatization and devaluation, the neoliberal iteration of accumulation by fabrication has provoked an especial theoretical interest in the conjoined problems of precarity and affect. In one simple definition, "precarity" names the "structure of affect," to borrow Lauren Berlant's phrase, of generalized insecurity. Though the forms and spaces of vulnerability to which "precarity" corresponds are in theory myriad—encompassing both the migrant farmworker and the free-lance graphic designer—its analytic currency is conditioned by the effects of neoliberalization upon formerly secure populations. It is continuous, Berlant has argued, with patterns of social and economic transformation that expose the bourgeoisie to "ordinary contingencies of material and fantasmatic life associated with proletarian labor-related subjectivity."[24] So if, in one sense, neoliberalism makes managers of us all—self-governing and self-surveilling—so too does it generalize the proletarian condition, the quotidian insecurities of working-class life. One expression of this is the way in which the material and affective labor of security is increasingly outsourced by the state. The unpaid work of "care" or "love" in the domestic sphere—a mode of exploitation long the target of feminist critique—has acquired a more universal dimension, as the low-waged sectors of "care" and "service" grow in social and economic significance.[25] This latter expansion of care work corresponds to the retreat of the welfare state, as capital abandons any attempt to mitigate its destructive effects. The theorists of "precarity" are interested in the political potentiality of this pervasive insecurity—the recognition of our shared vulnerability and ethos of mutual care that it provokes. "As bodies," Judith Butler writes, "we suffer and we resist and together ... exemplify that form of the sustaining social bond that neo-liberal economics has almost destroyed."[26] The Occupy movement worked, in this spirit, to render the insecurity of neoliberal crisis visible, and to enact the possibilities of a radical politics founded upon our shared precariousness. The term "affect" captures this duality—the individual and paralyzing burden of neoliberal disappointment, and the collective volition to which that waning optimism might give way (if not give rise).[27]

If processes of primitive accumulation are enabled by crude state violence, and if the expanded reproduction of capital is made possible rather by the "silent compulsion of economic relations" (the spirit or ideology that compels market participation), accumulation by fabrication is facilitated by a synthesis of coercion and consent. The consultants and managers that facilitate the downsizing of the firm are still keen to invoke the virtues of efficiency and flexibility. And the newly adrift worker might maintain a hopeful belief, however threadbare, in the liberatory possibilities of the "sharing economy." But growing insecurity inevitably gives rise to acute cultures of repression. In the advanced capitalist world, the increasing scarcity of secure employment and privatization of the social commons has coincided with the militarization of public and private police, who suppress the precariat's collective action, occupy communities left behind by capital—communities of color most especially—and facilitate the project of mass incarceration. As the authors of *Policing the Crisis* (1978), writing at the neoliberal end of the 1970s, put it, in the moment of crisis, "the masks of liberal consent and popular consensus slip to reveal the reserves of coercion and force on which the cohesion of the state and its legal authority depends."[28]

Today, in the context of pervasive and recurring economic and political crises, the temporality of "accumulation by fabrication" appears ascendant. And indeed, its core political and economic forms—heightened state repression, synthetic forms of dispossession—are often read as synonymous with neoliberalism broadly conceived. But as I am keen to stress, the distinctiveness of neoliberalism, as a global systemic phenomenon, lies not merely in the relative centrality of "accumulation by fabrication," but in the contingent articulation of the latter with the extant temporalities of primitive accumulation and expanded reproduction.

❖

To this point, I have sketched a kind of temporal succession. The moment of primitive accumulation prefaces and founds the moment of expanded reproduction, the crises of which then provoke—and are deepened by—processes of accumulation by fabrication. If we limit our geographic focus to one national space—to Marx's "classic" example of England, say—there is a certain, if limited, plausibility to this sequential narrative. But when we bring the broader world-system of capital into sharper focus, it becomes clear that these three temporalities are—historically and in the neoliberal context—synchronous.

Frantz Fanon, in a suggestive moment in *The Wretched of the Earth* (1961), contrasted the mechanisms of capitalist governance in the metropole and in the colony. In the metropole, he observed, exploitation of labor was enabled by the "structure of moral reflexes . . . [and] aesthetic expressions of respect for the established order," which create around the worker an "atmosphere of submission." In the colony, by contrast, "the policeman and the soldier, by their immediate presence and their frequent and direct action maintain contact with the native and advise him by means of rifle butts and napalm not to budge."[29] Put slightly differently, the primitive accumulation of capital in the colonies was enabled by the "language of pure force" (also Fanon's phrase); and the reproduction of capital in the metropole was made possible by various ideological apparatuses and ingrained moral sentiments. Fanon's account, though, implied the interrelation of and not simply the distinction between colony and metropole. Violent forms of colonial dispossession fueled processes of expanded reproduction within the metropole, and accelerated the social-democratic development therein of the ideological state apparatuses. The racialized negation of the colonized subject, meanwhile, helped guarantee the interpellation of the white worker back home. In the putative aftermath of the colonial period, these interrelations mutated in pace with the exigencies of accumulation, as synthetic forms of dispossession—what Guy Debord and Henri Lefebvre termed the "colonization of everyday life"—joined with neocolonial processes of extractive industry to renew the ideal and reality of economic growth.

In the late-neoliberal present, these dynamics persist. Expanded reproduction continues to be enabled by outright dispossession. And the efficacy of capitalist ideology in the global North continues to be ensured in part by the enactment of crude state violence in the global South (or peripheral spaces within the North). That the "reserves of coercion and force" are applied with an especial intensity on the other side of the tracks ensures the potency of the "structure of moral reflexes" on this side. Rendered insecure by processes of accumulation by fabrication, the "white working class" amplifies its appeal toward "law and order"—and the militarization of borders, impunity of racist police violence, and aerial bombardment of foreign lands appear as plausible forms of redress. But if this resurgent nativism is one expression of capitalist ideology, it is also symptomatic of its crisis. And as the compulsion of the market becomes yet less compelling and yet more audible, new political possibilities—the positive determination of a planetary rather than nationalistic precariat—might come into view.[30]

The Mexican small farmer driven off her land by NAFTA migrates toward the Maquiladoras of Juarez or the meatpacking plants, corporate fields, and service industries north of the border. The outsourced American worker, meanwhile, takes a job at Walmart, where she earns a fraction of her former wage selling the same commodities she used to produce. One urgent imperative of contemporary theory is to elucidate both the sameness and difference that define these emergent spaces of shared precariousness. The factions that might make up the collective subject of resistance to neoliberalism will enunciate a particular critical vocabulary, and deploy a particular tactical imagination, depending on the time-space of contemporary capital that they currently inhabit or from which they hail. Novels, to which I now turn, can help us distinguish the substance of these unique imaginaries of struggle—while also, perhaps, clarifying the potentiality of their affiliation.

Literature

When the contemporary novel engages the neoliberal reenactment of original methods of primitive accumulation, it most often does so obliquely, by way of analogy. But this analogic approach is possessed of a certain critical efficacy, as it evokes the routes of continuity between historical and latter-day forms of capitalist unfreedom. Novels such as Marlon James's *The Book of Night Women* (2009) and Amitav Ghosh's *Sea of Poppies* (2008) highlight the "language of pure force" that guarantees processes of primitive accumulation; and these texts evince in turn the Fanonian insistence that the violence of colonial dispossession will only yield when confronted with a reciprocal and greater violence.

In James's *Book of Night Women*, the Jamaican planter class dismisses the prospect of mass slave revolt as ontologically impossible. The black appeal to the ideal of freedom is unthinkable, to the plantation aristocracy, precisely because it marks the slave as a human being. The night women themselves, enacting G.W.F. Hegel's dialectic of master and slave, articulate their claim to freedom and personhood through violence. "We not getting free," the slave Homer puts it, "we taking free."[31] Freedom is understood here, that is, not as a political right bestowed or denied by the state—but as the reflexive affirmation of human selfhood that follows from the negation of a negation.

In *The Book of Night Women*, the faith of Jamaican planters in the infrahuman being of their slaves is shook by the news of revolution emanating from Saint Domingue. The reverberation of that event across the West Indies and planet at large, coupled with the subsequent abolition of the slave trade by the empires of Britain and France, encouraged the innovation of new forms of capitalist bondage. Ghosh's *Sea of Poppies* traces the latter transformation, shifting the focus from the late eighteenth century to the mid-nineteenth, from the Caribbean to the Indian Ocean, from the sugar plantation to the trade in coolies and opium. In the India of *Sea of Poppies*, the British reliance on opium—to balance its trade deficit with China and fuel its imperial expansion—has displaced practices of subsistence farming with monocultural production. The transition toward the latter is not voluntarily embraced by the farmers themselves, but imposed by the English sahibs, who force cash advances on small producers, demanding they grow only poppies to fuel the factory's "never sated" appetite for opium.[32] Many farmers struggle each year to repay this compulsory credit. Others who fail to do so exchange one form of indenture for another, joining the growing ranks of bonded migrant workers bound for southern Africa and the West Indies.

Ghosh's Mr. Burnham, a consummate exponent of the British Empire, laments the closure of the Middle Passage. "The African trade," he remarks in earnest, "was the greatest exercise in freedom since God led the children of Israel out of Egypt." But fortunately, "when the doors of freedom were closed to the African, the Lord opened them to a tribe that was yet more needful of it—the Asiatick."[33] Like slavery, indenture is freedom. As *Sea of Poppies* reveals, though, in the moment of primitive accumulation it is the overseer's lash, rather than his rhetoric, that ensures in the last instance the realities of capitalist unfreedom. And in the novel's penultimate scene, on board the *Ibis*, the whip is snatched from midair by the coolie Kalua and returned to the subedar who wields it, coiling around his neck and ending his life. In this novel too, then, freedom is conditioned by the absolute negation of an absolute negation.

Though drowned out by the report of the whip or rifle, Mr. Burnham's paean to the liberatory powers of capital does gesture toward the increasing efficacy of the market's "silent compulsion." The war with China looming on the horizon, he insists, will be waged, not for opium, but "for a principle: for freedom—for the freedom of trade and the freedom of the Chinese people."[34] One can hear, in Mr. Burnham's words, an anticipatory echo of ideology's preeminence in later capitalist eras—the conjoined ideals of "free labor" and "free trade" that today work to mask the violence of the wage relation and assimilate the individual subject to the rationalities of the commodity form.

The contemporary ascent of this ideological lexicon is illuminated with a particular clarity by novels that inhabit the time-space of expanded reproduction—texts that focus on the governing ideology of the workplace (the office or retail counter more often than the assembly line, in these post-Fordist times), and texts that evince more broadly the saturation of neoliberal rationality throughout the social sphere. Belonging to the latter category, novels such as Jonathan Franzen's *Freedom* (2010) or Benjamin Kunkel's *Indecision* (2005)—to summon two examples of an expansive corpus—bring into relief the often-invisible patterns of thought that orient our relationship to the market. The bourgeois characters that people theses novels experience freedom, the ethos of "choice," as a sort of oppression. Here, for example, is Franzen's Patty Berglund elaborating the implications of the novel's title: "By almost any standard, she led a luxurious life. She had all day every day to figure out some decent and satisfying way to live, and yet all she ever seemed to get for all her choices and all her freedom was more miserable. The autobiographer is almost forced to the conclusion that she pitied herself for being free."[35] Plagued by a similar ennui, the protagonist of Kunkel's *Indecision*, Dwight Wilmerding, is prone to meditating on the "Uses of Freedom." Faced with the possibility of a trip to Ecuador, in pursuit of an unrealized love, Dwight reflects that, "I was trembling. After all here was a new place, therefor a new life, and hence an occasion for some quaking at the prospect of doing right away, if you want to, and can make up your mind, a wide variety of things in this world."[36] The antidote to this conception of freedom as oppressive superfluity is, in Kunkel's novel, commitment to the conjoined ideals of love and democratic socialism—the reclamation and revivification of the demos invoked by Brown. *Indecision*, like *Freedom*, makes the compulsion of the market audible. But it also betrays a growing crisis of governmentality amongst not merely the working classes but the bourgeoisie as well.

This cultural crisis is today deepened by crises of accumulation that threaten to cast broad swathes of the middle classes into the realm of the insecure. A constellation of recent novels—texts such as Dave Eggers's *A Hologram for the King* (2013) and Raphael Chirbes's *On the Edge* (2016)—tell stories of redundancy and precarity amongst the bourgeoisie. These books illuminate forms of neoliberal devaluation. The temporality they inhabit and critique, then, is that of accumulation by fabrication. Set adrift by the whims of the market, the white men of a certain age that people these narratives struggle for psychological integrity and financial solvency. Freelance consultant Alan Clay, the hero of Eggers's novel, is "virtually broke, nearly unemployed," which is to say he's neither broke nor unemployed, but symbolic of each of these states and the existential as well as economic crises they signify.[37] Alan—having just missed out on a crucial deal to provide the blast-resistant glass to lower Manhattan's nascent Freedom Tower—finds himself in pursuit of a hypothetical IT contract for a chimeric city in Saudi Arabia. Alan's underemployment finds no cure in the Gulf though, and the aimless, idle days he spends waiting for a promised meeting with King Abdullah prompt him to reflect that: "This wasn't the freedom [he] sought. He wanted to be free to give his presentation, to get confirmation of the deal."[38] The freedom he imagines, in other words, can only be realized through capitalist belonging, rather than in the transcendence of commodity rationality or relations. For Alan, the silent compulsion of the market persists, even when he himself has been cast into the growing ranks of the lumpen bourgeoisie. But the fragility of that nostalgic fidelity—both its subject and its object—is, in Eggers's novel, made perfectly plain.

It is, too, in Chirbes's *On the Edge*, a novel of the economic crisis in Spain. *On the Edge* is set in the near-inland village of Olba, the current malaise of which is owed to the deflation of the housing bubble. The identikit developments recently thrown up along the coast—homes constructed with cheap materials and financed by fictive capital, now unoccupied or uncompleted—obscure the village's view of the sea. And they signal the redundant vocation of the novel's narrator, Esteban; dispossessed of his modest carpentry workshop after an ill-timed real estate investment, Esteban mourns the passing of a working life he had never embraced. He reflects,

> You discover the irritating calm of mornings with no alarm clock going off, the day like a meadow stretching out toward the horizon, limitless time, an unbounded landscape, no flocks graze in that infinite space, not a building to be seen, not even the silhouette of a tree. Just you walking in the void. Hell is a derelict warehouse, a silent hangar filled only with a terrible emptiness. In the end, the divine curse of earning our daily bread seems almost agreeable, the sound of alarm clocks, water gushing out of faucets or showers, the bubbling of the coffee pot, the hustle and bustle of morning traffic.[39]

Esteban shares this sense of emptiness with his former employees, whose resentment he feels acutely. "They hate me," he recognizes, "because I've smashed the milk jug they were carrying on their heads . . . but I'm not to blame for their dreams, I didn't encourage them. . . . I exchanged money for labor. . . . No dreams were in the contract."[40] Esteban highlights here the futility of his workers' ethical investment in their labor. And he perceives, more broadly, the declining efficacy of capitalist ideology in the current conjuncture. "A century ago," he reflects, "[business] signified action and progress, but now it's a synonym of other words heavy with negative energy: exploitation, egotism, wastefulness."[41]

Esteban's sensitivity to the ebbing spirit of capital is bound up in his own descent from security to insecurity. "What about *my* fragile state" he asks, "does anyone care about that?"[42] In the new order brought about by the crisis, there are two classes—one "proudly leave[s] the mall with bulging shopping bags," while the other "[rummages] around in the dumpsters"[43]— and Esteban increasingly feels a part of the latter. The crisis, he reflects, "has made us all equal again, brought us all down to the same level, everyone on the floor."[44] The "us" here excludes the rarified denizens of the mall. And it includes the underemployed migrant worker (compelled toward Spain by the consequences of primitive accumulation on the periphery), the exploited laborer, and the fallen members of the middle classes—the subjects, in other words, of neoliberal capital's three temporalities. This shared insecurity, though, does not, in *On the Edge*, translate into a politically effective solidarity. When Esteban invokes the class struggle—a deep element of his familial inheritance; his father was a socialist radical who fought for the Republican side in the Spanish Civil War—it is always with a question mark, and in the past tense: "Wasn't it the determining factor that impregnated and marked everything? The engine of world history?" If his father "still believes we're in the middle of a war and . . . the most interesting battle is yet to come," Esteban is rather more skeptical.[45] He is resigned to his nightly card game at the bar, and the constant litigation of how it all went wrong.

Though absent from *On the Edge*'s narrative, the potentiality of resistance is evinced by the novel's form. Esteban's testimony is occasionally interrupted by other voices, which join with, rather than displace, his own. As they accumulate, these solos acquire a kind of choral quality, even if the social realities they convey are defined by dissonance rather than harmony. A newly unemployed carpenter reflects that "I don't know exactly what I would be capable of doing to you—to you, who've got everything—but I do have a rifle at home."[46] "Where are the Euros of yesteryear?" the fallen entrepreneur laments: "What became of those lovely purple notes? They fell as fast as dead leaves on a windy autumn day and rotted in the mud."[47] Another of Esteban's former employees recounts his earlier turn as a garbage collector, a job that afforded him a privileged insight into the "smell of the twenty-first century," the overflowing trash can, which mingles and melds with the fragrances of gasoline and lush, floral gardens. Just as these distinct odors become "a single smell," the brief "I" interludes that intersect with Esteban's narrative constitute a differential unity that, while expressing (like the superfluity of waste) decay and decomposition, evokes, as well, the multiple vectors and dialects of contemporary anti-capitalist critique.

In Olba, this critique remains latent; the term "struggle" signifies, there, private suffering rather than collective rebellion. But as Esteban ruminates over his beer, the *Indignados*, in their multitudes, are occupying the squares of many Spanish cities—affirming the idea that the most interesting battle is still to come.[48] The possibilities of this imminent (or immanent) struggle are explored with a particular urgency by Rachel Kushner's novel *The Flamethrowers* (2013). Set against the backdrop of neoliberalism's 1970s emergence, *The Flamethrowers* connects processes of accumulation by fabrication in postindustrial Manhattan to crises of capitalist ideology in the Italian auto industry and the primitive accumulation of rubber in Brazil. Illuminating the three temporalities of contemporary capital, the novel brings into view as well the manifold modes of resistance that are articulated therein.

The abandoned industrial spaces of lower Manhattan have been converted into lofts occupied by artists and those keen to derive economic or cultural capital from their work. The crew of artists and gallerists that the novel's protagonist Reno run with all affect a vaguely anti-capitalist air. Sandro Valera—estranged heir to an Italian tire and motorcycle empire—works in a minimalist idiom, constructing large aluminum boxes, empty and gleaming. The objects evoke the assembly line, but also elide it. The boxes were fabricated by hand at a boutique facility in Connecticut and their exchange value has nothing to do with the labor that was put into them or any practicable utility they might have. Another artist, Sammy, completes a heroic performance piece, presumably designed to impress the tyranny of industrial time, in which he punches a clock every hour on the hour for a year. Gordon Matta-Clark (the actual historical figure), re-enchants abandoned factories, warehouses, and piers by carving holes into their exteriors—transforming them into "cathedral[s] of water and light."[49] Each of these artists critiques the violence of the commodity form from a position of self-conscious remove. "I don't make a *wage*," Reno's friend Ronnie puts it. "I'm an artist, I'm not part of the system."[50] None of them reckon with their complicity in the transformation of the cityscape—a process of social and economic dispossession, facilitated by financial elites and enabled by the city's bankruptcy in 1975, which pushed the underclasses to the margins of the metropolis. Nor do they meditate on the fate of those displaced or devalued by the city's deindustrialization. There is one exception: Burdmoore, erstwhile member of the real late-60s activist group the Motherfuckers, longs for the day "when the people of the Bronx wake up, the sisters and brothers out in Brooklyn," and reclaim their right to the city.[51]

When Reno, herself an aspiring artist, travels to Italy with her lover Sandro, the peripheral and dispossessed enter the foreground. Uncomfortably immersed in the Valera world, Reno begins to learn more about the history and present of the company and its cultures of production. In the postwar moment, "'everyone [had] his own little auto, put-putting around, well enough paid at Valera to buy a Valera, and tires for it, and gas."[52] As this Fordist idyll fades, its ideological armature is also diminished. Sandro's brother Roberto has instituted particularly punitive shop-floor policies. The workers live in squalor; and "their wives and children put together Moto Valera ignition sets at the kitchen table, working all night because they were paid by the piece, whole families contracted under piecework, which was practically slave labor."[53] Though many of the factories remain open, the post-Fordist paradigm—spatially and temporally diffuse forms of production; devalued labor—is taking hold. In response, the workers are in revolt—halting the assembly line and joining leftist youths in the streets.

The piecework performed in the home—"practically slave labor"—resembles the debt peonage of the Indians in Brazil who have long harvested the rubber for Valera tires. The Tappers run "from tree to tree, coated in sweat and jungle damp, zigzagging until . . . you are ready to collapse, feeling like your head is in a cloud of ammonia, dizzy, confused, pain shooting up your spine, muscles twisted into torn rags."[54] This brutal regime of labor—overseen by a patrão whose tools are "the cheap muzzle-loader, mock drownings with water poured over a facecloth"[55]—helped fuel the "postwar miracle" in Italy and furnished the Brazilian government with enough money to construct from nothing the "all-inclusive concrete utopia" of Brasilia.[56] While Fordism gives way to post-Fordism in Italy and across the advanced capitalist world, the primitive accumulation of rubber in the Amazon persists, and the ranks of the tappers continue to grow, as the conditions of indenture are passed from one generation to the next. The patrão has a monopoly on the instruments of violence—"by the laws of harmony, you cannot both have guns"—so the only route of resistance available to the tapper is escape: "The green tree ferns pound into and out of view, branches scrape you, your feet are numb. You trip, you fall, you get up, you keep running."[57]

The tappers themselves are not represented in the 1977 movement in Italy. But the subjects of primitive accumulation, and the methods of resistance available to them, are. Italy's Northern bourgeoisie, Antonio Gramsci observed in the 1920s, reduced the South to an "exploitable colon[y] . . . enslaved to the banks and the parasitic industrialism of the North."[58] The

Valera workers both within the factory and beyond it—on the assembly line and at the kitchen table—are migrants from the agrarian South, compelled toward the industries of the North by extractive forms of land rent. In the movement, industrial laborers—displaced by primitive accumulation, exploited by expanded reproduction, and increasingly degraded by accumulation by fabrication—are joined by a diversity of contingents: the university students ("bespectacled and grave"), and ragtag bands of youth from peripheral slums—kids who "have no part in bourgeois life." In keeping with the Autonomist tradition, members of the movement set their own prices for commodities and services—"their own rent, their own bus fare"—and occupy spaces abandoned by capital. The factory workers carry their tire irons to the barricades, using the tools of their trade to resist the creeping redundancy of their trade. The ragged youth paint their faces and chant ironic slogans: "We want nothing! More work, less pay! Down with the people, up with the bosses!"[59]

Finding herself entangled in the movement in Rome—after taking flight from the unfaithful Sandro—Reno is struck by "the 'we' of it," the adhesive intimacy of the disparate bodies that converge in the square. But she is sensitive too to the different demands invoked and different tactics deployed by the different "sections" that comprise the collective body of the demonstration. Some are more open to violence than others (though everyone is armed: "The gun was a tool like the screwdriver was a tool, and they all carried them").[60] Some desire the bourgeois security that has been promised them, and others work—in spiritual accord with the fleeing tapper in Brazil—to evade capture by any capitalist rationality.

The neoliberal present is composed of multiple temporalities, wherein different forms of accumulation and governance are paradigmatic. The contemporary critique of capital is limited when it elides this complexity and assumes instead one unitary neoliberal rationality. As I have argued here, we need to clarify both the distinction between and interrelation of the moment of primitive accumulation, the moment of expanded reproduction, and the moment of accumulation by fabrication. Defining this interrelation is less a question of synthesis than of "articulation"—a joining wherein the constitutive elements maintain their difference. The three temporalities of neoliberalism form, in this sense, what Althusser termed a "complex unity," and this phrase also captures the dynamics of any pan-temporal opposition to the logics of capital. The dispossessed small farmer in Bengal and laid-off carpenter in Spain—the indentured tapper in Brazil and underemployed IT contractor in the United States—are separated by thousands of miles, as by divergent experiences and aspirations. However stark, these contradictions do not occlude the possibility of meaningful solidarity. In our eagerness to conjure the latter, we appeal to the universalisms of the "precariat" or the "multitude," anticipatory imaginaries that carry an urgent resonance. But even as we enunciate this provisional vocabulary of collectivity, we must remain attuned to the unique languages of critique emanating from the unique moments of contemporary capital—the discordant and accordant sounds of their articulation.

Notes

1. Though the historiographic literature tends to locate the political and economic origins of neoliberalism in the 1970s, Michel Foucault, in his 1978–1979 lectures at the Collège de France, notably highlighted the proto-neoliberal significance of the ordoliberals in postwar Germany, who imagined the market and its rationality as the foundation for the reconstituted German state. The intellectual history of neoliberalism, meanwhile, has even deeper origins. In the 1930s, economists and philosophers such as Friedrich Hayek and Ludwig von Mises formulated a critique of Keynesianism that associated the latter with "totalitarian" forms of collectivism such as Nazism and communism. Government planning, these "Austrian School" thinkers avowed, ultimately led to the negation of individual freedom. The realization of that freedom, Hayek, von Mises, and the other attendants at the famous 1947 Mont Pelerin meeting insisted, required the liberation of market forces and generalization of market logics. While the Keynesian consensus prevailed in the immediate postwar period, neoliberal thinking took root in and spread throughout think tanks and other ideological state apparatuses; when the postwar political-economic order was thrown into crisis in the early 1970s, the already insidious ideology of neoliberalism found concrete political expression.

2. Karl Marx, *Capital* Volume One, trans. Ben Fowkes (London: Penguin Books, 1990 [1867]), 915.

3. Marx, *Capital*, 874.

4. Marx, *Capital*, 875.

5. J. Arbuthnot, *An Inquiry into the Connection between the Present Price of Provisions, etc.*, 124, 129, cited in Marx, *Capital*, 888–889.

6. John Locke, *Two Treatises of Government* (New York: Hafner, 1947 [1689]), 139.

7. Marx, *Capital*, 918.

8. Marx, *Capital*, 899.

9. Hannah Arendt, *Origins of Totalitarianism* (New York: Schocken Books, 1951), 148.

10. Pratyush Chandra and Dipankar Basu, "Neoliberalism and Primitive Accumulation in India," *Radical Notes*, February 9, 2007. http://www.countercurrents.org/chandra090207.htm.

11. Marx, *Capital*, 896.

12. I borrow the term "wageless" from Michael Denning; see Michael Denning, "Wageless Life," *New Left Review*, 66 (November–December 2010), 79–97.

13. Marx, *Capital*, 899.

14. Michel Foucault, *The Birth of Biopolitics: Lectures at the Collège de France, 1978–1979* (New York: Picador, 2008), 120.
15. Foucault, *Biopolitics*, 270–271.
16. Wendy Brown, *Undoing the Demos* (New York: Zone Books, 2015), 31, 35.
17. Brown, *Undoing the Demos*, 35–36.
18. Brown, *Undoing the Demos*, 41.
19. Luc Boltanski and Eve Chiapello, *The New Spirit of Capitalism*, trans. Gregory Elliott (London: Verso, 2005), 8, 58.
20. In keeping with this rhetorical shift, one common anti-union tactic of contemporary firms is to reclassify jobs as "managerial" so that they exist outside of the bargaining unit.
21. Rosa Luxemburg, *The Accumulation of Capital*, trans. Agnes Schwarzschild (New York: Routledge Classics, 2003 [1913]), 257.
22. See David Harvey, *The New Imperialism* (Oxford: Oxford University Press, 2003), 137–82.
23. Marx, *Capital*, 919, 1125.
24. Lauren Berlant, "Precarity Talk: A Virtual Roundtable with Lauren Berlant, Judith Butler, Bojana Cvejić, Isabell Lorey, Jasbir Puar, and Ana Vujanović," Jasbir Puar, ed., *TDR: The Drama Review*, 56:4 (Winter 2012): 166.
25. Gabriel Winant, "We Found Love in a Hopeless Place: Affect Theory for Activists," *n+1* 22 (Spring 2015). https://nplusonemag.com/issue-22/essays/we-found-love-in-a-hopeless-place/.
26. Judith Butler, "For and Against Precarity," *Tidal* 1 (December 2011). http://tidalmag.org/pdf/tidal1_the-beginning-is-near.pdf.
27. see Laurent Berlant, *Cruel Optimism* (Durham, NC: Duke University Press, 2011), 1–51.
28. Stuart Hall, Chas Critcher, Tony Jefferson, John Clarke and Brian Roberts, *Policing the Crisis: Mugging, the State, and Law and Order* (London: The MacMillan Press, 1978), 217.
29. Frantz Fanon, *The Wretched of the Earth*, trans. Constance Farrington (New York: Grove Press, 1963 [1961]), 38.
30. Some of the phrasing in this paragraph is reproduced in another essay of mine "Historicizing Repression and Ideology," *Mediations*, 30: 2 (August 2017).
31. Marlon James, *The Book of Night Women* (New York: Riverhead, 2010), 71.
32. Amitav Ghosh, *Sea of Poppies* (New York: Picador, 2008), 28–29.
33. Ghosh, *Sea of Poppies*, 78.
34. Ghosh, *Sea of Poppies*, 112.
35. Jonathan Franzen, *Freedom* (New York: Farrar, Straus, and Giroux, 2010), 181.
36. Benjamin Kunkel, *Indecision* (New York: Random House, 2005), 10–11.
37. Dave Eggers, *A Hologram for the King*, 4.
38. Eggers, *A Hologram for the King*, 184.
39. Raphael Chirbes, *On the Edge*, trans. Margaret Jull Costa (New York: New Directions, 2016), 210–211.
40. Chirbes, *On the Edge*, 268.
41. Chirbes, *On the Edge*, 212.
42. Chirbes, *On the Edge*, 225.
43. Chirbes, *On the Edge*, 224.

44. Chirbes, *On the Edge*, 225.
45. Chirbes, *On the Edge*, 225, 273.
46. Chirbes, On the Edge, 73.
47. Chirbes, On the Edge, 397.
48. The Spanish boom of the early 1990s was concentrated in cities such as Barcelona and Seville; "all the money," Esteban observes, "flowed down those two great drains" (246). The cities themselves, though, are not simply sites of generalized prosperity, but spaces wherein the contradictions of capital are clarified and contested. The absorption of the surplus through urbanization, as David Harvey highlights, has always depended upon processes of "creative destruction" that evict and degrade the city's poorer residents. In the city, in other words, the intimacy of expanded reproduction and accumulation by fabrication is brought into stark relief. And it precisely this intimacy, and the inequities of its effects, that the *Indignados* are resisting.
49. Rachel Kushner, *The Flamethrowers* (New York: Scribner, 2013), 97.
50. Kushner, *The Flamethrowers*, 201.
51. Kushner, *The Flamethrowers*, 166.
52. Kushner, *The Flamethrowers*, 266.
53. Kushner, *The Flamethrowers*, 250.
54. Kushner, *The Flamethrowers*, 215.
55. Kushner, *The Flamethrowers*, 214.
56. Kushner, *The Flamethrowers*, 367.
57. Kushner, *The Flamethrowers*, 217.
58. Antonio Gramsci, *The Southern Question*, trans. Pasquale Verdicchio (Chicago: Guernica, 2005 [1926]), 70.
59. Kushner, *The Flamethrowers*, 275–276.
60. Kushner, *The Flamethrowers*, 288.

[3] STEPHEN SHAPIRO

FOUCAULT, NEOLIBERALISM,
ALGORITHMIC GOVERNMENTALITY,
AND THE LOSS OF LIBERAL CULTURE

Neoliberalism as a New Epoch of Historical Capitalism

Even by 1978, Michel Foucault was aware of claims that *neoliberalism* was not anything new or different from *liberalism*, and that "hidden beneath the appearances of a neo-liberalism," there was "just a way of establishing strict market relations in society" or a "cover for a generalized administrative intervention by the state."[1] These responses "ultimately make neo-liberalism out to be nothing at all, or anyway, nothing but always the same thing, and always the same thing but worse."[2] Against these dismissals, Foucault contended that neoliberalism was a new, significantly different, and epoch-making, phase of historical capitalism.

Understanding liberalism as emerging around 1750 and continuing, more or less, as a dominant mode of social organization until the 1970s, Foucault felt that neoliberalism challenged the three main characteristics of liberalism: the marketplace as a site that delivered the "natural" truth of prices, a place of "veridiction," wherein supply-demand equilibrium would reveal the true value of commodities; a State that limited its involvement in the marketplace based on the notion that greater social utility would result from the State's self-restraint; and a geography, wherein Europe (later the West, more broadly) was considered to be a "region of unlimited economic development" that could expand and control the "world market."[3] Additionally, liberalism construes the need for "already given political [civil] society" as a necessary mediating feature that would both separate the State from the marketplace, while also allowing for their buffered inter-connection.[4]

Neoliberal perspectives, in contrast, make no claims for the marketplace's naturalism, the State's inactivity, or any need for a prophylactic civil society. Instead, advocates for neoliberalism see competition as an artificial "structure with formal properties," one that *can* and *must* be created, established, and promoted by the State's "permanent vigilance, activity, and intervention," to ensure "economic regulation through the price mechanism."[5] Unlike liberalism, which saw the marketplace as ultimately harmonizing and equalizing, satisfying the needs of both parties through the act of exchange, so long as it remained free from the corrupting influence of governmental actors, neoliberalism has a "theory of pure competition." While liberalism told itself that all could prosper in a commercial society, neoliberalism is not merely comfortable with the presence of consequential inequality after commodity exchange, it often seeks the creation of disparity in order to spur disruptive innovation. Unlike Joseph Schumpeter, who felt that cyclical downturns would help motivate entrepreneurial investment, neoliberalism, in Foucault's eyes, wants the State to catalyze permanent transformation without regard to the business cycle. Neoliberals are reluctant to accept the temporality of the market's internal rhythms, which they believe to be yet another form of naturalism. Instead they want the State to endlessly promote the marketplace.

Neoliberals do not share classic liberalism's fear of an overly intrusive State. Instead, they fear the reverse, contending that the State has become too sedentary and submissive before a bureaucracy that was historically created to contain and domesticate its (absolutist) desire for action. Because neoliberal economists saw a capitalist market in crisis from the 1920s, they sought to reawaken the State, by infusing it with the marketplace's activity, so that the State could be used, in turn, to reinvigorate the capitalist market by expanding its domain to civil society and other lifeworld realms that were previously incompletely financialized.

Foucault's definition of neoliberalism as the search for an active State, rather than liberalism's passive or recused one, helps answer what has often been felt as a riddle about the recent period as dominated by neoliberal policies. On the one hand, neoliberalism insists on the necessity of relying on the competitive market as the normative model for all institutions, while on the other, it vastly amplifies the State's institutional violence, as seen in the United States with the renewal of imperial adventures and punitive domestic acts, not least with the onset of the prison industrial complex and aggressive metropolitan policing against non-white citizens and denizens.[6]

In their project to reconstitute the State, Foucault claimed that neoliberals' overarching "problem[atic]" was "how the overall exercise of political power can be modelled on the principles of a market economy." Neoliberalism is, therefore, a "government style," not its absence, as classic liberalism insisted. Here Foucault uses the term "government" in a wider way, "not in the narrow and current sense of the supreme instance of executive and administrative decisions in State systems, but in the broad sense ... of mechanisms and procedures intended to conduct [wo]men, to drive their conduct, to conduct their conduct."[7] Neoliberalism is not merely a set of economic beliefs about capitalism, but is instead to be seen in a larger sense as a sociocultural project that seeks to reconfigure the State, civil society, and marketplace trinity by directing its attention to that which had separated the State from the marketplace: civil society. Neoliberals sought to erase liberalism's public and private distinctions, along with its attendant features of a disinterested public sphere, bourgeois sociability, and cultural institutions, exemplified in the early nineteenth-century ideal of an autonomous research university and an enlightened republic of letters. As we will see, the end of liberal culture has implications for the function of contemporary American writing, especially for the form of the novel, as a mode of cultural expression that, from the eighteenth century onwards, emerged from and often exemplified liberal civil society.

If neoliberalism is understood as the replacement of liberalism's ideal of *homo oeconomicus*, human as civilizing commodity exchanger, in favor of what we might call *homo astutus*, human as cunning speculator and competitive entrepreneur, one fundamentally hostile to civil society, the challenge that Foucault poses in *The Birth of Biopolitics*, his 1977–1978 lecture series on neoliberalism, is three-fold.

Firstly, Foucault suggests that much of his past writing will have little contemporary efficacy, as he argues that we have moved to a new dominant mode of power that is significantly different from what most of his prior work has described. Throughout the 1970s, Foucault elucidated a large-scale historical sequence that contrasted the historic regime of what he called sovereignty from its replacement, which he initially called discipline, but eventually also named as liberalism. The sovereign system was one fundamentally grounded on issues of repressive juridicality, especially with regards the relationship between the sovereign and a *subject of rights*. The liberal system was based on productive truth-formation, what Foucault called veridiction. Liberalism was grounded on a "set of practices and a regime of truth" that created "an apparatus (*dispositif*) of knowledge-power," wherein the naturalized "division between true and false" established a "transactional reality" (or social construction) that produced a different form of subjectivity, a subject based on interests rather than rights.[8] This historical shift involved a different target, operation, and set of tactics. While sovereignty worked on the outside (of the body, for instance) and dealt with acts, liberalism shifted gears to work on the inside (of the soul or psyche) and construct identities based on binarized oppositions, such as that between normality and deviance.

Neoliberalism, according to Foucault, dispenses with liberalism's veridicatory project in favor of a competitive ecology. If we accept Foucault's periodization, then our neoliberal moment is one that is neither primarily juridical nor epistemological in orientation, but agonistic in ways best characterized by game theory's notion that actors must calculate their selfish activity based on the tactical assumption that all other actors are simultaneously calculating how best to maximize their self-interest. If we exist in a neoliberal lifeworld that is not based on liberalism's regime of truth formation, then the often-elegiac commentary on the current condition of a post-truth, post-pluralist consensus society is wrong to assume that a damaged liberalism might still be repaired. Instead, Foucault suggests that this entire formation has become largely superseded within the contemporary reconfiguration of the capitalist world-system. Hence, if Foucault claimed that liberal power operated in *productive*, rather than the *repressive* modes dominant in the age of sovereignty, his discussion of neoliberalism as the new dominant implies *the need for yet a new understanding of power*, one that is neither repressive, nor productive, but something else entirely. In this search, Foucault's prior writings are mainly useful more for providing terms of contrast in order to better discern the shape of the emerging contemporary.

Secondly, Foucault's discussion of neoliberalism's competitive-power raises the question not only of culture in general, but literary form specifically. While Foucault rarely ventured into literary studies, his understanding of genre treats it by highlighting an exemplary form as enmeshed within the dominant tendencies of each period. Considering tragedy, he saw it as "always, essentially . . . about right . . . there is a fundamental, essential kinship between tragedy . . . and public right" and, inferentially, the question of sovereignty.[9] In a period when sovereignty is no longer dominant, another cultural form emerges—the novel: "there is probably an essential kinship between the novel and the problem of the norm."[10]

Foucault's assumption about the links between liberalism and the novel mirror several influential accounts of the novel, such as those by Ian Watt and Lionel Trilling.[11] Similarly, the claim matches accounts that the novel helped enable liberalism's constellation and manner of constructing group and individual subjectivity. Extending Marx and Engels's discussion in *The German Ideology* (1932) of civil society as an "illusory community" [*illusorische Gemeinschaftlichkeit*], Benedict Anderson influentially argued that the novel's rise within print capitalism helped bind readers together within a liberal, national, imagined community.[12] No matter its formal differences or periodizing styles, the novel magnetized and cemented readers together into a collective identity through their shared reading experience. Within American literature, the goal of creating a "Great American Novel" became a particular shibboleth throughout the twentieth century as part of the search for the cultural glue that could hold together a liberal pluralist consensus for a nation of immigrants. On the other hand, the notion that the novel was different from prior forms of long fiction due to its modelling and rehearsing of the liberal subject's developmental interiority through examples like the *Bildungsroman* has been commonsensical ever since Georg Lukács's claim that the novel is separate from epic because "the novel tells of the adventure of interiority, the content of the novel is the story of the soul that goes to find itself."[13]

If the novel stands as one of liberalism's great cultural achievements, as a form hewn from and indicative of its intrinsic tensions between self and society, then what is its fate in a neoliberal era that dispenses with that contradiction? Does neoliberalism portend the end of the novel-form as a cultural dominant, or, at least, the novel as still conventionally practiced, in favor of other genres of expression, media, and manner of organization? Similarly, does neoliberalism also put into question the ideal of the liberal university and its seminar room as a site that both stages the expression of individuality and rehearses the process of coming to amiable consensus through conversational interplay? Can these institutions and cultural forms hold together in the same way as formerly if the motivating compacts of liberalism are no longer upheld?

Finally, do Foucault's claims from the 1970s remain useful in the current moment? Should they be discounted or extended in ways unforeseen by even Foucault himself? Does the recent return of the far right, epitomized by Trump's US election and the UK's Brexit vote mark a periodizing end to comfort with globalizing markets as calls emerge for neo-mercantilist, insular ethno-nationalist protectionism that seem directly to replace neoliberalism's commitment to the free trade of goods, services, and labor? Or are these *cri de coeurs* simply a tactical deployment that looks to smash definitively the last remnants of liberalism's civil society? Is anti-globalism just a means to further erode the rational-critical public sphere's counterweight to the State's activity by accelerating a politics that casts suspicion on institutional truth claims based on the expertise of a disinterested bureaucracy and deflates the university's discussion protocols through social media trolling?

In what follows, I will contend that the relatively recent implementation of advanced computational equations, activities clustered under the name "algorithm," not least within the retail and service sectors of experiential consumption, including social media platforms, indicates the arrival of a new form or phase of neoliberalism, through what Antoinette Rouvroy calls algorithmic governmentality, wherein she yokes Foucault's insights on neoliberalism with an awareness of the role of big data.[14] The characteristics of this new phase could not be easily charted by Foucault in the 1970s, as he was not in a historical position to be fully aware of the new computational techniques resulting from the massification of increasingly cheaper and more powerful hardware and software, and their deployment in State-assisted deregulation and financial derivatives. Hence any search for our current form of neoliberalism means that while Foucault's writings from the 1970s might be a necessary starting point, they no longer remain a sufficient conclusion. To paraphrase Fredric Jameson, we need to comprehend the emerging cultural logic of late neoliberalism in its algorithmic modality.

Here I want to pursue Rouvroy's arguments to see what impact they may have on our registration of contemporary American writing and culture. Since Rouvroy's arguments self-consciously deploy Foucault's terminology, which he, in turn, used as the framework for his comments on neoliberalism, it is necessary to revisit his concepts of government and governmentality as he developed them through the mid to late 1970s Collège de France lectures to best gauge his own understanding of neoliberalism.[15] While Foucault's arguments have been a frequent touchstone for many discussions of neoliberalism, they have not been clearly deployed, for reasons explained in the text to follow, even by his otherwise dedicated advocates. Therefore, a somewhat patient exegesis of Foucault's claims can still provide a fruitful direction for considering the state of American writing and culture.

Situating Governmentality

Despite prior discussions of governmentality, a brief look backwards is necessary for several reasons before we can fully understand Foucault's comments about the rise of neoliberalism and Rouvroy's about neoliberal algorithmic politics and culture.[16]

Firstly, until the complete publication of his posthumously edited lectures, anglophone critics have often been misled by their unavoidable partial and incomplete reception of Foucault's work throughout the 1970s. As a consequence of the lectures' inaccessibility, scholars were left to extrapolate larger claims from highly discrete publications of single lectures outside of their context within an annual set of usually twelve lectures, which Foucault clearly orchestrated as a coherent unit. The deduction of the whole from scattered parts has meant that many prior discussions of the lectures' claims depended on assumptions that could not be firmly grounded once their larger horizon over several years was finally made visible.

Even with these lectures now almost completely before us, important caveats remain. In what cannot be over-estimated, Foucault never brought these inquiries into (book) publication. Between 1976 and 1980, Foucault used the lectures to investigate an aspect of social management that he considered to be categorically different from the techniques of discipline, which he had mainly detailed in *Discipline and Punish* and *The History of*

Sexuality, Volume 1.[17] Yet this project was going to be difficult to perceive for his print readers, as it remained largely absent from his publications. The last chapter of *History of Sexuality, Volume 1* is mainly a revision of his final lecture from the 1975–1976 series, *Society Must Be Defended*, where he announces a new concept of *biopower*.[18] Because Foucault uses that chapter to mark the distinction between the early modern sovereign's right to take life against the modern production of life, many readers would have necessarily assumed that the schematic was simply meant to reinscribe the prior pages' opposition of (absolutist) sovereign repression to disciplinary production of deviance.

The intervening lectures make clear, however, that this discussion of biopower was meant to *announce* and *initiate* Foucault's exploration of a set of techniques that are distinct from discipline in fundamental ways. Hence, in terms of the monograph's coherence, the last chapter is misplaced and might have been better left out entirely. Nonetheless, this turn to something that is not discipline began a sequence that led up to and included his lectures on neoliberalism, and continued into the following year's lectures, published as *On the Government of the Living* (1979–1980).

After the 1976 publication of *History of Sexuality, Volume I*, Foucault's next book publication, in 1984 (the year of his death) was the second volume of *History of Sexuality*, named *The Use of Pleasure*. Translated into English the next year, this volume begins by acknowledging an entirely different turn from the ones "his auditors at the Collège de France" would have expected and had the "patience to wait for its [published] outcome."[19] From 1980, the lectures entitled *Subjectivity and Truth* signal his research's turn to post-classical Greek and Roman treatments of the ascetic self that ran, alas, until his premature decease. In other words, not only does Foucault use *The Use of Pleasure* to announce the end of his sequence from 1975 to 1980, but also its effective silencing, as he seems to have decided to never bring its research into the wider circulation through book publication.[20] So apart from a few isolated lectures that were published before his death, the overarching concerns, terminology, and historiography that Foucault used in the second half of the 1970s would remain substantively unknown to those who were not consistent auditors (even at a distance) of his annual lectures. Even when finally published, the lectures were not published consecutively.[21] The consequence of this jumbled publication has been that the step-by-step trajectory of Foucault's argument has not been easily intelligible.

One reason for the necessity of reading the development of his claims in sequence comes from Foucault's own indecision about terminology. For a writer who is often usefully schematic in his claims based on a precise and consistent use of terms, Foucault seems to have had difficulty in deciding on these to his satisfaction. With each year's lectures, his highlighted keyword slightly shifts, as if Foucault was unhappily searching for the best framework. His first published term, for instance, is *biopower*. With this term he meant the means by which "the basic biological features of the human species became the object of a political strategy ... from the eighteenth century."[22] Yet, the term is functionally deployed in only one 1976 lecture, the lecture that would be revised and published as the last chapter of *History of Sexuality, Volume I*. Biopower is briefly mentioned in the first lines of the next lecture (given in 1978 after an intervening sabbatical year) before it is abandoned in favor of the term, *security*. In ensuing years, *security* is then substituted by *regularization*, which is, in turn, replaced in later years by *governmentality*, and then more simply, *government*.

Although Foucault *did* bring the term biopower into publication, thus giving it a certain authority, he swiftly abandoned it in ways that few of his non-Parisian students knew. *Biopolitics* became his first preferred replacement keyword, chosen perhaps because Foucault decided that the process of knowledge formation was a more central definitional aspect to this new mode of power, since the biological was merely the object for its strategy and techniques. Without having access to the lectures, anglophone readers further utilized the concept of biopower beyond its validity within Foucault's own writing, often intermixing biopower and biopolitics indiscriminately.

The flickering terminology means that Foucault's discussion of neoliberalism, as itself a term that only appears in a single year's lectures, has to be embedded within his prior lectures in order for it to appear as something other than an anomalous topic. The context is important for the *Birth of Biopolitics* is exceptional in several ways within Foucault's corpus. The discussion of neoliberalism stands as one of his few focused discussions of post-1945 Euro-American history, let alone contemporary politics (of the 1970s). This seemingly unexpected treatment of the modern and contemporary, however, has a logical presence within Foucault's work only to the degree that it is placed within the trajectory of the prior years' lectures on the rise and operation of historical liberalism from the mid-eighteenth century onwards.

The discussion of liberalism and neoliberalism also marks another shift for Foucault. For he now moves his mode of historiography away from the manifesto opening of *The Archaeology of Knowledge* that announced the study of micro-history and ruptures.[23] The temporal units within his 1970s lectures become increasingly ones of greater durations and historical overlaps, rather than sequential breaks. His use of longer historical phases also accepts the role of persistent national particularities. Just as Foucault acknowledges the difference between the Austrian and English strategies after 1815, he understands German ordo/neoliberalism as having a different emphasis, cause, and temporality than the American version, in ways implying that anglophone and German-speaking cultural differences endure, no matter what governmental form may be used at any moment.[24] While there are overlaps, transmissions, and linkages between various national emphases, they also have noteworthy differences that Foucault acknowledges in ways significantly different from *Discipline and Punish*'s assumption that French evidentiary material could stand in unremarkably for "the West" in his history of penality.

The turn to longer historical phases may be conjoined to his discussion of the contemporary moment as likewise an end of a long run. Near the end of *Discipline and Punish* (1975, English translation 1977), Foucault suggests that, "the specificity of the prison and its role as link [to the disciplinary network] are losing something of their purpose."[25] Likewise, in a 1978 interview, Foucault claimed that discipline was in crisis. He felt that it was losing its efficacy as contemporary industrialized societies were becoming "more diverse, different, and independent" and that there were, increasingly, groups who were less willing to be captured or held back by disciplinary protocols (he may have been thinking specifically of the gay sado-masochism milieu).[26] In *Discipline and Punish*, Foucault went on to say that prison was not "indispensable to our kind of society" and was being superseded, in two ways.[27] Firstly, prison's production of delinquency in order to widely cast a net of normalization over the non-incarcerated was proving "ineffective" due to "the growth of great national or international illegalities directly linked to the political and economic apparatuses (financial illegalities, information services, arms and drug trafficking, property speculation)." Secondly, the specific need for the penal apparatus was declining as its function was subject to a "massive transference" to a wider disciplinary network of "medicine, psychology, education, public assistance, 'social work.'"[28]

These claims read today as simultaneously misplaced and prescient for contemporary readers. On the one hand, the claim for imprisonment's decline seems basically wrong, especially for North Americans, who saw the vertiginous expansion of the prison industrial complex from the 1980s onwards. On the other hand, Foucault's insight into the rise of what has been commonly called the FIRE industries of finance, insurance, and real estate matches most accounts of the period's turn to financialized and speculative economic processes often taken as hallmarks of neoliberalism. The hint that these forms of illegality have become diffused through a wider circulatory network has an implicit corollary that (neoliberal) finance and informatics are also becoming imbricated within the wide template of "social work," welfare, and culture, more broadly, from the 1970s onwards.

This passage has been wrongly inferred as indicating that discipline was being replaced by something, which he would later call governmentality. Yet Foucault goes to lengths in the lectures to assert that while governmentality is categorically different from discipline, it is not its sequential replacement. By the late 1970s, he was also becoming more comfortable with allowing for the presence of overlapping modes: "We should not see things as the replacement of a society of sovereignty by a society of discipline, and then of a society of discipline, say, of government. In fact, we have triangle: sovereignty, discipline, and governmental management."[29]

Thus, a more precise understanding would see that while discipline is fading, or becoming more residual, this metamorphosis does not necessarily mean that it is replaced by biopower-governmentality (here used to cover the scansion of his 1970s lectures). If governmentality is not discipline's substitution, but a simultaneous occurrence, then what *does* stand in the space that had been occupied by discipline in a world that is no longer as clearly disciplinized (or liberal governmentalized) as was the case in the nineteenth century? This is neoliberalism.

Foucault suggests that neoliberalism's governmentality does not depend on protocols of disciplinary normalization, but a behaviorism dedicated to subjects orienting themselves to rules that are constantly adjusted. In light of Foucault's suggestion that discipline and its production of a normalized subject was vanishing in the 1970s, Gilles Deleuze proposed the emergence of a society of *control*, but his comments on this are equally foresightful and impressionistic.[30] We will see that Rouvroy's commentary on algorithmic governmentality suggests that even Deleuze's initial description is inadequate.

The last, but not least, motive for placing Foucault's work on neoliberalism within the larger scansion of the work between that which focused on discipline in the early 1970s and the later ones on the technology of the self, from the 1980s onwards, involves the role of culture, as understood with reference to the cultural materialism of Raymond Williams and British Cultural Studies, exemplified, but not monopolized by, Stuart Hall and his implementation of Gramsci. In his introductory lecture of the 1979–1980 series that begins his post-governmentality phase, Foucault explains that he is seeking a "word that corresponds, not to the knowledge useful for those who govern, but to that manifestation of truth correlative to the exercise of power," Foucault chooses alethurgy.[31] If "there is no exercise of power without something like an alethurgy," Foucault adds that if "hegemony is just the fact of being in the position of leading others, of conducting them, and of conducting, as it were, their conduct," then "hegemony cannot be exercised without something like an alethurgy." The use of hegemony in this way is immediately familiar to readers of Gramsci and Gramscian-inflected Cultural

Studies as the term he positioned against rule by (repressive) force and coercion. If there is no "hegemony without alethurgy," we might then place some pressure on Foucault's phrase of the "manifestation of the truth" to read it in a more Gramscian light, at a time when Foucault was actively seeking dialogue with Gramscian members of the Italian Communist Party (PCI, Parti Communiste Italien). Hence Foucault's terms here might be read as meaning that which Gramsci treated with his use of hegemony, as the creation of a sociocultural "common sense."[32] Viewed in this way, the later Foucault can be taken as suggesting that no exercise of power is possible without establishing a manifestation of hegemonic culture. Additionally, when Foucault discusses neoliberalism as a form of "conducting the conduct" of humans, it needs insisting that these are the terms that Gramsci also used in his analysis of how "intellectuals" direct and conduct individuals.[33] Foucault's notion of counter-conduct can similarly be easily replaced with the Gramsci's idea of counter-hegemony.[34] Seen in this way, Foucault's object of analysis from the mid-1970s through the 1980s is fundamentally on the role of culture as a field that allows governmentality's manifestation and operation.

The significance of Foucault's under-recognized turn to cultural studies then brings up yet another aspect of the lectures that will ultimately remain pertinent for any discussion of neoliberalism, datalogics, and American culture and writing. The lectures are far more historically grounded than the book publications, which often are stripped of their magnetizing social class context. For instance, the 1970–1971 lectures on penal theory and institutions has a lengthy discussion of the role of rural grain riots as one of the primary factors leading to the creation of sovereignty. Yet this social history is erased when *Discipline and Punish* opens with the terrific execution of Damiens, the would-be regicide, as the avenue to his explication of sovereignty. Similarly, the 1980–1981 lectures on subjectivity and truth explain that classical-era technologies of the self arose as a tactical response by urban aristocratic elites in 2 CE Rome who were experiencing decline, as their power was eroding due to the arrival of countryside factions demanding an end to oligarchic rule. In all these cases, the ostensibly more philosophical categories of the publications have an attendant history of social crisis charted out in the lectures. This is also the case for Foucault's understanding of why neoliberalism emerged as a response to the crisis of liberalism in post-war Germany and then the 1970s economic crisis in the United States. For Foucault, the establishment of techniques of control and the search for a new hegemony is always catalyzed as a reaction to the demands of more demotic forces and pressure from the lower classes.

The question of culture within historical transformation catalyzed by class struggle, what we might call historical materialism, raises two interlinked questions about resistance. In passing, Foucault suggests that one reason for neoliberalism's ability to replace liberalism was that the socialist movement, broadly defined, ultimately failed to produce a durable alternative lifeworld, despite its initial possibility through Keynesian and New Deal formations, as a result of the left's over-reliance on a nineteenth-century textual canon, rather than instantiating oppositional (institutional) forms. If "there is a really socialist governmentality, then it is not hidden within socialism and its texts. It cannot be deduced from them. It must be invented."[35] Whatever position we take on Foucault's correctness on this claim that lived socialism cannot simply be extrapolated from a dedicated reading of Marx on capital, it might provide the rationale for Foucault's turn to the study of (ancient Greek) fashioning of the self. Foucault might have chosen this otherwise unexpected turn to examine the process of how governmentality was made (or disassembled) in the past, rather than for any desire to emulate the ancient content of that process. This search for the dynamics of a past governmentality transformation might have been investigated in order to find an alternative path beyond neoliberalism. His death, however, foreclosed that avenue.

Secondly, Foucault's suggestion that neoliberalism was carried over into America from Germany because both the American left and right were simultaneously attacking the Fordism of military Keynesianism throughout the 1960s and 1970s.[36] Had the left been more tactically sophisticated in its attack on State bureaucracy, it might have foreseen a course of action that would not ultimately benefit the right. In the space provided by lost opportunities to confront neoliberalism, Rouvroy can be likewise read as suggesting that a similar conjunctural opportunity was lost after the 2008–2011 crisis, which created a vacuum that was filled by the mass onset of the datalogical, which has created a more insistent version of neoliberalism, rather than its replacement. To see the rhythm of historical transformation that Foucault narrates, it helps to review the historical sequence that Foucault charted towards neoliberalism.

Towards Neoliberalism: Foucault's History of the West

The moment for neoliberalism's arrival comes through the longer tale of (Western) Europe and American history that Foucault charts through his 1970s lectures. What Foucault calls the system of suzerainty fell into crisis roughly about and through the Peasants' War (1524–1526).[37] For "the movements of urban revolt and peasant revolt, the conflicts between feudalism and the merchant bourgeoisie," conjoined with concerns about "the status of women, the development of a market economy, the decoupling of the urban and rural economies, the raising or extinction of feudal rent, the status of wage-earners, the speed of literacy" that all became causes for the ensuing Wars of Religion (1562–1598).[38] The general crisis of the sixteenth century thus conclusively ended the medieval dream of reconstituting a universality that would be epitomized by the monolithic rule of the Roman Catholic Church and various national attempts to reconstitute the Roman Empire. As suzerainity unraveled, the system of sovereignty appeared in order to constitute and legitimize "monarchical, authoritarian, administrative, and, ultimately, absolute power."[39]

Sovereign power "is bound up with a form of power that is exercised over the land"—a territory—and it seeks to extract commodities and wealth through "chronologically defined," but discontinuous "systems of taxation and obligation."[40] The "implicit identification of people with [the] monarch, and nation with sovereign" was enabled by the (domestic) marketplace being configured as the site of the monarch's justice, wherein the sovereign protects purchasers from being cheated in weights, measures, and pricing.[41] While the sovereign's majestic authority allows for spectacular displays of consumption and the terrific power to take life, the sovereign State was constructed less through irrational force, than with "apparatuses, institutions, and rules" involving a "theory of the [social] contract and the reciprocal commitment of the sovereign and subjects" that was used "both to restrict and to strengthen royal power."[42] On the one hand, "power as a primal right" by the subject is "to be surrendered, and which constitutes sovereignty."[43] On the other, if the sovereign "oversteps the limit," this transgression is understood as a delegitimizing act of oppression. Juridical limits to what a sovereign might not do are established by a combination of constraints based on claims of natural law and a social contract that will be guided by a *Raison d'Etat*, overseen by governmental advisors who will protect social nature from the State's over-reach.

Largely as a result of pressures from the mid-eighteenth century's "demographic explosion and industrialization," a "new mechanism of power" arose that was "absolutely incompatible with relations of sovereignty."[44] This new, non-sovereign power is the disciplinary one that applies "primarily to bodies," and seeks to "extract time and labor" through "constant surveillance," as "one of the basic tools for the establishment of industrial capitalism."[45] While the theory of sovereignty and public right continues well into the nineteenth century, this endurance was, in the first instance, simply a tactical move through which the promoters of discipline "concealed its mechanism" before it had become more self-sufficient.[46] Unlike the sovereign code of law, discipline invokes a code of normalization through veridiction. This code is not based on juridical mechanisms, but on the formation of truth claims within the human sciences and medicine that were used to buttress a theory of constant struggle against threats to civil society. In this way, nineteenth-century discipline helped advance notions of racialized nationalism, which eventually become interiorized through the concept of a subject's self-division between private desire and public action. Here Foucault's argument about the historical inter-relation of nationalist racism and liberalism's public-private divide echoes Marx's *On the Jewish Question* (1844).

By 1976, Foucault shifts from discussing the "rationalizing and strictly economizing" disciplinary techniques over the individual body to consider a massifying biopolitics that uses the species of population as its unit of analysis.[47] Focusing on "periods of time" involving "forecasts, statistical estimates, and overall measure," biopolitics takes as its starting point the statistical computation of "the birth rate, the mortality rate, various biological disabilities, and the effects of the environment" in order to establish knowable, regular patterns of life.[48] Biopolitics is different from discipline's construction of threatening deviancy or abnormality as it is instead a "reassuring or regulatory . . . technology of security," which seeks "to establish a sort of homeostasis, not by training individuals, but by achieving an overall equilibrium that protects the security of the whole from internal dangers."[49]

The focus on a statistics of safety means that when in 1978 Foucault replaced the term *biopower* with *security* as his overarching category, the new term acts to further highlight the control of danger by recourse to a mathematically enabled knowability. Features of security involve population (as a space of security distinct from sovereignty's territory or discipline's body), the management risk, and a form of normalization different from discipline, one that does not operate like discipline's "binary division between the permitted and the prohibited," but instead "establishes an average considered as optimal," through a "bandwidth of the acceptable that must not be exceeded."[50]

Security stands as the obverse of discipline, both in its scale and operation. While discipline is centripetal, as it "concentrates, focuses, and encloses," the "apparatuses of security" are centrifugal, allowing for the development of ever-wider circuits. Rather than fixing and congealing space through segmentation, security takes the maintenance of circulation as its target. It seeks to use an already given environment in order "to plan a milieu in terms of events or a series of events or possible elements that will have to be regulated within a multivalent and transformative framework" in order to minimize the negative.[51] Discipline pores over details in order to tell "you what you must do at every moment"; security sees these details as neither "good or evil in themselves," but as a "necessary inevitable process," wherein the action is to "respond to a reality in such a way that this response cancels out the reality to which it responds–nullifies it, or limits, checks, or regulates it."[52]

Discipline works by a process Foucault had previously defined as normalization, but now suggests it should be called *normation*. *Normalization*, Foucault argues, should now be used to describe security's distribution of cases with a "population circumscribed in time or space" in order to posit "an optimal model that is constructed in terms of a certain result" and "to get people, movement, and actions to conform to this model."[53] Security seeks to "an interplay between these different distributions of normality . . . the norm is an interplay of differential normalities."[54]

Just as Foucault had argued for the necessary relationship between capitalism and discipline, the same is true of biopower~government: "the development of capitalism would not have been possible without bio-power [security/regularization/governmentality]." The rise of statistical institutions ensured "the adjustment of the accumulation of men to that of capital, the joining of the growth of human groups to the expansion of productive forces and the differential allocation of profit."[55] In this, discipline and biopolitics~governmentality intersect with one another, even though Foucault argues that disciplinary action emerges historically earlier than biopolitics, since the latter requires "complex systems of coordination and centralization" that are more complicated to establish. Similarly, the calculation of the social "distributions around the norm" must wait on the development of apparatuses, like statistics, that can deliver these "scientific" truths.[56] The discipline and governmentality pair can be considered as linked and different in the same way that Marx used the first volume of *Capital* to detail the cross-class conflict over the production of surplus-value, while the second and third volumes details infra-capitalist competition in the entire circulation of capital and its expanded reproduction. Governmentality is analogous to capitalism's use of competitive pressures to ensure the flow and turnover of capital circuits.

Additionally, Foucault describes the turn from sovereign systems to disciplinary and biopolitical~governmental ones by a similar passage of economic theories from cameralism and mercantilism through physiocracy and towards (liberal) political economy. Foucault sees mercantilism as tied to sovereignty and its subject of rights. With the loss of the universalizing dream of the Roman Empire and Church after 1648, the mercantilists sought a "series of controls on prices, storing, export, and cultivation" to address the problem of food scarcity.[57] While they sought the creation of a large population, which would allow a nation to produce cheap goods for export, mercantilists faced the problem of feeding this population. Because mercantilism was unable to solve this riddle, physiocratic thought came to replace it.

The physiocrats consequently sought the "free circulation of grain," rather than the mercantilist concern for a nation's segmentation and trade barriers. Thus, the physiocrat's unit of analysis was not market scarcity, but "the entire cycle" of production, distribution, and the marketing of grain.[58] By acknowledging and working *with* price fluctuations, rather than seeking to prevent them, as did the mercantilists, the physiocrats were able to move away from mercantilism's belief in spatial boundaries to a perspective that focused more on flows, rather than discrete territories.[59] Yet the physiocratic model faced the challenge of seeking to prolong the survival of sovereignty in the face of increasingly insurmountable anti-sovereign pressures, like the economic and "demographic expansion of the eighteenth century, which was linked to the abundance of money," due to the influx of precious metals from the Americas and "the expansion of agricultural production."[60] As an incoherent or internally contradictory approach that could not respond to these changing conditions, physiocracy was destined to be a transitional moment before the rise of (liberal) governmentality, the term that by this point in the lectures has replaced biopower, security, and regulation. Foucault now encapsulates the prior terms within his definition of governmentality as "the ensemble formed by institutions, procedures, analyses and reflections, calculations, and tactics that allow the exercise of . . . power that has the population as its target, political economy as its major form of knowledge, and apparatuses of security as its essential technical instrument."[61]

Liberal thought continues with aspects of the physiocrats as it considers the population as a "set of processes . . . not a primary datum . . . [but] a series of variables."[62] What separates liberalism from physiocracy is that the former considers these variable as forming constants and "regularities even in accidents." The search for norming patterns occurs in order to "identify the universal of desire regularly producing the benefit of all," the average utility on which the pastoral State should act.[63] This turn thus replaces the subject of (sovereign) right for a subject of (liberal, collective) interests that may be heterogeneous, but also calculable. For the (bourgeois) individual, (class) interest becomes understood as personal desire that is interiorized in order to protect it from the public force of a larger (proletarian) population.

In order to maintain equilibrium between the State and the market, liberals insisted on the necessary presence of civil society. As a result of this configuration, liberalism creates a public/private divide, where the population is also a *public* (sphere) with "opinions, ways of doing things, forms of behavior, customs, fears, prejudices, and requirements; it is what one gets a hold on through education, campaigns, and convictions."[64] The State's pastoral care of this multiplicity is made easier, though, by the production of a disciplined subject, one who is "subjected in continuous networks of obedience, and who is subjectified through the compulsory extraction of truth."[65] Discipline and liberal governmentality form a centaur-like yoking of coercion and consensus made possible only in the wake of sovereignty's decline as a dominant force. Yet it is the ensuing crisis of liberal governmentality that creates the conditions for the rise of neoliberalism, much as sovereignty arose as a response to the crisis of feudal suzerainty.

Foucault on Neoliberalism

Foucault's historical narrative on the rise of neoliberalism begins with the Freiburg School of ordoliberals who initially developed their ideas through the Weimar and Nazi years, but eventually came to respond to the conditions of post-war Germany.[66] Here, the pressing question was to answer the riddle of what might legitimize a State in a land that had so clearly failed to maintain liberal predicates and was, in any case, suffering from the devastation of the war and hemmed in by the Allied occupiers' oversight. Consequently, unlike classical liberalism, ordoliberals did not seek to protect the marketplace from the State, since, given Germany's popular conditions, the State was barely in existence, let alone a threat. Instead, these economists looked to the marketplace to "have a state-creating function and role, in the sense that it will really make possible the foundation of the state's legitimacy."[67]

In part due to the legacy of the Nazi concentration of powers, the German economists rejected the legacy of Bismarckian state socialism and centralized economic planning that they saw resurrected in the Keynesian policy of a protected economy.[68] Their rejection of State bureaucratic planning and reconstruction came because they saw the monopolizing centralization of capital as resulting from liberalism's failure to keep its promise, rather than as an intrinsic feature of capital. Moreover, the ordoliberals believe that liberalism's ideal of the marketplace's naturalism was a naïve fantasy. Instead, they concluded that the State's role is to ensure *and* create entrepreneurial competition, and to lead the population into accepting the market's infiltration into other new, ostensibly non-market areas. In this light, they sought the creation of an "enterprise society," rather than a "civil" one, where subjects are neither consumers with sovereign-backed rights, nor exchangers with liberal interests, but entrepreneurs and speculative investors of personal resources.[69] Unlike the Keynesians, the ordoliberals did not seek to ensure consumers' purchasing power through full employment, price controls, or support for a particular sector.[70] Their main instrument would be to control the price of goods and labor by instigating competition among workers.

Foucault sees the advent of neoliberalism in the United States as coming later than Germany and as having its own national particularities, such as the more radical unwillingness to accept aspects of social welfare. While the German crisis of liberal governmentality was a feature of the immediate postwar condition, the crisis of American liberal governmentality came in the late 1960s and early 1970s, when both the left and the right mutually sought to unravel the military Keynesian State. The left saw the State as the realm of soul-killing, one-dimensional bureaucratic massification complicit with imperial adventurism, while the right was upset about the multiform challenges to a longstanding social stratification due to various civil rights and anti-war movements. In contrast to what happened in America, Foucault suggests that German ordoliberals were ultimately held back in the 1960s because European social democracy remained too strong and was able to continue to ensure the State's protections. Without any group advocating for center-left policies in the United States, there was little to block the onset of neoliberalism when it proposed itself as the solution to the perceived failures of Keynesianism in the face of 1970s stagflation. Unlike in continental Europe, where the primary concern was to cultivate anti-centralizing competition in collective society, the US neoliberals (anarcho-liberals is Foucault's preferred term for this group) focused more on promulgating the individual as an "entrepreneur of himself," one who would calculate all their life behavior through the lens of investment decisions and opportunities.[71] This idea of human capital seeks to place all "non-economic behaviour through a grid of economic intelligibility."

Thus, the American neoliberals abandoned liberalism's unit of the population and looked instead for individuals to seek to learn the constructed rules of an economic and social game. Unlike disciplinary techniques, neoliberalism does not seek "a standardizing, identificatory, hierarchical individualization, but an environmentalism open to unknowns, freedoms of [interplay] between supplies and demands."[72] In this, neoliberal governmentality sought to manage individuals by modifying "the terms of the game, not the player's mentality." Hence, the neoliberal subject exists as an entirely different entity than that of liberalism. As a subject of calculation, rather than one of (collective) interest or right, the neoliberal subject requires neither a collective morality of natural (human) rights, nor the evaluative norms of liberal civil society. Furthermore, it abandons the interiority of liberalism in favor of something that looks more like the historically prior exteriority of sovereignty and its right to take life. This homology may explain why discussions of neoliberalism often do so with reference to ideas of the exceptional State (Carl Schmitt), bare life (Giorgio Agamben), or necropolitics. By abandoning liberalism's tension between danger and security, neoliberals sought a game that was based on endless risk. As Rouvroy will argue, the knowability looked for in statistics becomes obsolete as a different kind of mathematical directive will emerge, one based on constantly dynamic and automated algorithms.

Partly because Foucault then turned his work away from these contemporary concerns after 1979, he left the question as to what would replace the element of discipline in an age of neoliberal governmentality largely unexplored. Within this conceptual vacuum, Deleuze scripted a "Postscript on Control Societies" (1990), in which he, both presciently and superficially, argued that a "mutation of capitalism" had shifted beyond the earlier form of discipline.[73] He considered this new form of society by "control" as having three noteworthy features. Firstly, control was not purveyed through professional examination and disciplinary oversight against a norm, but through institutions that enabled marketing or sales perspectives. Secondly, as part of the shift from a (Fordist) productive manufacturing economy to one based on (post-Fordist) consumerist service sectors and prefabricated assembling, control dispenses with discipline's spaces of compartmentalization in favor of modulations "continually changing from one moment to the next."[74] Lastly, Deleuze argues that it is no longer possible to be disciplined because no one can now have an integral individuality or belong to a "mass" society. For that which was previously called civil society is now simply the interrelationship of sub-integral agents, what Deleuze "dividuals," that are found within "samples, data, markets, or *banks*," with the latter meaning both hardware servers of digital informatics as well as finance capitalists arbitrating floating exchange rates.

Deleuze's outline, however, is also short and sparse, making it easier to read as a set of poetic intimations about computation than as a fully blown critical intervention. These initial claims can now be more completely understood through what Rouvroy calls *algorithmic governmentality*. Rouvroy's work suggests that the advent of the datalogical not only completes the logic of neoliberal competition, but also significantly leaps beyond it to develop a new phase of neoliberalism.

Algorithmic Governmentality

Legal scholar Antoinette Rouvroy argues that the computational turn involving algorithms marks a further turn of the screw in the "neoliberal mode of government which produces the subjects it needs."[75] Following Guillaume Le Blanc, she understands neoliberalism as that which conjoins its subjects to a "maximization of performance" (production) and enjoyment

TABLE 3.1 Foucault's Historical Epochs and Beyond Neoliberalism

Epoch	Period	Dominant Means of Power	Target	Dominant Form of Subjectivity	Dominant Mode of Power
Suzerainty	early 1500s				
Sovereignty	early 1500s–late 1700s	Terror	Acts	Subject of right	Law's repressive power
Physiocracy	early 1700s–1750/1780	Punishment	Representation	Subject of sentiment	
Liberalism	1750–1970s	Discipline	Identity	Subject of interests	Knowledge's productive power
Neoliberalism	1930/40s–1970s	Enterprise	Human capital	Subject of speculation	Game's competitive power
Algorithmicity	2010s–	Datalogic	Digital profile	Subject of data mining	Data's algorithmic power

(consumption) through a "continuously reiterated project of 'becoming themselves.'" Yet for all the claims of sousveillance—self-control, self-evaluation, self-entrepreneurship—Rouvroy argues that because of the constantly altering shape of the data profile through algorithmic feedback loops, algorithmic governmentality does not allow for the creation of either an intentional subject or one who might be addressed or interpellated in the Althussarian-Lacanian sense or normalized in the disciplinary Foucauldian one.

If liberal "governing" was the production of "a certain 'regularity' of behaviors (among citizens, customers, patients, students, employees, etc.) it consists—at least in liberal countries—in inducing individuals to choose, in the range of things they may do or may not abstain from doing," as well as the role of (bureaucratic) expertise in making resource allocation evaluations.[76] Algorithms, however, are basically created to dispense with the need to choose or supervise decision making, since the fundamental goal of autonomic computing is to achieve efficiency by shrinking, if not entirely removing, the time between the user's desired outputs and the IT "implementation necessary to achieve those goals—without involving the user in that implementation."[77] IBM's defining characteristics of autonomic computing, in which algorithms are used, includes the system's ability to remove the friction of the user's interpretive presence by having the system able to recognize and identify its own components, dynamically reorganize itself for maximal optimization, prevent against malfunctions by having context awareness and adaptability to a changing environment, and "anticipate and optimize resources consumption while keeping its complexity hidden."[78] Without the need for intentional agency or interpreting analysis, autonomic computing diminishes the need for a buffering medium, such as was the analogous function of civil society in the liberal State-market system.

These technologies form a different kind of governmentality than that of liberalism, one conveying what Rouvroy calls "data behaviourism," a governmentality based on the "implicit belief . . . that provided one has access to massive amounts of raw data . . . one might become able to anticipate most phenomena (including human behaviours) . . . thanks to relatively simple algorithms . . . without having to consider either causes or intentions."[79] The purpose of data mining among vast sets of information inputs is not to discern the interested choices of integral subjects, but instead to locate fragments of actions that exist below the "signature" of individual awareness. These non-integral fractions will be used to create a larger datalogic profile, formed by capillary bits of activity that are bundled to make intelligible otherwise imperceptible correlations of activities that are weakly intentional. Rather than have an integral subject that can be hailed or disciplined, algorithms create what might be called a *wave-particle* subject, one that is simultaneously microscopic and a protean aggregate that is constantly changing through real-time feedbacks. Consequently, "algorithmic governmentality is without [a] subject: it operates with infra-individual data and supra-individual patterns without, at any moment, calling the subject to account for [her or] himself."[80]

In this datalogic turn, a different kind of mathematics becomes dominant. Foucault argued that the human sciences throughout the late eighteenth and nineteenth century used the mathematical knowledge of statistics to construct liberal subjectivity. Statistics were deployed to render "heterogeneous situations and accomplishments *commensurable*," for the sake of comparing risk.[81] By creating a, more or less, static and stable object (or category) of knowledge, like Quetelet's "average man," statistical claims could be used to validate a "hypothesis about the world," which can then be used for utilitarian, liberal decision-making.[82] In contrast, Rouvroy contends that algorithmic neoliberalism now dispenses with statistics as a form of knowledge production. The real-time instantaneous feedback of an algorithm, which constantly adjusts itself with regard to *all* data inputs, forgoes the goal of stability, not least since algorithms are not designed to establish an ideal utility or equilibrium, but to respond interactively with their environment... Consequently, an algorithmic system "simply exempts from the burden... of organizing interpretation or evaluation process... [it] *spares* the burden of testing, questioning, examining, evaluating actual facts... it avoids [the need] to make objects or persons" appear.

In this sense, Rouvroy's discussion of algorithms for the sake of a new kind of post-liberal governmentality shifts our understanding of prior goals of neoliberalism in two significant ways. Firstly, the locus has been moved from heroic entrepreneurial investment into the self as speculative human capital to one of non-stop consumption, as seen with Charles Duhigg's exemplary article on the shopping retailer Target and their early adoption of algorithmic profiling.[83]

Duhigg showed that Target was able to deposit its shoppers' individual purchase choices into a data mine from which they could extract new correlations across all the other sets of personal checkout events. This process then allowed Target to use the derived profile to very successfully indicate the presence either of a consumer's pregnancy or its location within the consumer's immediate family based on the purchasing choices. While the story gained notoriety for the creepiness of its collapse of public-private boundaries, this profiling's larger goal was lost to readers who encounter the article outside of its place within Duhigg's book, which advances a larger claim about the ability to rewire habit through alterable behavioral trigger mechanisms.[84]

The target of Target's profiling was not ultimately a relatively small subset of consumers associated with pregnancy, but as a means of discovering how to erase preexisting integral patterns in *all* its shoppers in order to increase their purchasing of Target's goods. Because time-conscious consumers quickly create their own habit-trail through a store that takes them to the location of their desired goods as quickly as possible, Target looks to alter these set patterns that make many of their shelves functionally invisible to shoppers who have trained themselves to see only their sought for goods.

For as a big-box retailer of everything, from furniture and interior furnishings to outdoor leisure equipment, electronics, groceries, and drugstore goods, Target not only needs to get shoppers into their shopping space, but to then have them walk through as much of their floor display as possible, so that they view as much as possible of the shelved inventory. Target's project was their response to the falling rate of profit facing all "monopoly" stores. On one hand, their attraction to consumers is the good of time efficiency by standing as a one-stop superstore that has everything. On the other hand, Target must reduce the unprofitable time that goods remain on their shelves, as well as lower warehousing costs for goods that cannot be stocked until the current shelf space becomes empty.

The attraction of understanding the algorithms of pregnancy purchasing for Target is that given pregnancy's relatively unique purchasing requirements, the life-event stands as a privileged habit-altering event in ways that allows the store to *distribute* the necessary goods widely throughout the store, rather than clustering them, in order to force consumers to search the shelves for where these might be located. Target hopes that by forcing fresh eyes on previously ignored aisles, consumers will end up buying goods other than the ones they were looking for in the first place. By deploying the governmentality of dispersion, rather than isolation of discipline (in the sense that no section is now signposted for pregnancy needs), Target sparks consumption, while also saving money by working on consumer flow, rather than going through the expense of altering what must be for them a nationally standardized store layout. What Target sought to learn from the data patterns gained from pregnancy shopping was how to discern (or create) a host of other habit-altering events. In this sense, algorithmic marketing is not interested in making a "disciplinary" evaluation of one's object choices. It is amoral and does not care, in any disciplinary instance, what shoppers specifically desire, be it Chopin's etudes, NASCAR racing video games, or strap-on dildos. It merely seeks to ensure customers keep shopping, and thus keep providing more data to be mined that might be recursively used to instigate even more shopping. This shopping, though, is not for the "investment" of human capital, as was sought for in earlier forms of neoliberalism.

Instead, it is designed to create an endless consumption that is never meant to "realize" profit or conclude the circuit of consumption.

Secondly, Target's algorithmic shopping is *anti-developmental*. It seeks to make shoppers approach the store every time like it is their first time, and be constantly alert and curious as to what the store is offering. This, too, marks a significant shift within neoliberal techniques. Early neoliberalism sought to encourage subject to embrace risk by learning the dictated rules of a constant game, yet the ever-changing nature of the algorithm, due to its own internal feedback of data input, means that the game is always changing its outputs and has no clearly advertised rules by which it does so. Hence, a player can never gain experience or skill based on past performances, because it is never possible to know in advance the effects of any action in this moment's ecology. Unlike liberal supply and demand, the algorithmic market has no "natural" price setting equilibrium. Prices can constantly surge or fall based on unknowable events or momentary conditions. In this way, the market produces no "truth" about a commodity's value in the way imagined by liberalism's political economy. This radical uncertainty makes it easier to achieve nudging the shopper into consuming by providing hints, but not conclusive answers, to the moment's underlying rules, not least by guiding shoppers into spontaneous "likes" of correlative purchasing of goods that they never knew they had desired before and, importantly, might not ever again. No act contains any preparation for how one might perform in the future.

By forcing the consumer to be constantly alert, but also uncertain of the effect of their moves, algorithmic occasionality means that purchasing becomes increasingly separated from the development of a subjective personality. Pierre Bourdieu's claim about the construction of a cultural field of taste within liberal societies is thus undermined.[85] An algorithmic network is not organized through a chart a syntagmatic series of commodity choices that can be placed in a grid of oppositions in order to construct markers of (class) difference. Because one never gains a complete directory of known qualities that can be taken as indexing one's status position within the algorithmic field, it becomes less possible to fashion a statement about identity through the symbolic codification of purchasing. "High" and "low" cultural differentiations vanish, not in a spirit of egalitarianism, but because these markers of identity formation through aesthetic choices are no longer stable or visible within the algorithmic matrix.

Within the algorithmic ecology, not only do the players not know what is permissible, neither do the referees. For example, within predicative policing by algorithm, the authorities are themselves unaware of what they are looking to incriminate, since they, too, must wait on the screen's commands to guide them, much like a driver relying solely on the GPS. Claims for a prejudiceless law enforcement are utopian, since algorithmic policing does incorporate (racialized, gendered, class-oriented) disciplinary norms.[86] Yet, while Rouvroy admits the possibility that "the pre-emptive powers of algorithms are over-estimated," the larger point is that older forms of embodied profiling overlap and may ultimately be subsumed within the newer, disembodied or cybernetic, algorithmic ones.

Such a radical separation from development or judgment gained through past performance experience then creates a psychic condition that Rouvroy compares to postwar traumatic syndrome disorder, where individuals find that they cannot express their experience, since they have no readily available representational code or symbolic medium to do so.

Algorithm's complete removal of truth-formation, personal development, coherent sense of belonging within a civil society (or fractions therein), and investment-less consumption can stand as distinguishing features of a new phase of neoliberalism, a phase that may have been called upon to save earlier forms of neoliberal governance from its own failures. Philip Mirowski, among others, has wondered why neoliberal policies were not abandoned after the crisis of 2008–2011? If the crisis of the early 1970s put an end to liberal macroeconomics, then why have the last few years not done the same for neoliberalism?[87] Here it might not be coincidental that it was precisely at this time that the algorithmically organized consumer portals involving social networks (Facebook), information delivery (Google), online retailing (Amazon), urban transport and delivery (Uber, Deliveroo), and streaming entertainment (Netflix) became popularized. The massification of algorithms within daily life, rather than as a tool for relatively elite financial and scientific practice, may have been as much a factor in neoliberalism's post-2008 survival as were State bailouts and fiat currency creation through qualitative easing, both of which were, after all, tactics that momentarily resurrected otherwise distasteful Keynesian interventions. The rise of algorithmic capitalism is thus linked to, but also different from, the neoliberalism of the 1970s, much as postwar military Keynesianism was linked to, but also different from, New Deal-era liberalism. It is this new environment that frames the challenge for American writing and culture.

The Cultural Forms of Algorithmic Governmentality

If Foucault argued that each regime of governmentality has its own dominant genre, then what cultural form(s) should emerge to become influential in our current moment? What are the cultural registrations of the loss of disciplinary individuality and liberal social governmentality before the force of algorithmic governmentality? If the current algorithmic condition manifests an extreme existential uncertainty that creates a crisis of linguistic exhaustion and voiding of semiotic representation, then perhaps the claims of post-critique literary criticism unwittingly registers a contemporary reality involving the loss of a Habermasian rational-critical public sphere? If we are said to exist in a post-truth political age, the possibility for this appears when the institutionalized cultural apparatuses of the liberal era have not simply become conjuncturally damaged, but are now made nearly obsolete. Rather than social media feeds being seen as the corruption of public sphere communication, it might be more apt to recognize how they have been shaped in the first instance through algorithms that were never designed to operate through liberal principles, since the ensuing algorithmic profile is not a collective public, or even a counterpublic, but an entirely different entity altogether.

Perhaps the new awareness about racialized and gendered micro-aggression involving unintentional statements that reveal a persistent milieu of prejudice in forms otherwise too inconsequential for intervention by a law-evaluating judiciary is also the appearance of attempts to understand the infra- and supra-individual profiling by which our societies are being contoured. Rather than seeing complaints about micro-aggression and the assumption of (racial or gendered) privilege as a turn away from juridically enforced civil rights or critiques of (economic) power inequalities, these concerns may capture a reality and recognition that older forms of redress are faltering, given that these older forms were forged according to liberalism's specifications.

In a larger sense, can the institutions and cultural forms of liberalism continue to hold together in a post-self, post-collective realm of wave-particle subjectivity? Given that the novel-form arose through liberalism's long duration, and that the American novel in particular was conjoined to New Deal and military Keynesian desires to instantiate pluralist consensus, then what is left of this cultural form in the era of algorithmic neoliberalism? What of the novel's long-standing project to cement an imagined community through the creation of a readership shaped by disciplinary interiority and liberal regulatory governmentality? When the system of sovereignty was bypassed by that of liberalism, the form of dramatic tragedy did not vanish, but it lost its preeminent place as a consecrated mediator of social and cultural energies. Will a similar act of declining status also be the fate of the (liberal) novel in the age of algorithmic neoliberalism? This riddle about the efficacy of its longstanding form and social function is one of the primary questions that contemporary American writing today must seek to answer.

Notes

1. Michel Foucault, *The Birth of Biopolitics: Lectures at the Collège de France, 1978–1979* (Basingstoke: Palgrave, 2008), 130.
2. Foucault, *Biopolitics*, 130
3. Foucault, *Biopolitics*, 61.
4. Foucault, *Biopolitics*, 131.
5. Foucault, *Biopolitics*, 131, 132.
6. Loïc Wacquant, *Punishing the Poor: The Neoliberal Government of Social Insecurity* (Durham, NC: Duke University Press, 2009).
7. Foucault, *Biopolitics*, 131; Michael Foucault, *On the Government of the Living: Lectures at the Collège de France, 1979–1980* (Hampshire, UK: Palgrave Macmillan, 2014), 12.
8. Foucault, *Biopolitics*, 19, 297.
9. Michel Foucault, *"Society Must be Defended": Lectures at the Collège de France, 1975–1976* (New York: Picador, 2003), 175.
10. Foucault, *Society Must Be Defended*, 175.
11. Ian Watt, *The Rise of the Novel: Studies in Defoe, Richardson, and Fielding* (Berkeley: University of California Press, 1957); Lionel Trilling, *The Liberal Imagination: Essays on Literature and Society* (Garden City, NY: Doubleday, 1953).
12. Benedict Anderson, *Imagined Communities: Reflections on the Origin and Spread of Nationalism* (London: Verso, 1983). See also, Guido Mazzoni, *Theory of the Novel*, trans. Zakiya Hanafi (Cambridge, MA: Harvard University Press, 2017).
13. Georg Lukács, *The Theory of the Novel*, trans. Anna Bostock (Cambridge, MA: MIT Press, 1971), 89.
14. Antoinette Rouvroy, "The End(s) of Critique: Data Behaviourism Versus Due Process," in *Privacy, Due Process and the Computational Turn: The Philosophy of Law Meet the Philosophy of Technology*, Eds. Mireille Hildebrandt and Katja De Vries (Abingdon: Routledge, 2012), 143–167; Antoinette Rouvroy, "Technology, Virtuality and Utopia: Governmentality in an Age of Autonomic Computing," in *Law, Human Agency and Autonomic Computing: The Philosophy of Law Meet the Philosophy of Technology*, Eds. Mireille Hildebrandt and Antoinette Rouvroy (Abingdon: Routledge: 2011), 119–140; Antoinette Rouvroy and Thomas Berns, "Le Nouveau Pouvoir Statistique," *Multitudes* 40 (February 2010): 88–103. For a more complete list of her French language publications, see https://works.bepress.com/antoinette_rouvroy. Rouvroy's work has been implemented in Bernard Stiegler, *Autonomic Society: The Future of Work, Volume I* (Cambridge: Polity, 2016) and John Cheney-Lippold, *We Are Data: Algorithms and The Making of Our Digital Selves* (New York: New York University Press, 2017).
15. For useful accounts of neoliberalism, see citations in this volume's introduction.
16. For indicative works, see *The Foucault Effect: Studies in Governmentality*, Eds. Graham Burchell, Colin Gordon, and Peter Miller (Chicago: University of Chicago Press, 1991) and Thomas Lemke, *Foucault, Governmentality, and Critique* (Boulder, CO: Paradigm Publishers, 2011).
17. Michel Foucault, *Discipline and Punish: The Birth of the Prison* (New York: Pantheon, 1977); Michael Foucault, *The History of Sexuality, Volume I* (New York: Pantheon, 1978).

18. Foucault, *Society Must be Defended*, 239–264. This material is revised in *History of Sexuality*, 135–159.

19. Michael Foucault, *The Use of Pleasure* (London: Penguin, 1990), 7. The third volume of *The History of Sexuality* was also published in 1984. The English publication of this volume appears as *The Care of the Self* (London: Penguin, 1990).

20. According to a self-published journal by Foucault's Berkeley students, he was planning to conduct a research project with them on "the 1920s, and the rationalities of government that made possible the Welfare State, fascism, and Stalinism," Had Foucault lived and actually led this project, this might have been the place where the work on governmentality might have found publication. Anonymous, "Foucault in Berkeley," *History of the Present* 1 (February 1985): 6–14. See also, Keith Gandall and Stephen Kotkin, "Governing Life in the U.S.A. and the U.S.S.R.," *History of the Present* 1 (February 1985): 4–6.

21. The four lectures from 1975–1976 to 1979–1980 (no lectures were given in 1976–1977) appeared in French in 1997, 2004, 2004, and 2012, with the English translations in 2003, 2007, 2008, 2014.

22. Michael Foucault, *Security, Territory, Population: Lectures at the Collège de France 1977–1978* (Basingstoke, UK: Macmillan, 2009), 1.

23. Michael Foucault, *The Archaeology of Knowledge and the Discourse on Language* (New York: Harper and Row, 1976), 3–6.

24. Foucault, *Biopolitics*, 60.

25. Foucault, *Discipline and Punish*, 306.

26. Michel Foucault, "La Sociéte disciplinaire en crise," in *Dits et Écrits: 1954–2008*, Vol. 3 (Paris: Gallimard, 1994), 532–533.

27. Foucault, *Discipline and Punish*, 305.

28. Foucault, *Discipline and Punish*, 306.

29. Foucault, *Security, Territory, Population*, 107.

30. Gilles Deleuze, "Postscript on Societies of Control," in *Negotiations: 1972–1990*, trans. M. Joughin (New York: Columbia University Press, 1995), 178–182, originally published in *L'Autre Journal* l (May 1990). Other brief discussions are: Deleuze, "Control and Becoming" in *Negotiations*, 169–176 (originally published as a conversation with Toni Negri, *Futur Anteneur* 1 (Spring 1990) and Gilles Deleuze, "Having an Idea in Cinema" in *Deleuze and Guattari: New Mappings in Politics, Philosophy, and Culture*, Eds. Eleanor Kaufman and Kevin Jon Heller (Minneapolis: University of Minnesota Press, 1998), 14–19. Although not explicitly linked to these claims, see also his philosophical study of modulations, *The Fold: Liebniz and the Baroque*, trans. Tom Conley (Minneapolis: University of Minnesota Press, 1992).

31. Foucault, *Government of the Living*, 6–7.

32. Michel Foucault, *Remarks on Marx: Conversations with Duccio Trombadori*, trans. R. James Goldstein and James Cascaito (New York: Semiotext(e), 1991).

33. Compare the first passage from Foucault's *Biopolitics* (186) to one by Antonio Gramsci:

1) "The term itself, power, does no more than designate a domain of relations which . . . I have proposed to call governmentality, that is to say, the way in which one conducts the conduct of men, is no more than a proposed analytical grid for these relations of power. So, we have been trying out this notion of governmentality

and, second, seeing how this grid of governmentality, which we may assume is valid for the analysis of ways of conducting the conduct of mad people, patients, delinquents, and children, may equally be valid when we are dealing with phenomena of a completely different scale, such as an economic policy, for example, or the management of a whole social body, and so on."

2) "In practice, this problem is the correspondence 'spontaneously and freely accepted' between the acts and the admissions of each individual, between the conduct of each individual and the ends which society sets itself as necessary-a correspondence which is coercive in the sphere of positive law technically understood, and is spontaneous and free (more strictly ethical) in those zones in which 'coercion' is not a State affair but is effected by public opinion, moral climate, etc." Antonio Gramsci, *Selections From the Prison Notebooks*, trans. Quintin Hoare and Geoffrey Nowell Smith (New York: International Publisher, 1971), 195–6.

34. Foucault, *Security, Territory, Population*, 201–202.
35. Foucault, *Biopolitics*, 94.
36. Foucault, *Biopolitics*, 218.
37. Foucault, *Security, Territory, Population*, 229.
38. Foucault, *Security, Territory, Population*, 215, 216.
39. Foucault, *Society Must Be Defended*, 25.
40. Foucault, *Society Must Be Defended*, 35.
41. Foucault, *Society Must Be Defended*, 69.
42. Foucault, *Security, Territory, Population*, 103; Foucault, *Society Must Be Defended*, 27, 35.
43. Foucault, *Society Must Be Defended*, 16–17.
44. Foucault, *Society Must Be Defended*, 249, 35.
45. Foucault, *Society Must Be Defended*, 36.
46. Foucault, *Society Must Be Defended*, 37.
47. Foucault, *Society Must Be Defended*, 242.
48. Foucault, *Society Must Be Defended*, 246, 245.
49. Foucault, *Society Must Be Defended*, 249.
50. Foucault, *Security, Territory, Population*, 6, 11.
51. Foucault, *Security, Territory, Population*, 44, 20.
52. Foucault, *Security, Territory, Population*, 45, 47.
53. Foucault, *Security, Territory, Population*, 57, 60.
54. Foucault, *Security, Territory, Population*, 63.
55. Foucault, *History of Sexuality*, 141.
56. Foucault, *Society Must Be Defended*, 250; *History of Sexuality*, 144.
57. Foucault, *Security, Territory, Population*, 32.
58. Foucault, *Security, Territory, Population*, 40.
59. Foucault, *Security, Territory, Population*, 342.
60. Foucault, *Security, Territory, Population*, 103.
61. Foucault, *Security, Territory, Population*, 108.
62. Foucault, *Security, Territory, Population*, 70.
63. Foucault, *Security, Territory, Population*, 74.
64. Foucault, *Security, Territory, Population*, 76.
65. Foucault, *Security, Territory, Population*, 185.

66. For a longer discussion of ordoliberalism in postwar Germany, see this volume's introduction.
67. Foucault, *Biopolitics*, 95.
68. Foucault, *Biopolitics*, 107–109.
69. Foucault, *Biopolitics*, 147.
70. Foucault, *Biopolitics*, 139.
71. Foucault, *Biopolitics*, 226.
72. Foucault, *Biopolitics*, 261.
73. Deleuze, "Postscript on Control Societies."
74. Deleuze, "Postscript on Control Societies," 179.
75. Rouvroy, "Data Behaviourism," 153.
76. Rouvroy, "Data Behaviorism," 153.
77. Rouvroy, "Governmentality," 120.
78. Rouvroy, "Governmentality," 120.
79. Rouvroy, "Data Behaviourism," 143.
80. Rouvroy, "Data Behaviourism," 144–145.
81. Rouvroy, "Data Behaviourism," 149.
82. Rouvroy, "Data Behaviourism," 149.
83. Charles Duhigg, "How Companies Learn Your Secrets," *New York Times*. February 12, 2012. http://www.nytimes.com/2012/02/19/magazine/shopping-habits.html.
84. Charles Duhigg, *The Power of Habit: Why We Do What We Do in Life and Business* (New York: Random House, 2014). For Google's discussion of group modification through algorithms, see "The Selfish Ledger," Accessed July 10. 2018. https://www.theverge.com/2018/5/17/17344250/google-x-selfish-ledger-video-data-privacy.
85. Pierre Bourdieu, *The Field of Cultural Production* (Cambridge: Polity Press, 1983) and *Distinction: A Social Critique of the Judgment of Taste* (London: Routledge, 1986).
86. Frank Pasquale, *The Black Box Society: The Secret Algorithms That Control Money and Information* (Cambridge, MA: Harvard University Press, 2015); Cathy O'Neil, *Weapons of Math Destruction: How Big Data Increases Inequality and Threatens Democracy* (New York: Penguin, 2016); John Cheney-Lippold, *We Are Data: Algorithms and the Making of Our Digital Selves* (New York: New York University, 2017); Virginia Eubanks, *Automating Inequality: How High-Tech Tools Profile, Police, and Punish the Poor* (New York: Macmillan, 2018); Safiya Umoja Noble, *Algorithms of Oppression: How Search Engines Reinforce Racism* (New York: New York University Press, 2018).
87. Philip Mirowski, *Never Let a Serious Crisis Go to Waste: How Neoliberalism Survived the Financial Meltdown* (London: Verso, 2010).

[4]

MYKA TUCKER-ABRAMSON

THE FLAMETHROWERS AND THE MAKING OF MODERN ART

RACHEL KUSHNER'S *THE FLAMETHROWERS*[1] is a novel about neoliberalism's emergence in the 1970s and its crash in the financial crisis of 2008. At its center are two sites and struggles that were crucial to both the post-World War II reconstruction and expansion of US-led global capitalism under Keynesianism, and its consolidation under neoliberalism. First is the explosion of social and artistic movements that emerged in the lead up to, and fall out from the radical restructuring of New York City as a result of the fiscal crisis of 1974–1975 that culminated in what David Harvey and others have termed a "financial coup."[2] Second are the student and worker movements of Operaismo and Autonomia that shook Italy from 1962 to the late 1970s that formed in response to the so-called *miracolo italiano*, or Italian Miracle, the recapitalization and reconstruction of Italy that was carried out through the Marshall Plan.[3] *Flamethrowers* connects these two spaces through its protagonist, Reno, an aspiring land artist and motorcycle racer, and her relationship with the well-known minimalist artist, Sandro Valera, whose family owns the Valera motorcycle company—one of the automotive factories at the center of the novel's vision of this time of unrest in Italy.

It is perhaps surprising, then, that the myriad reviews this novel generated had so little to say about these two emblematic political moments (or even their relationship to the New York art scene that Reno stumbles into), instead focusing almost exclusively on how this bracingly masculine New York arts scene silences Reno, and in turn how today's equally bracingly masculine arts scene silences Kushner. Laura Miller's *Salon* review drew an analogy between the effacement of Reno's voice within the novel and contemporary critics effacement of Kushner's voice, reading the novel as being "concerned with the dilemma faced by female artists."[4] The *LA Review of Books*' Nicholas Miriello argued that the book's theme is "the deaf ears that receive a woman's mind, a woman's ambition,"[5] and Geoff Mak audaciously claimed that *The Flamethrowers* is essentially "a feminist novel, [rather] than a political novel, or a novel about art."[6]

Even those reviews that situated *The Flamethrowers* within its political moment of the 1970s ultimately effaced the novel's engagement with the politics of that moment. While, for instance, Nicholas Dames reads *The Flamethrowers* as part of a "burst" of nostalgic "fictional resurrections of the Seventies," his vision of the 1970s is ultimately a pastiche of stagflation and 1960s nostalgia. Thus, he suggests that what is at stake in these novels' nostalgia for this miserable time—"How sad does one have to be to want to resuscitate the era of stagflation?" he asks—is a contemporary desire to relish the "bygone experiments" of the 1960s while still being able to comfort ourselves with the "fate of consecration that befell them."[7] Both these feminist and periodizing readings of Kushner efface the underlying focus of the novel—the ascendancy and as I will argue in the conclusion, decline, of a US-led global capitalism—and instead treats its vision of the 1970s as a set piece, implicitly casting the novel as an example of what Georg Lukács diagnosed as "so-called historical novels," that is, novels that treat history as "mere costumery" (19). In these novels, Lukács argued, while the setting may be historical, both "the psychology of the characters [and] the manners depicted are entirely those of the writer's own day" (19). Dames sees Kushner staging the cultural anomie of our present; Miller sees Kushner staging the misogyny of the contemporary art world. In both readings, the novel appears to project localized present-day characters and concerns against a 1970s backdrop.

What is at stake in these reviews, however, is not just the status of the 1970s, but also the status of art. That is, they raise the spectre of the art and autonomy debates, the question of whether art—both the 1970s art world the novel presents, as well as the novel itself—has become wholly "subsumed" by capital.[8] For Miller, *The Flamethrowers*' 1970s art world is a misogynist, cultural industry that fails to valorize Reno's work and voice, while for Dames, *The Flamethrowers*, like the numerous other 1970s novels he catalogues, is a parodic aestheticization of the past that transforms the 1970s into a consumable commodity. In both cases, this novel, like the art it depicts, appears to have become wholly subsumed. To a certain extent, this vision of both the novel and the world it depicts makes sense. Reno, after all, walks through the 1970s like a spectator through a set of famous historical photo stills of the 1970s and perceives the art world of the 1970s as free floating, a machine of commodification that she hopes will one day valorize her work.

But the positions heralded by these reviews depend upon a collapsing of the novel's perspective with that of Reno's. In this chapter, I want to offer a reading of *The Flamethrowers* against Reno, a reading that identifies Reno and her constant tendency to flatten, commodify, fragment, and misread the political and artistic world of the 1970s not as the operation, but the problem of the novel. In doing so, I aim to make an argument for *The Flamethrowers* as a properly, though necessarily revised, Lukácsian historical novel, that is a novel that transforms history, and particularly the 1970s, from a set piece into "a *mass experience*,"[9] an experience in which men and women shape history, though not as Marx famously wrote, "as they please [. . .but] under circumstances existing already, given and transmitted from the past."[10] By disarticulating the novel's standpoint from that of Reno, we can see how the novel ultimately refuses Reno's perspective and instead stages the 1970s as a fraught and explosive period in which the struggle over the uneven processes of global neoliberalism that created our present moment was being waged: a moment marked by stagflation, urban crisis, and decline, but also by the explosive and intertwined artistic and social movements that imagined and worked to create new kinds of societies from the ruins of Fordist-Keynesianism. And it suggests that key to resurrecting this *other* 1970s—not one of stagflation, decline, and disillusion, but of struggle and possibility—is the reclamation of art's potential to critique and historicize the present.

In "Wages Against Artwork," Leigh Claire La Berge puts forward the idea of decommodification as an alternative to autonomy. While, La Berge argues, "one cannot locate a new, uncommodified ground of that long hoped for 'outside' [. . .] one can] take objects, processes, anxieties out of circulation, making them available once again for the generation of a different value, and provide a model for doing so."[11] It is not my intention to delve into the aesthetic autonomy and immaterial labor debates, but rather to consider how *The Flamethrowers* raises these debates—both the meaning of the 1970s alongside the autonomy of the role of art debates—in order to stake a claim for the political and critical potential of art, culture, and, particularly, the novel as able to operate both "within and against capital"[12] in our post-2008 moment.[13]

Specifically, I argue, *The Flamethrowers* puts forward what can best be understood as a theory of combined and uneven subsumption, a process that understands art as "caught," to borrow from Ericka Beckman's formulation in a somewhat different context, "between capitalist and non-capitalist modes of production [. . . in which] they are at different moments in history alternately brought into and thrown out of circuits of accumulation."[14] It is precisely this space of caughtness—never fully in or out—the novel suggests, that makes art an ideal site with which to understand the intertwined landscapes of industrialization and industrial abandonment that marked the

1970s, and the social and political uprisings that emerged in response. In reclaiming and repoliticizing the art practices of the 1970s as engaged in the process of decommodification, *The Flamethrowers* also models this process: that is, the novel itself reveals the role that art can play as tools of critique and revelation in our current moment at the end of neoliberal capitalism.

I

The Flamethrowers' historical referent is the moment of transformation between the post-World War II era of Fordist-Keynesian and that of neoliberalism. This novel focalizes this uneven, yet global transformation through the novel's three primary locales: New York City, abandoned by industry and the tax dollars of the white middle class, which triggered its fiscal crisis; Reno, Nevada where many of these corporations fled to in search of cheaper land and labor; and Italy during the period of the Italian Miracle, a moment marked by an unprecedented industrialization and urbanization, and then as a result of the 1973 oil shock, deindustrialization, structural reform, and unemployment. The novel centers these historical and geographical contexts repeatedly. Sandro, for instance, provides this historical context when he shoots down Reno's romantic visions by explaining that Italy is not the fantasy an American woman experiences on her year abroad to Florence (109), but a place bankrupted by the oil shock, of an "IMF loan. Inflation. Unemployment. [. . .] Work stoppages. Sabotage. Wildcat strikes." (108). Similarly, the New York City that the novel gives us is marked by the garbage piling up as a result of a 1975 wildcat garbage strike and the 1977 blackout that leads to a fire at a chemical bank that kills three employees because "There had been no available fire truck to come and put out the fire" (353).

How, the novel asks, can we understand the connections between these three spaces? What connects Nevada, New York City, and Italy in the 1970s, as well as the Italian flamethrowers and motorcycle battalions of 1917, and the Brazilian rubber plantations of the 1940s? *The Flamethrowers* offers us two models, two ways to map this connection.[15] First is the model given by Reno, whose sentimental search for love takes both her and the reader from Nevada, to New York, and Italy, thus providing the window through which the reader is able to see the highways of the Southwest, the abandoned and impoverished spaces of New York City, and the protests and strikes of Italy. Reno provides us a map early on when she explains, "Flip recaptured the world record, the season after the Watts riots and kept it until last year, 1975, when an Italian stole it away in a rocket-fuelled vehicle and Flip officially retired. Now he does television commercials for after-market shocks. The Italian, Didi Bombonato, is sponsored by Valera Tires, which is where the lines begin to cross. Didi Bombonato would be at the Bonneville Salt Flats to set a record. Sandro is Sandro Valera, of Valera Tires and Moto Valera motorcycles" (23). Reno's map is both geographical and sentimental, tracking the journey from her childhood crush on the racer Flip in Nevada to her first grown up love, Sandro in New York. For the novel, however, this map to Reno's heart is also a map of the uneven geographies of the post-war deal. In this reading, what connects these spaces and moments is not love or attraction, but rather the automobile. It is the rise of the automotive-fuelled white flight of the 1950s to places like the Sunbelt that at once caused the rise of motorcycle racers like Flip Farmer to become the heartthrobs of suburban teenagers like Reno, and that catalyzed urban unrest of the 1960s across Northern cities like Watts and New York, by hollowing out their tax bases. And it is the Marshall-plan backed explosion of the automotive industry as part of the Italian Miracle that lay at the center of the worker and student movements of Italy in the 1960s and 1970s.

More specifically, it is the automobile as a symbol of both the period of post-war national reconstruction and recapitalization and its undoing in the 1970s that led to some automobile workers (Flip) becoming subsumed into the US-backed culture industry, and other workers (those, for instance, left in Watts when the automobile factories left LA) becoming surplus populations in revolt. What connects these spaces, in other words, is not love, but the domestic and international strategies deployed by the United States to maintain political hegemony and expand and restabilize global capitalism, first through Keynesianism, and then, following its crash in 1973, through neoliberalism.[16]

This crash at once forms the backdrop of the novel—it is this crash that creates the "thoroughly abandoned" New York that Reno finds (44)—and is concretized within the novel through the oft-discussed scene of Reno's motorcycle crash. Early in the novel, Reno enters a competition, racing her new model Valera in the Bonneville salt flats in Nevada. Reno heeds the "timing official's" warning of "wind gusts" and irregular section of track around "mile three [...that] didn't get smoothed out" (29), and sets off. However, part-way through the race, a sudden gust of wind knocks Reno over, "cracking and pulverizing" the "fiberglass bodywork," turning the bike's "beautiful teal fairing [to] sudden garbage" (113). As images for the crashing of the Fordist-Keynesianism into a new era of neoliberal financialization goes, the sudden transformation of Reno's beautiful teal motorcycle into mangled garbage as a result of fragile surfaces, speed, and a gust of wind, is not a bad one.

By now the story of this transformation from Fordist-Keynesianism into neoliberalism has become all but gospel. Following the Great Depression,

Washington turned to Keynesian policies that attempted to regulate and prevent the excesses of capitalism and to stabilize the global economic system under its leadership. Defined by the Bretton Woods system, which created a system of fixed exchange rates, the assumption of a manipulable trade-off between inflation and employment rates, and the belief that the government could strike a balance between labor and capital ensuring prosperity for all, Keynesianism became the new common sense, but throughout the 1970s the Keynesian-inspired post-war deal stopped working. Corporate profit rates began to decline and a crisis in US global hegemony, as well as growing student and worker militancy, threatened the delicate compromise struck between capital and labor.

This crisis of profitability was at least partially solved by a shift in focus from revolutions in production and labor productivity to circulation and the shortening of what Marx calls "turnover time," that is, the time in which capital valorizes itself (97). The so-called "revolution in logistics,"[17] that is revolutions in transportation such as containerization, and just-in-time production, and new instruments of credit allowed corporations to leave the traditional industrial centers to places where tax breaks and weaker or no unions or labor laws promised a reduction in costs. The economic shift from the industrial, urban north to the suburban Sun Belt of the South was a precursor to this process. Building on the industrial base secured by Roosevelt's 1940's announcement that most wartime production would occur not in the north, but in places like Georgia, the postwar period saw a flourishing of business, industry, and population in the South and Southwest. The combination of racist federal housing policies that subsidized middle-class homeownership for millions of white families, national highway acts that facilitated automobile-based commuting, Cold War spending policies and tax breaks that facilitated corporate relocation to areas with cheaper taxes, and less powerful unions, as well as numerous local initiatives carried out by boosters and businesses, led to a massive shift in economic power from industrial cities to the south and southwest.[18]

Reno embodies both the specific transformation from the industrial North to the Sun Belt South and the larger transformation from production to circulation. Not only is Reno from one of those working class families in Nevada, but her very desire to race motorcycles across the highways and landscapes of the United States mimics the shift from production to circulation. However, while Reno is both a product of and embodies these shifts, and while she sees that Nevada, New York, and Italy are connected, that the lines "cross" (23), she is unable to map these connections. She cannot see how the industrialization of Nevada, the deindustrialization of New York, and the eruption of student and worker movements in Italy are all part of this global reorganization of capital. For her, as I've argued, the lines that cross and intersect are not connected by these deeper political, ecological, and economic shifts, shifts in larger processes of life-making. They are simply connected by love and by coincidence. It is because of Chris Kelly that she moves from Nevada to New York; it is because of Sandro she ends up in Italy; it is because Sandro cheats on her and his chauffeur, Gianni, is there that she ends up at the center of the protests in Italy. For Reno, life is a series of singularities. As she explains, "Like all people who fall in love, I took the attraction between me and Sandro as singular and specific, not explainable to types and preferences" (94). The same reason she can't see Sandro for who he is, she can't figure out the larger social and political transformations that shape her movements. Hers is a world governed by chance and by singularities.

What looks like a love story, a story about a scorned lover who can't read her lover's infidelities and patterns because she is too deeply in love, might more accurately be read as a political allegory for the subject position that is unable to adequately map their surroundings for the simple reason that they have been subsumed in the system, their subjectivity has come to mirror the logics of capital. For Marx, "the analysis of the real, inner connections of the capitalist production process is a very intricate thing and a work of great detail" (144) and those inculcated within the system are unable to engage in such an analysis because their ideas were necessarily distorted: the ideas of those capitalists, he explains, involved in circulation "are necessarily quite upside-down" while those connected to manufacture are "vitiated by the acts of circulation to which their capital is subject" (145). Both subject positions, in other words, see the world upside down. Reno, encapsulated within and embodying the logic of circulation, sees the world in an upside-down way. And while Sandro, with his firm grounding in the production of automobiles, seems to offer a clearer vision of the world—we can think for instance of his lecture to Reno that aims to show her that Italy is not the romantic place of Venetian canals and Florentine piazzas, but of economic precarity, structural adjustments, and worker unrest—he too can only see part of the picture. One way to think about this novel's aim, then, is to help the reader turn the world right side up by helping them to make these connections.

If neither Reno nor Sandro is able to turn the world right side up, Kushner wages that the art of the 1970s, or at least some of it, can. And the novel offers a panoramic view of 1970s art practices—the feminist conceptual art of Valie Export (fictionalized in that of Sandro's ex-girlfriend, Gloria), the land art of Robert Smithson, the anarchitecture of Gordon Matta-Clark, and the anarchist and dada-influenced political art of the Motherfuckers—all of which are similarly engaged in trying to map this rapidly transforming world. And it is, perhaps, no coincidence that these works of art are also engaged in one of the central aesthetic questions of the period: the extent to which art can be said to resist the real subsumption of capital, or the extent to which art is able to resist being wholly absorbed by the culture industry.

The Flamethrowers raises the spectre of this question in order to ask a larger question: can art offer us a form capable of mapping and critiquing the uneven modes of development that characterized the shifts and transformations of the 1970s? And *The Flamethrowers* aims to answer this question in the affirmative, to show the potential of art as a site of critique, both in the 1970s and, as I will argue shortly, in our present moment. That is, while *The Flamethrowers* undoubtedly mocks the overindulgent bluster of the New York art scene, it takes the art itself quite seriously as an important and critical mode of mapping. While we could turn to many of the examples of emblematic art, the novel focuses its gaze on two particularly resonant examples: Smithson's "Spiral Jetty" (1970), located in Great Salt Lake in Utah, and Matta-Clark's "Day's End" (1975). The Spiral Jetty is located in Reno's hometown in Nevada. Reno learns about Smithson, she tells us, not from her art school, but from an obituary in which Smithson is quoted as "declaring that pollution and industry could be beautiful and that he chose this part of the Great Salt Lake for his project, where the lake's supply of fresh water had been artificially cut, rising the salt content so high that nothing but red algae grow" (7). Reno's imagination is seized by this description. "I had immediately wanted to see this thing made by a New York Artist in leather pants," she explains, "who described more or less the slag-heap world of the West I knew, as it looked to me, and found it worth his attentions" (23).

Kushner frames the Spiral Jetty within the history of de/industrialization. The Jetty, as Reno points out, could only have been built both because of the high salinity of the water and because of the building of a causeway by the Southern Pacific Railway in 1959, which isolated the lake from fresh water sources. Put differently, it is made possible by the postwar infrastructure projects that would soon help facilitate the movement of capital from the northeastern industrial cities and to the Southwest. The Spiral Jetty is a site where New York meets the Southwest—where the flagging industrial cities of the North meet the newly burgeoning economies of the Southwest. Deindustrialization meets industrialization.

Its counterpoint, also present within the novel, is the site of deindustrialization itself: New York through the work of Matta Clark, and specifically his 1975 piece, "Day's End." Matta-Clark's artistic method famously consisted of him finding buildings that had been abandoned—largely from industry leaving New York—like this warehouse, but also apartment buildings that have been condemned, and he would make temporary installations that he knew would be destroyed with the building. In "Day's End," Matta-Clark made sail-shaped cuts in the wall and roof of the derelict Pier 52 on Manhattan's West Side, creating what the novel describes as a "cathedral of water and light" (97) for the gay cruising scene that gathered there. And just as Reno stumbles upon Smithson's obituary, so too she stumbles upon Day's End, though as she archly comments, it was not so much stumbling as her being led by Sandro who led "by seeming to wander when he wasn't, we weren't" (97). The novel describes Matta-Clark's process: "Matta-Clark had cased the building quietly and with discipline for weeks before sneaking in and changing the locks, then slowly, stealthily, he'd moved in equipment, power saws, acetylene, torches, pulleys, and ropes to make his cuts. He had noted when, if ever, there was security around the pier. When, if ever, the building was in use. He had learned that its only use was for discreet sex acts between men" (98).

Like Smithson, Matta-Clark made art out of the waste products of capital; he turned the spaces abandoned by capital into art, and often he focused on buildings that were to be condemned and destroyed. This was art that could not be bought or even preserved; it was art that was meant to disappear. Taken separately, these are pieces that register, engage with, and are made possible by, industry's destruction of the Great Salt Lake on the one hand and the deindustrialization and abandonment of New York on the other. When brought together, however as the novel does, these two works ask us to think about how these seemingly opposed spaces are connected by the dialectic of development and neglect that characterizes the uneven processes of neoliberalization.

But ultimately the artworks most capable of mapping and critiquing the processes that heralded the neoliberal globalization of the 1970s are the fictional artworks of Sandro and Reno. Sandro, Reno explains, is a minimalist who made "large aluminum boxes" (93). These boxes, while produced in a factory in Connecticut, "had little to do with the assembly line imagery they implied: the factory, Lippincott, only fabricated artists' works, by hand, and very, very carefully" (93). While the novel finds much to be mocked in minimalism, it also suggests that minimalism's own simultaneous mimicking of, and withdrawal from industrial production (its refusal to have a use value) allows it to act as a site for the critique of these dual processes of amped up industrial exploitation and deindustrialization. Sandro's fascination with industrial objects produced under artisanal conditions stands as an expression of, and rebellion against, the highly exploitative industrial production his family is engaged in that also funds the production of his art. His art, within the novel at least, allegorizes the politics of minimalism's withdrawal from, as well as its implicit dependency on, global industrial production. Sandro is trying to escape the market and his family by using industrial processes to create products with no use value, and thus that are not commodities, while Reno, on the other hand, makes art out of the very industrial commodity, the motorcycle, that Sandro's family produces, and that created the landscapes of her childhood.

While Reno's art is tied to the production of the Valera motorcycle, that *ur* symbol of Fordist production within the novel, her art, as I've argued, is focused on speed itself: it consists of documenting the marks that speed leave on the earth. She explains that as a child "the two things I loved were drawing and speed, and in skiing I had combined them. It was drawing in order to win" (9). Her movement from skiing to motorcycle racing, we're meant to understand, is a continuation of this fusing. Sandro describes her art this way, her art practice as a motorcycle racer is the acting of "draw[ing] a line across the salt flats" (7). Reno's artwork literally concretizes the processes of speed up and the shift from production to circulation that characterized the 1970s. In other words, the very art Reno deploys to escape her home also replicates the processes that created Nevada in the first place. Like Sandro, Reno's art both attempts to escape and recreates the conditions of their class and geographic positions. Reno's friend Giddle tells Reno repeatedly that Sandro likes her because she's an ingénue, but the novel suggests that Sandro's attraction to her is also tied up in her fetishization of the very objects he disavows. Reno's art both takes as its object and requires the real industrial machinery produced by Sandro's family, even as it deploys it for completely abstract aims. There is something in each of them that requires the other.

Like with Smithson and Matta-Clark, read together, Sandro and Reno's artwork allow us to see the two sides of circulation and production within this new mode of production. They allow us, to return to Marx, to turn the world upside down. In one of the more oft-quoted passages of *Capital*, Marx writes:

> The consumption of labour-power is completed, as in the case of every other commodity, outside the limits of the market or of the sphere of circulation. Accompanied by Mr. Moneybags and by the possessor of labour-power, we therefore take leave for a time of this noisy sphere, where everything takes place on the surface and in view of all men, and follow them both into the hidden abode of production, on whose threshold there stares us in the face "No admittance except on business." Here we shall see, not only how capital produces, but how capital is produced. We shall at last force the secret of profit making. (195)

Marx's point is that we need to see both circulation and production to understand "the secret of profit making." In *The Flamethrowers*, it is through the art of Reno and Sandro, and through their love story, that we are able to see both, to link circulation and production.

Kushner's depictions of these art works, both real and fictional, is not invested in arguing for the autonomy of 1970s artwork. Rather, Kushner's depictions of the 1970s art scene appear to be caught between capitalist and non-capitalist modes of production, both caught up within and about the mobility of capital and the fixity of the soil; they are works that reveal the impossibility of autonomy, showing how different art movements, like the spaces in which their art is carried out, are alternately incorporated into and ejected from the circuits of accumulation. But in that sliver of autonomy, that caughtness, Kushner is also invested in showing how, through their very attempt to grapple with their own conditions of production, these artistic practices are able to offer critical maps of the processes of economic globalization that join the slavery of the Brazilian rubber workers with the art economy of New York and the factory work of Italy, all existing within a single, uneven whole.

What, then, are the stakes of this recuperation of the 1970s artistic landscape as a critical practice and why is *The Flamethrowers* so invested in it? Hal Foster offers one suggestion in "The Crux of Minimalism" when he argues that the dismissal of minimalism in the 1980s was rooted in a desire of "rightists" to "cancel the cultural claims and to reverse the political gains of the 1960s, so traumatic were they to these neoconservatives."[19] For Foster, the contemporary rejection of the 1970s is part of an effacement of the radical culture of the 1960s and 1970s. This is the project that allows Dames to comment—and many to agree—"How sad does one have to be to want to resuscitate the era of stagflation?" *The Flamethrowers* response is that whatever the numerous flaws of the art world and the political movements it was connected with, art offered a crucial site of critique.

But for all the pieces of art that Kushner points to that are able to maintain that limited autonomy and that are able to critically map the world around them, there is one object of art that is ultimately unable to do so, and that is the novel's protagonist, Reno herself. Reno is also the one character whose psychology and manners turn out to be, to return to Lukács, "those of the writer's own day" (19). I want to suggest that the novel addresses the problem of art and the commodity, and more sharply the problem of art's potential as a site of and space for critique, not through a defense of Reno, but rather by distancing itself from her. And it is within this context of distancing rather than identification that we need to consider the novel's feminist politics. Numerous critics have pointed out that Reno is a woman in a man's world. Or in men's worlds. From the motorcycle racing of her youth to the New York art scene she is trying to break into, Reno constantly struggles to prove herself their equal. And Reno's frustration at the machismo she experiences is more than justified. From the New York art scene to her attempt to break into motorcycle racing to Sandro's Italian Villa, Reno is alternately terrorized by women and ignored or sexualized be men, and in each case she becomes entirely commodified: her success as a motorcycle racer is effaced as she is transformed into a poster girl, a stylized image of a girl and a motorcycle; her work as an artist is effaced and she becomes a China Girl. Read within this context, Miller's claim that the novel's tragedy is that only Reno can hear her voice makes sense. We as the reader want to rescue Reno from the margins of commodification. We want others to hear her voice.

And yet, there is something peculiar about this narrow focus on the commodification of Reno as the locus of the text's feminist politics, particularly given Kushner's attempt to redefine the 1970s as an era of insurgency. The process through which Reno is flattened into a poster girl is, of course, not unique to Reno. It is the same process that has flattened the intellectual and political movements of the 1970s into the iconography of armed masculine virility that endlessly circulate today. As Kushner herself wrote in her essay on the research and writing of *The Flamethrowers*, "I looked at a lot of photographs and other evidentiary traces of downtown New York and art of the mid-1970s" and what "I kept finding were nude women and [men with] guns."[20] But these images of naked women and men with guns are not the truth of the 1970s, but rather one story that is told of the 1970s, and the problem of the novel is not simply that Reno has been transformed into one of these nude women in love with endless men with guns, but that Reno has been so interpolated into this commodified vision of the 1970s that she too can only read the 1970s through these images. It is her vision that ultimately presents us a vision of the 1970s as mere set piece.

If we read the text through Reno and a desire to save Reno, we end up enacting the very problem the novel attempts to address: that is, we read the 1970s as a period of nude women and men with guns and not as a tumultuous, fraught, and turbulent period of revolt that produced the present. The feminist movements of the 1970s is crucial to this story. After all, the 1970s was also a high water mark of the feminist liberation struggles and thought, particularly in Italy and across the cities of the northern United States. This is the period of Valerie Solanas' SCUM *Manifesto* (1967), Shulamith Firestone's *The Dialectic of Sex* (1970), Mariarosa Dalla Costa and Selma James's *The Power of Women and the Subversion of the Community* (1972), the formation of the National Black Feminist Organization (1973–1976), Autonomia, the international Wages for Housework movement with its manifesto, *Wages*

Against Housework (1975), and the *Combahanee River Collective Statement* (1977), to name just a few.

One question worth asking is, given the novel's feminist politics, why aren't these movements within the novel and, more to the point, why aren't people like Valerie Solanas, the Italian feminists, or even more pressingly absent, black feminists and activists, among the cast of characters Reno encounters? Solanas, after all, shot and almost killed Andy Warhol for many of the reasons that reviewers of the novel are so frustrated with Reno's treatment at the hands of a patriarchal art scene.[21] Moreover, while Solanas isn't in *The Flamethrowers*, both the Motherfuckers—the one group of artists who supported Solanas—and Warhol are. Why can the novel see the Motherfuckers and particularly the misogyny of the Motherfuckers—the novel has Burdmoore explain "We hated women. Women had no place in the movement unless they wanted to cook us a meal or clean the floor or strip down. There are people who've tried to renovate our ideas, claim we weren't chauvinists" (158)—but not Solanas, who is making these critiques at that very moment in New York?

I want to suggest that the *seeming* absence of this militant feminism is a deliberate one that serves to highlight Reno's own blind spots. While there is no explicit mention of Marxist feminism in *The Flamethrowers*, no mention of the feminist thinkers such as Luisa Passerini, Mariarosa Dalla Costa, and Sylvia Federici or movements like Lotta Femminista or the Committees for Wages for Housework that emerged out of militant groups like Lotta Continua and which spread to the United States in the 1970s,[22] there are traces of these movements and intellectual currents. For instance, when Ronnie discusses a *Time* article about random events, such as when a meteor fell on a housewife, Reno muses, "The job of a housework is a little vague [...] The woman senses that time is more purely hers if she squanders it and keeps it empty" (149). In both content and style, this passage evokes the *Wages Against Housework* manifesto and its demand that we place reproductive labor at the center of our understanding of work. However, this is just a passing thought, one that is quickly folded into the main point: Ronnie's seriality and Sandro's singularity. It is part of a point to do with love.

And yet the spectre of Italian workerism, and particularly its feminist iterations, keeps resurfacing in the love story of Reno and Sandro, but it does so not through Sandro's singularity—his "one pair of work boots, one nice jacket [...] one girlfriend" (149)—but rather through his decidedly less singular pattern of infidelity. When Sandro takes Reno to Italy to visit his family, Reno catches him kissing his cousin, Talia, in the alley behind his factory (where all the workers are on strike). To get revenge, Reno runs off with his chauffeur, Gianni, who it turns out is a spy for the movement and his job has been to gain access to the Valera family (presumably to carry out the kidnapping of Sandro's brother). Gianni takes her to a communal apartment where she meets Gianni's maybe girlfriend or lover, Bene.

The novel emphasizes that the radicalism of 1970s Italy operates outside of Reno's comprehension. She repeatedly attempts to import her distinctly New York conceptual frameworks, an attempt that fails. When she first enters the apartment, for instance, she surveys everyone and notes "They weren't a type I could place [...] They reminded me of the plainclothes cops in Tompkins Square Park, who were always too severe and ominous despite their efforts to pass for hippies" (267). Similarly, she cannot decipher the role she plays in this scene, assuming that as in New York, her role is that of the ingénue, the eventual love interest of whoever she perceives to be the group's leader, in this case Gianni. One day, after she goes out with Gianni, Gianni and Bene get into a massive fight in their bedroom. Storming out of her room, Bene walks into kitchen, calls "Gianni various names" and then turns to Reno and says "Go ahead. Just go with him" (292). Reno, in typical fashion, misinterprets their fight, assuming that Bene is jealous because Gianni wants to sleep with her. Right up until the end, Reno remains bewildered by Bene's rage, explaining that "It wasn't at all like Bene seemed to think [...] It was all extremely proper" (376). But it is not Bene, but Reno who gets it wrong. Bene knows that Gianni is about to use Reno to help drive him to the Alps to escape from Italy. What specifically Bene's anger is about—is it a political disagreement about tactics? Is it simply fear of losing her lover?— we never get to find out, but clearly it has nothing to do with jealousy or Reno. Bene is a revolutionary—likely a feminist revolutionary—but we never get to find out more about her because Reno can only think of the personal; she can only see the singular, she can think about love and jealousy, about infidelity and desire. She cannot see the political or the patterns around her.

To read the novel with Reno is to precisely miss the novel's point. Reno is not the hero, but the idiot of the novel. The novel opens with Sandro's father, Valera, reading Gustauve Flaubert's *A Sentimental Education* (33), a novel about a similarly guileless young man who finds himself in the middle of the 1848 French Revolution—but of course, as James Wood and others have pointed out, it is Reno who is Frederic Moreau.[23] Like Frederic, Reno is a passive figure, unengaged and largely ignorant of the existing world-historical social and political crises that surround her. Lacking independent ideas, Reno simply parrots a pastiche of the ideas of the artistic societies she aims to inhabit.

While Reno doesn't get it—she doesn't get what's going on with Sandro (who is cheating on her with lots of women), she doesn't get the political situation in New York that leads to the blackouts and garbage strikes, she doesn't get what's happening in Italy, and she certainly can't assimilate these events or mark the connections—the novel does. The novel ends with Reno waiting at the bottom of a ski hill in the French Alps, waiting for Gianni to arrive. He doesn't. Because of the temporally jumbled nature of the novel, we know that Reno will return to New York where Sandro will have another girlfriend, and where Ronnie will break her heart again. There will be a blackout, riots will erupt, Reno will think back to Gianni and muse "he's either hurt, or possibly dead, or he has deceived me, and I won't ever know which" (353), and three chemical bank employees will die, and Reno will never connect any of these events except as a sentimental pastiche of aestheticized images that may or may not appear in her next art project.

This is the error that Andrew Strombeck makes when he reads the different parts of the novel, or what he terms the "two responses to crisis" (452)—namely the artistic response of New York artists and the autonomist Marxism of Italy—as "inassimilable" (452). In Strombeck's Latour-inspired reading, the novel's use of the motorcycle as the detached and untimely event linking and delinking the novel's many contexts serves to "rework the project of the historical novel by emphasizing historical discontinuity" through the motorcycle's many fractured meanings (472). But such a claim depends on aligning Reno's failure to link and assimilate these diverse events as part of an interconnected, if uneven, global economic system, with the novel's failure or refusal. It is a claim that is based on a US-centered model of history, one that ignores Italy's cultural and economic entanglements with the United States—as Jaleh Mansoor points out, the Economic Miracle was accompanied by the sudden hegemony of American artists within Italy such that "thanks to the CIA . . . the Venice Prize was awarded to Robert Rauschenberg" in 1964 (20)—and the central role that US global policy played in shaping the motorcycle's diffuse meanings as symbols of both global production and then circulation. What then does it mean that the main response to *The Flamethrowers* has been, to borrow again from Miller, that it is a tragedy that the only character who can hear Reno's "potent" voice is Reno herself, when Reno's voice misses the very connections and histories the novel traces?

By way of conclusion, I want to suggest that this valorization of Reno is itself a symptom of the 2008 global financial crisis. The economist Mirowski argues that this crisis was not just economic, but ontological, "inflict[ing] a breakdown in confidence that we can adequately comprehend the system within which we are now entrammelled. After the crisis, professional explainers from all over the map were throwing up their hands and pleading that the economy was just *too complex* to understand."[24] For Mirowski, "professional explainers" could find no standpoint from which to analyze the system, consistently concluding that the market was too smart for them, and they, in turn, are just part of a global market that wasn't meant to be understood, but that would hopefully self-correct and keep on going.

I argued earlier that Reno's art—her desire to go faster and faster—symbolized the larger transformations in the 1970s global economy, in which the crisis in corporate profitability was resolved, at least partially, through developments in logistics and transportation technology that in turn allowed a rapid speed up of capital's circulation. If Reno's motorcycle racing exemplifies this new form of neoliberal economics, her crash doubles as the crash of that system. That is, in the weird structure of the novel that intertwines temporal and narrative threads, her crash both heralds the beginning and the end of neoliberalism. "What seemed like endless perfect white on white," the novel explains, "was only a very thin crust of salt" (114), a crust that she ultimately "breaks through" (114). What seemed solid and stable, the ground on which Reno could go faster and faster, turns out to be thin and fragile, far less stable than it initially appears. And as with the crash to which it refers, nothing changes. Reno learns nothing from the crash and continues living life trying to skim the surfaces of things.

One of the reasons, then, that so many reviewers love Reno is that her inability to understand what is happening in the 1970s both valorizes the incomprehension many of us felt in the wake of the 2008 housing crash and subsequent financial crisis, *and* offers a fantasy of the repair of that economic system. This suggests that the valorization of Reno is profoundly entangled with post-2008 fantasy about the future of circulation-capital within a US-controlled system of global capitalism. Read as a love story, The Flamethrowers narrates the fantasy of production (Sandro) catalyzing circulation (Reno) and, in turn, circulation (Reno) revivifying production (Sandro). Read as a *künstlerroman*, it is a story of circulation (Reno) valorizing her/itself. In both of these fantasies, the system continues as is. Nothing has to change. But this, of course, is not what actually happens in the novel. The love story remains broken, Reno's own aesthetic career remains uncertain, and social and economic crises continue both within and outside of the novel. How then should we read *The Flamethrowers*?

I opened by making the claim for *The Flamethrowers* as a properly historical novel, that it is a novel about history as a mass experience, and a novel that is explicitly about the necessity of understanding the rebellious mass experience of the 1970s if we are to understand the development of neoliberalism. And yet, as the above claim suggests, this isn't exactly true, or at least Kushner's historical novel doesn't function quite as it did for Lukács. For Lukács, the historical novel was directly focalized through its "mediocre" (35) protagonist whose participation in the making of history is allegorical of the democratization of history, and thus of the potential of the reader herself to participate in the making of history. In *The Flamethrowers*, this can't happen because the main characters are not so much allegorical of people or even "the people," as they are of fantasies about capitalist regeneration under US hegemony. And yet for all of this, the mass experience of history is not calcified or commodified, nor does it form the set piece of the novel, but it does move into the background. I thus want to maintain my insistence that we understand *The Flamethrowers* as a properly historical novel, but with the caveat that we do so, only insofar as we read the novel *against* the foreground and the main characters, and *with* those characters and movements that form the backdrop of the novel. In *The Flamethrowers*, it is the fantasies of capital that form the surface of the novel, while its histories and struggles form the background. It is this background that *The Flamethrowers* asks we turn our gaze to.

Notes

1. Rachel Kushner, *The Flamethrowers* (New York: Scribner, 2013). Hereafter cited parenthetically.

2. Sasha Lilley, "On Neoliberalism: An Interview with David Harvey," *MR* Zine (June 19, 2006), http://mrzine.monthlyreview.org/2006/lilley190606.html. For more on the fiscal crisis and the following coup, see David Harvey, *A Brief History of Neoliberalism* (Oxford: Oxford University Press, 2005); Jamie Peck, *Construction of Neoliberal Reason* (Oxford: Oxford University Press, 2010); William Sites, *Remaking New York* (Minneapolis: Minnesota University Press, 2003); Alice O'Connor, "The Privatized City: The Manhattan Institute, the Urban Crisis, and the Conservative Counterrevolution in New York," *Journal of Urban History* 34:2 (2008): 333–353; and Kim Moody, *From Welfare State to Real Estate. Regime Change in New York City, 1974 to the Present* (New York: The New Press, 2007).

3. For more on the rise of Operaismo (or workerism) and Autonomia in Italy, see Georgy Katsiaficas, *The Subversion of Politics: European Autonomous Social Movements and the Decolonization of Everyday Life* (Oakland, CA: AK Press, 1997), Sylvère Lotringer and Christian Marazzi, *Autonomia: Post-Political Politics* (Cambridge, MA: MIT Press, 2007), and Mario Tronti's "Our Operaismo" *New Left Review* 73 (January/February 2012): 119–139.

4. Laura Miller, "Rachel Kushner's Ambitious New Novel Scares Male Critics," *Salon* (May 5, 2013), http://www.salon.com/2013/06/05/rachel_kushners_ambitious_new_novel_scares_male_critics/.

5. Nicholas Miriello, "What is this review interested in?: On Frederick Seidel's Review of Rachel Kushner's *The Flamethrowers*," *LA Review of Books* (July 13, 2013), https://lareviewofbooks.org/essay/what-is-this-review-interested-in-on-frederick-seidels-review-of-rachel-kushners-the-flamethrowers/.

6. Geoff Mak, "Art, Revolution, and Echoes of the Present: A Review of Rachel

Kushner's *The Flamethrowers*," *Vol 1 Brooklyn* (April 25, 2013), http://www.vol1brooklyn.com/author/geoff-mak/.

7. Nicholas Dames, "Seventies Throwback Fiction," *N+1* 15 (Winter 2015), https://nplusonemag.com/issue-21/reviews/seventies-throwback-fiction.

8. Michael Hardt and Antonio Negri, *Empire* (Cambridge, MA: Harvard University Press, 2001), 24.

9. Georg Lukács, *The Historical Novel* (Lincoln: University of Nebraska Press, 1983), 19. Hereafter cited parenthetically.

10. Karl Marx, *Capital: A Critique of Political Economy, Volume 1*, Trans Ben Fowkes (New York, Penguin, 1992), 161. Hereafter cited parenthetically.

11. Leigh Claire La Berge, "Wages Against Artwork: The Social Practice of Decommodification," *South Atlantic Quarterly* 114:3 (July 2015): 574.

12. Jaleh Mansoor, *Marshall Plan Modernism: Italian Postwar Abstraction and the Beginnings of Autonomia* (Durham, NC: Duke University Press, 2016).

13. See for instance, Nicholas Brown's "The Work of Art in the Age of its Real Subsumption Under Capital," *Nonsite* (March 13, 2012), http://nonsite.org/editorial/the-work-of-art-in-the-age-of-its-real-subsumption-under-capital, Boris Groys' "On Art Activism," *e-flux* 56 (June 2014), http://www.e-flux.com/journal/56/60343/on-art-activism/, Steven Shaviro's "Accelerationist Aesthetics," *e-flux* 46 (June 2013), http://www.e-flux.com/journal/46/60070/accelerationist-aesthetics-necessary-inefficiency-in-times-of-real-subsumption/, and Stewart Martin's "The Absolute Artwork Meets the Absolute Commodity," *Radical Philosophy* 146 (November / December 2007): 15–25.

14. Ericka Beckman, "Unfinished Transitions: The Dialectics of Rural Modernization in Latin American Fiction," *Modernism/Modernity* 23:48 (2016): 813–832, 816.

15. Andrew Strombeck offers a third, and somewhat bewildering model in the form of the motorcycle, which does "its unruly, unintegrated work" (453) and serves not, ultimately, to connect these sites but reveal them in their discontinuous, undefined paths and histories (454). I will take up this reading in the essay's conclusion. Andrew Strombeck, "The Post-Fordist Motorcycle: Rachel Kushner's *The Flamethrowers* and the 1970s Crisis in Fordist Capitalism," *Contemporary Literature*, 56:3, (2015): 450–475.

16. What is missing from this map, but which the novel makes clear underpins all these spaces, is the rubber plantation in Brazil where Sandro's father travels in 1942 to source rubber after the Japanese overran the previous global rubber frontier, Malaysia, cutting Italy off from its rubber supply (130). Geographer Jason Moore argues that revolutions in productivity, like that which occurred in the postwar period, fuse together the plunder and "enclosure of new geographical frontiers (including subterranean resources) and new scientific-technological revolutions in labor productivity" (228). While absent from Reno's vision, the rubber frontier of Brazil, and specifically the violent control and extraction of cheap labor from the Brazilian workers that produced the rubber necessary to fuel this period of relative prosperity and freedom in the global north, is also central to the novel. Its enclosure is the precursor to the rise of Valera tires and thus, the absent cause of the entire network that shapes the novel's form. See Jason W. Moore, "Cheap Food & Bad Money: Food, Frontiers, and Financialization in the Rise and Demise of Neoliberalism," *Review: A Journal of the Ferdinand Braudel Center*, 33:2–3 (2010): 225–261.

17. Deb Cowen, *The Deadly Life of Logistics: Mapping Violence in Global Trade* (Minneapolis: University of Minnesota Press, 2014), 23.

18. See Elisabeth Tandy Shermer, "Sunbelt Boosterism: Industrial Recruitment, Economic Development, and Growth Politics in the Developing Sunbelt," in *Sunbelt Rising: The Politics of Place, Space, and Region*, eds. Michelle Nickerson and Darren Dochuk (Philadelphia: University of Pennsylvania Press, 2011), 31–58, Matthew Lassiter, *The Silent Majority: Suburban Politics in the Sunbelt South* (Princeton, NJ: Princeton University Press, 2006), Kevin Kruse, *White Flight: Atlanta and the Making of Modern Conservatism* (Princeton, NJ: Princeton University Press, 2007), Blaine Brownwell, "Introduction," in *Searching for the Sunbelt: Historical Perspectives on a Region*, ed. Raymond A. Mohl. (Knoxville: University of Tennessee Press, 1990).

19. Hal Foster, "Crux of Minimalism," *The Return of the Real*. (Cambridge, MA: MIT Press, 1996), 35.

20. Rachel Kushner, "Curated by Rachel Kushner," *The Paris Review* 203 (Winter 2012), http://www.theparisreview.org/art-photography/6197/curated-by-rachel-kushner-the-flamethrowers.

21. See Dana Heller, "Shooting Solanas: Radical Feminist History and the Technology of Failure," *Feminist Studies* 27:1 (Spring 2001): 167–189.

22. For more on the Italian Feminist movements of the 1970s, see Luisa Passerini, *Autobiography of a Generation: Italy 1968* (Middletown, CT: Wesleyan University Press, 1996), Mariarosa Dalla Costa, "The Door to the Garden: Feminism and Operaismo," *Libcom*, https://libcom.org/library/the-door-to-the-garden-feminism-and-operaismo-mariarosa-dalla-costa, 2002. For more on Wages Against Housework, see Sylvia Federici, *Revolution at Point Zero* (Oakland, CA: PM Press, 2012), and Selma James and Mariarosa Dalla Costa, *The Power of Women and the Subversion of the Community* (Bristol, UK: Falling Wall Press, 1975).

23. James Wood, "Youth in Revolt: Rachel Kushner's *Flamethrowers*," *New Yorker* (April 8, 2013), http://www.newyorker.com/magazine/2013/04/08/youth-in-revolt.

24. Philip Mirowski, *Never Let a Serious Crisis Go to Waste: How Neoliberalism Survived the Financial Meltdown* (New York: Verso, 2014), 11.

[5]   HAMILTON CARROLL

"ON THE VERY EDGE OF FICTION": RISK, REPRESENTATION, AND THE SUBJECT OF CONTEMPORARY FICTION IN BEN LERNER'S *10:04*

WHILE IT IS GENERALLY unwise to judge a book by its cover, the US hardback edition of Ben Lerner's 2014 novel *10:04* has a particularly interesting story to tell. The dust jacket consists of an aerial photograph of New York City, taken from a helicopter by the Dutch architectural photographer Iwan Baan on the night of October 31, 2012, two days after the storm surge from Hurricane Sandy wiped out electrical power across much of lower Manhattan.[1] The photograph is disconcerting, not only because of its subject matter (lower Manhattan plunged into almost total darkness in the aftermath of a devastating storm), but also because it has been reversed (the buildings on the banks of the West River standing in for their equivalents on the Hudson; a black and empty expanse of water where the Brooklyn Bridge should be; etc.). There is a doubled relationship at work here; the event depicted in the photograph is itself uncanny, the world's most famous cityscape is made strange by being plunged into darkness, but at the same time, the reversal of the image on the cover of *10:04* compounds that estrangement and—crucially—does so at the level of visual representation. The familiar is rendered unfamiliar and the prospective reader struggles to make sense of the image. If the historical moment depicted in the photograph is uncanny in and of itself, the reversal of the photograph both heightens that sense of estrangement and changes its source by altering the relationship between the photographic representation and the thing being represented. No longer "merely" a photographic document of an historical event—and therefore a "straightforward" figurative representation—the photograph reversed becomes non-figurative and its representational capacities are transformed. As such, if what the cover image offers is a moment of cognitive estrangement for the prospective reader, it also offers a key with which she can unlock the novel's meaning. While *10:04* does indeed end with a depiction of the events of Hurricane Sandy sometime around the time at which the photograph was taken, rendering it a figurative representation of the novel's time and place, the cover image does more than merely suggest to the reader what the subject or setting of the novel might be; it also provides a representation of its cognitive framework, one in which, to paraphrase the novel's epigraph, everything is as it is, just a little different.[2]

The photograph used on the cover of *10:04*, for example, is not just a more-or-less realist illustration of the novel's temporal and spatial settings, or a key to the intellectual concerns of its contents, for it appears also as a described representational object within its pages. Five pages from the end of the novel, as the protagonist-narrator, a young author called Ben, and his close friend Alex return to Brooklyn from a storm-sieged Manhattan, he states, "It was getting cold. We saw a bright glow to the east among the dark towers of the Financial District, like the eye-shine of some animal. Later we would learn that it was Goldman Sachs, see photographs in which one of the few illuminated buildings in the skyline was the investment banking firm, an image I'd use for the cover of my book—not the one I was contracted to write about fraudulence, but the one I've written in its place for you, to you, on the very edge of fiction."[3] There is a great deal of work taking place in this late passage from Lerner's novel: it exemplifies the novel's consistent referencing of real-world visual cultural objects; the description of Baan's photograph anchors the novel's action to the real-world time and place that serve as its setting; and the mention of the photograph's use as the cover image of the book, and the direct address to the reader, suggest the novel's metafictional qualities, and begin to conclude its considerations of lived experience under millennial conditions. As both a paratextual object and the subject of ekphrastic representation, Baan's photograph says much about the complex work that *10:04* performs as it charts the relationships between literary and visual representation, between memory and perception, and between risk and catastrophe—all as they are represented through the thoughts and actions of the novel's young male narrator-protagonist.

In these representations, Lerner's novel suggests that contemporary writers have cast off some of the constraints of the by-now-traditional formal modes of postmodernism and have turned to reinvigorated—but no longer straightforward—modes of realism, informed but not constrained by postmodernism's distrust of realist narrative representation. Of the recent return to realism evident in contemporary American fiction, Madhu Dubey suggests, "given that the material conditions that gave rise to postmodernism still pertain and, if anything, have intensified, the problem that postmodernism posed for the social novel—the challenge of mapping a new form of social totality—cannot be solved on formal grounds, by reviving narrative realism."[4] As this essay will show, *10:04* has taken this problem as one of its central concerns and, as such, is exemplary of a recent cycle of novels that attempt to wed postmodern formal considerations to a reinvigorated sense of the value of realism as a mode of literary representation.[5] This relationship has produced novel-length fictional narratives that seek to maintain the formal complexity of high postmodernism, but with the aim of invigorating—rather than critiquing—the capacity of literature to act as a conduit for communication between writer and reader. For Mitchum Huehls, there has arisen under neoliberalism "a body of contemporary fiction that deploys post-structural concepts to innovate new, more experimental literary forms, all while refusing to turn those concepts against the fictional texts themselves."[6] He calls this deployment an "unreal realism . . . that contribute[s] to the composition rather than the deconstruction of the world."[7] Such novels, he suggests, "self-consciously consider and reveal [their] own conditions of possibility."[8] Or, as Huehls puts it elsewhere, "contemporary fiction writers are increasingly rejecting critique in favor of a post-normative, post-critical politics."[9] And this is certainly the case for *10:04*, a novel that is profoundly concerned with questions of representation and the capacity of literature not only to represent the real world, but also to forge lines of communication between subjects. Highly aware of its own fictionality, *10:04* nevertheless insists that meaningful communication between author and reader is possible.[10]

In this essay I argue that, in its descriptions of the workings of a system rendered all but invisible—and therefore all but indescribable—by the high-tech informational technologies that enable it, Lerner's novel makes visible the social and technological structures of contemporary neoliberalism while also charting the increasingly tight interconnections between the risk cultures of contemporary finance capital, the era of global terrorism and of the superstorm, and contemporary forms of citizenship and subjectivity. Disparate though these various facts of contemporary life may seem, they are all connected in their positioning of the subject in a position of precarity or potential threat. Bad weather, global terrorism, and finance are all risks to be borne by the contemporary subject.[11] As such, they thematize one of the core components of neoliberalism, which—as Mark Fisher has suggested—requires that the subject "develop a capacity to respond to unforeseen events [and] to live in conditions of total instability, or 'precarity'" (34). For Fisher, as for others, this precarity is felt most acutely in relationship to time. As he suggests, "the old disciplinary segmentation of time is breaking down. The carceral regime of discipline is being eroded by the technologies of control, with their systems of perpetual consumption and continuous development" (23). Under what Fisher calls the "increased cybernetization of the working environment" (33), the subject is unable to "synthesize time into any coherent narrative" (24). Or, as Richard Sennett has it, "the militarization of social time is coming apart" (24). For many, this "coming apart" structures much of contemporary life. As Benjamin Kunkel puts it in *Utopia or Bust*, "global capitalism or neoliberalism under US hegemony ... has inflicted economic insecurity and ecological anxiety on the young in particular" (19). Attending to these conditions, I argue, *10:04* produces a narrative of the present that foregrounds the powerful matrix of risk, fear, and insecurity that have come to dominate much contemporary lived experience in the United States, and of neoliberal subject formation more generally.

In David Harvey's formulation, "neoliberalism is in the first instance a theory of political economic practices that proposes that human well-being can best be advanced by liberating individual entrepreneurial freedoms and skills within an institutional framework characterized by strong private property rights, free markets, and free trade. The role of the state is to create and preserve an institutional framework appropriate to such practices" (2). Speaking on the relationship between citizenship and the state, Eva Cherniavsky suggests, "neoliberalism [is] a specific resolution to the duplicity of the modern nation-state, constituted in the double imperative to advance the public good and to secure private property in its myriad and proliferating forms. Neoliberalism abdicates the former imperative in favor of the latter, and in so doing frees the state from the compulsion to realize a national-popular interest that it can claim to uphold" (17). Neoliberalism's greatest trick has been its ability to cast that abdication as a form of common good in which any individual's failure to capitalize on it is precisely that: individual. "It has been part of the genius of neoliberal theory," Harvey observes, "to provide a benevolent mask full of wonderful-sounding words like freedom, liberty, choice, and rights, to hide the grim realities of the restoration or reconstruction of naked class power, locally as well as transnationally, but most particularly in the main financial centres of global capitalism" (119). Or, as he puts it in *The Enigma of Capital*, neoliberalism "refers to a class project that coalesced in the crisis of the 1970s. Masked by a lot of rhetoric about individual freedom, liberty, personal responsibility and the virtues of privatization, the free market and free trade, it legitimized draconian policies designed to restore and consolidate capitalist class power" (10). Furthermore, Harvey points out, "Redistributive effects and increasing social inequality have in fact been such a persistent feature of neoliberalization as to be regarded as structural to the whole project" (16).

If, as Harvey explains, "the neoliberal project is to disembed capital from [social and political] constraints" (11), one of the primary means through which that disembedding has taken place is through the recasting of the individual as a thoroughly financialized subject, on the one hand, and the absolute normalization of neoliberalism's dominant discursive modes. For Harvey, "neoliberalism has ... become hegemonic as a mode of discourse.

It has pervasive effects on ways of thought to the point where it has become incorporated into the common-sense way many of us interpret, live in, and understand the world" (3). The neoliberal subject is produced through a process of internalization in which, as Peter Fleming has it, "character," "personality," and "emotional infrastructure" became the means by which "everyday people act like capitalist enterprises in most facets of their lives" (5). For Randy Martin, moreover, "how individuals come to think about themselves, take stock of how they are doing and what they have accomplished, and how they know themselves to be moving forward through the measured paces of finance, yields a particular subjectivity" (9). As such, and as Harvey suggests, "neoliberalization has meant, in short, the financialization of everything" (33). In what follows, then, I read Lerner's novel as an examination of the pressure placed on the subject (and in this case particularly the male subject) under neoliberal conditions. Narrated in the first person, *10:04* uses the representational techniques (the tropes, forms, and structural conventions) of contemporary realist fiction; of thinly veiled autobiography, or autofiction; and of metafiction to make sense of the sorts of neoliberal social, capital, and political formations that I have outlined. *10:04*, I argue, is a millennial novel.[12] It is, in other words, an exemplary work of neoliberal realism, highly attuned to the postmodern formal concerns of the previous era but heavily invested in literature's capacity to represent contemporary lived experience.

"Some Impossible Mirror": Ekphrastic Representation

"The relationship between representation and reality under capitalism has always been problematic." David Harvey, *The Enigma of Capital*

If the cover photograph, as discussed, is exemplary of Lerner's treatment of visual culture in *10:04*, it is by no means unique. Visual representation is a vital aspect of the novel's meaning-making apparatus. Including Baan's photograph, the novel contains 13 different illustrations, ranging from paintings and photographs to film stills and postage stamps. Each of these illustrations serves to supplement or to develop an idea made in the novel, and, like Baan's photograph, many of them are also described objects in the narrative. Moreover, in addition to these illustrations and the attendant descriptions of them in the text, *10:04* contains many other references to the visual arts that are central to its meaning-making apparatus. A rough count yields references to over thirty discrete works of art, visual objects, or named artists in the novel's pages—ranging from Jules Bastien-Lepage and Donald Judd to Pablo Picasso and Jeff Koons; from Robert Zemeckis's

Back to the Future to Carl Theodor Dryer's *The Passion of Joan of Arc*—a number of which get sustained and repeated attention in its pages. At the same time, the novel contains references to a wide range of poets and novelists—Virginia Woolf, Ezra Pound, William Bronk, Franz Kafka, John Keats, Geoffrey O'Brien, and Walt Whitman, to name but a few. *10:04* is saturated with cultural intertexts and derives a great deal of its meaning from the description, analysis, and critique of them; epistemological knowledge is derived from engagement with visual and literary culture—and this is the case both for the novel's characters and for its readers. At the same time, knowledge is also a question of ontological engagement, and the novel is concerned with the relationship between representation and being.

One early example illustrates the interconnected relationship between the novel's ontological and epistemological registers. In it, Lerner compares French artist Jules Bastien-Lepage's oil painting *Joan of Arc* (1879) to the Hollywood blockbuster *Back to the Future* (1985). Both painting and film are significant cultural touchstones in the novel and appear within it repeatedly; as such, they reward sustained attention.[13] The first reference is to Bastien-Lepage's painting. Describing a visit to the Metropolitan Museum of Art with his friend Alex, the narrator states, "that day we were standing before Jules Bastien-Lepage's *Joan of Arc*—Alex looks a little like this version of her—and she said, apropos of nothing: 'I'm thirty-six and single.'"[14] At this point, the painting is already performing important work. It provides a location and a focal point for the reader, who can place the characters before the painting in the museum, a real-world location. As such, it suggests not only the real world outside of the fictional world of the novel, but also a cultural milieu into which the characters can be placed. "We often visited [the Met] weekday afternoons," the narrator tells the reader, "since Alex was unemployed and I, a writer."[15] But the painting also substitutes for narrative description. The reader can find a copy of the painting on the Internet (for example) and see who "Alex looks a little like." As such, the painting explicitly stands in for narrative description. This use of Bastien-Lepage's painting is doubly significant because the narrator repeatedly states his refusal to describe faces. Therefore, the painting performs representational work that the narrator (and, by extension, the author) refuses or rejects. It is a real-world intertextual supplement performing a task that literary narrative is deemed inadequate to execute.

But the painting is also used to set up one of the novel's primary concerns: the relationship between visual representation, human perception, and ontological being. After this opening description of the painting, the narrator describes a conversation the friends have while standing in front of the painting, in which Alex tells him that she wishes to have a child and proposes that he become a sperm donor for her. What follows next, however, is not further detail of that conversation (or any sense of the narrator's response to this request), but a paragraph-length description of Bastien-Lepage's painting. Because of its complexity, and its importance both to the novel and to my understanding of it, I will provide it in full:

> Three translucent angels hover in the top left of the painting. They have just summoned Joan, who has been working at a loom in her parents' garden, to rescue France. One angel holds her head in her hands. Joan *appears* to stagger toward the viewer, reaching her left arm out, *maybe* for support, in the swoon of being called. Instead of grasping branches or leaves, her hand, which is carefully positioned in the sight line of one of the other angels, *seems* to dissolve. The museum placard says that Bastien-Lepage was attacked for his failure to reconcile the ethereality of the angels with the realism of the future saint's body, but that "failure" is what makes it one of my favorite paintings. It's *as if* the tension between the metaphysical and physical worlds, between two orders of temporality, produces a glitch in the pictorial matrix; the background swallows her fingers. Standing there that afternoon with Alex, I was reminded of the photograph Marty carries in *Back to the Future*, crucial movie of my youth: as Marty's time-travelling disrupts the prehistory of his family, he and his siblings begin to fade from the snapshot. Only here it's a presence, not an absence, that eats away at her hand: she's *being pulled into the future*.[16]

This is a rich and complex paragraph, but it can be divided into three clearly-distinguishable epistemological registers: a straightforward description of the painting ("her hand ... is carefully positioned in the sight line of one of the other angels"); an analysis of it by the narrator ("it's *as if* the tension between the metaphysical and physical worlds, between two orders of temporality, produces a glitch in the pictorial matrix"); and, finally, a comparison of it to another visual cultural artifact ("I was reminded of the photograph Marty carries in *Back to the Future*"). This progression from comprehension, to analysis, to comparative analysis is both commonplace and part and parcel of epistemological understanding, but it is important to observe just how much even the seemingly straightforward description offered here is already an interpretive act. As they do throughout the novel, interpretive phrases such as "appears," "seems," "as if," and "maybe" dominate. *10:04* is a novel about the relationship between how things seem and how they are. But even this observation is complicated further by the fact that the paragraph offers at least three different interpretive registers: that of the narrator-protagonist, that of the museum (via the description of the informational placard), and that of the painter's contemporaries (again, via the placard). These three different registers locate interpretation both in time (then and now) and in space (real and fictional).

One hundred and sixty pages after this first description, the novel returns to its analysis of the interrelationship between *Joan of Arc* and *Back to the Future*, this time in the form of a long free-verse poem, composed while the protagonist is resident at the Chinati Foundation, a real-life writer's and artist's retreat in Marfa, Texas. Quoted piecemeal throughout the novel's fourth section, which depicts the narrator's residency at Chinati, the poem re-describes much of its narrative content and returns to many of its key intellectual questions.

While the description of the painting given in the poem closely resembles the one provided in prose at the start of the novel and discussed in this text, it is not precisely the same, and the differences between the two are highly significant. The poem chooses not to name the film, as it does in the first description, and makes new claims about the relationship between representation and the medium. For example, in the poem's description of Joan's hand, which was described in the first instance as 'dissolving' and "produc[ing] a glitch in the pictorial matrix," the loss of straightforward representational realism denotes a shift from epistemological to ontological meaning, thereby developing and refining the earlier interpretation:

> But from our perspective it's precisely
> where the hand ceases to signify a hand
> and is paint, no longer appears to be warm
> or capable, that it reaches the material
> present, becomes realer than sculpture because
> tentative: she is surfacing too quickly.[17]

No longer "warm or capable," the hand has shifted from a realist representation of the human body to the representation of another order of materiality. The "glitch in the pictorial matrix" produces a temporal shift into the "material present" in which meaning shifts from an epistemological to an ontological understanding of subjectivity. What is emphasized is not the thing being depicted (a human body) but the medium (paint). This is a temporal shift produced by a failure of genre. What fails the painting is its realism and, for both Bastien-Lepage's contemporaries and the narrator looking at the painting over 100 years later, realism is not a fixed condition, but a historically contingent set of genre conventions.

As it does throughout the novel, the materiality of the specific medium gains significance as the representational capacities of genre wane. As Bastien-Lepage's contemporaries bemoan his inability to stick to generic conventions—to reconcile the spiritual with the actual—the narrator of the novel applauds the painting's materiality. This waning or confusion of genre specificity is evident in the description of the painting given in the poem, in which the first-person speaker states "her hand, / in what for me is the crucial passage, partially / dissolves."[18] The description of the painting in the poem describes it as if it were a piece of prose: paintings do not have "passages," but novels do. Moreover, this second description of *Joan of Arc* and *Back to the Future* operates recursively. Because it is offered towards the close of the novel, it exists not only as a repetition of the previous description, but also in light of all that comes in between. The full meaning and significance of the first instance becomes clear following the second, and only in hindsight.

The novel's descriptions and interpretations of objects of visual representation are supplemented with illustrations that perform equally important work. Immediately following the first description of Bastien-Lepage's painting discussed above, for example, the novel's first two illustrations appear: one, captioned "the presence of the future," is a detail of Joan of Arc's hand from the painting; the other, captioned "the absence of the future," is a still from *Back to the Future* (although not, interestingly, of the photograph described in the text, but of Marty watching as his hand loses it corporeal, material solidity).[19] Because they follow directly from the novel's narrative description of the painting and of the film, these illustrations provide the reader with visual evidence of the claims that the narrator is making about them and ground the discussion of them in the real world. As such, they are exemplary; they prove the veracity of the claims that the narrator is making about them. But these illustrations are also evidentiary of the narrator's claims about time and of the world outside the novel in which those claims are being made; they are, in this regard, illustrative and referential. They speak to the world of the novel and the world of the reader; they are a bridge between the fictional and the real worlds, but they also call into question the capacity of literature to represent the world of the real. Like every single image included in the pages of *10:04*, they speak most clearly to the subject of representation and perception. While the novel itself suggests the necessity for new forms of narrative representation to suit current conditions, the illustrations included in its pages further trouble the relationship between representation, perception, and the world, and suggest the problematic status of literary narrative under millennial conditions.

"A Kind of Palimpsestic Plagiarism:" Fraudulent Authority

"Most of my youth went by during the end of history, which has itself now come to an end." Benjamin Kunkel, *Utopia or Bust*

"On the Very Edge of Fiction" [101]

Just as *10:04* uses ekphrastic representation and the inclusion of illustrations to negotiate the relationship between ontological and epistemological registers of subjectivity and to interrogate the representational capacities of literary and visual genres alike, it also devotes considerable attention to questions of fraudulence and authority. Examples of plagiarism and of the willful ignoring of "facts" abound and are essential to the novel's representation of culture under millennial conditions. The novel understands various registers of representation—visual, literary, political—to be profoundly interconnected, such that questions of authorship are disturbed by the saturation of information that has become a signal feature of contemporary lived experience. That saturation is evident in *10:04* in a number of ways, but occurs most clearly in the novel's representation of facts that have long been known, but have been commonly disavowed, and in its discussion of real-world examples of plagiarism and fraudulence. It is also a key component of the precarious relationship between protagonist and author that troubles the novel.

The clearest and most sustained example of the novel's engagement with the precarious status of facts in the real world is that of the brontosaurus. In an early subsection of the novel, which follows immediately on from the prose description of Bastien-Lepage's *Joan of Arc* already discussed, the narrator describes an after-school project about the brontosaurus that he is working on with Roberto, a young Hispanic student at a Brooklyn elementary school where the narrator's friend teaches. The brontosaurus, the narrator informs the reader, is a dinosaur that never existed. As such, it is one of a number of examples from the novel (the former planet Pluto being another) in which 'facts' from the narrator's childhood are revealed to have been false. Of the brontosaurus, the narrator states, "in the nineteenth century a paleontologist put the skull of a camarasaurus on an apatosaurus skeleton and believed he'd discovered a new species, so that one of the two iconic dinosaurs of my youth [the other presumably being the tyrannosaurus rex] turns out not to have existed, a revision that, along with the demotion of Pluto from planet to plutoid, retrospectively struck hard at my childhood worldview, my remembered sense of both galactic space and geological time."[20]

This unmooring of facts from their evidentiary base is a consistent feature of the novel and illustrates its representation of millennial subjectivity battered by an overabundance of information, on the one hand, and the loss of a previous sense of certainty, on the other. As any and all information becomes seemingly just a Google search away, the narrator begins to lose a firm sense of the solidity of being that, as I will discuss shortly, is related to questions of corporeal determinacy. The brontosaurus dinosaur is a fake, created by the comingling of the fossilized remains of two different species, thereby raising questions about the status both of factual evidence and of expertise. The brontosaurus exists because of an error created by an expert who, in his haste to best a rival, misread the geological evidence available to him. However, there is a further relationship being highlighted here in which the revelation that purported "facts" turn out to have been anything but is set against the all-but-willful refusal of many to "remember" that shift in status. As the narrator points out in the pages of Roberto's report on the event, which is entitled "To the Future" and is included towards the end of the novel, while scientists discovered the fact that the brontosaurus was a "fake" in 1903, "most people didn't know about their new discovery [and] thought that the brontosaurus still existed because museums kept using the name on their labels—and because the brontosaurus was really, really popular!" So popular, in fact, that the United States Postal Service went so far as to produce a brontosaurus stamp in 1989.[21] As such, the narrator positions the continued existence of the brontosaurus as a lie perpetuated by experts (in the form of museum labels), the public (who love them), and the government (who perpetuate the purported lie of their existence on releases) alike. As this example makes clear, facts in *10:04* are shown to be contingent, open to interpretation, and—in the era of Google—under a constant process of revision.[22]

In a further example of the rejection of known factual information, the narrator repeatedly refers to pigeons as "stout-bodied passerines" before confessing later on that "I just Googled pigeon and learned that they aren't true passerines" but are *Columbidae*, the name by which he refers to them on subsequent occasions.[23] As with the example of the brontosaurus, the awkward phrase "stout-bodied passerine" is insisted upon even after the narrator learns of his taxonomical error, thereby rendering the truth subordinate to other competing imperatives. Moreover, this insistence on using the incorrect term emphasizes the ambiguous genre status of the novel itself. While the narrator uses the correct name after admitting to his Google search, he does not go back and revise the earlier pages of the manuscript upon making the discovery. Further, because the fictional novel that the narrator is writing is also the actual novel that the reader is holding in her hands, the narrator's refusal to correct the error is also a decision made by the novelist that has the effect of highlighting the troubled relationship between facts and fiction. As the fictional first-person narrator does not revise his fictional manuscript to correct an error, the actual author places that decision on display; the novel becomes a novel about the writing of a novel, thereby placing it in an unusual temporality—a perpetual state of becoming. As such, the conscious misnaming of pigeons in the novel constitutes a further example of Lerner's

"On the Very Edge of Fiction" [103]

desire not to call into question the status of facts per se but to interrogate how—and to what effect—we reorganize the world, and to underscore the tenuous hold fictional narrative has on representation, in which all that can be accurately represented is the act of representation itself.

The novel's engagement with the cultural relevance of facts and with the representational capacities of literature are brought together in an extended discussion of the *Challenger* space shuttle disaster of 1986 (the year after the release of *Back to the Future*), in which the topic of literary plagiarism comes to the fore. As with the example of *Joan of Arc* and *Back to the Future* that has just been analyzed, the novel's discussion of the *Challenger* disaster takes place in an extended fashion in two different sections of the novel, and to similar effect. Five pages after the illustrations from the painting and film are provided, and immediately following the discussion of the brontosaurus, the first example occurs. In it, the narrator describes walking down a deserted hallway in Roberto's school and experiencing the sensation of being transported in memory back to his own time as a young student. In the description of his elementary school classroom that follows, the narrator references the disastrous *Challenger* space shuttle mission of 1986 when he highlights the "letters addressed to Christa McAuliffe in exaggerated cursive, wishing her luck on the *Challenger* mission, which was only a couple of months in the future."[24] Nothing else is said about the *Challenger* mission in the narrative at this point, or about the disaster that struck moments after liftoff. As such, it exists in the narrative merely as an example at this stage, a possible foreshadowing of a disaster to come, and its relationship to the subject matter of the novel is not clear.

However, the next paragraph of the novel consists of an unattributed excerpt, given in italics, from Ronald Reagan's speech to the nation on the evening of January 28, 1986, the day of the disaster: "*And I want to say something to the schoolchildren of America who were watching the live coverage of the shuttle's takeoff. I know it is hard to understand, but sometimes painful things like this happen. It's all part of the process of exploration and discovery. It's all part of taking a chance and expanding man's horizons. The future doesn't belong to the fainthearted; it belongs to the brave. The* Challenger *crew was pulling us into the future, and we'll continue to follow them.*"[25] While the quote is provided without context or attribution, included at this point is the novel's third illustration, which bisects the paragraph: a photograph of Christa McAuliffe in training, captioned "*pulling us into the future.*"[26] While the link is not made explicit at this point, a direct relationship is being produced here between McAuliffe and Joan of Arc. The direct quote from Reagan's speech that is used for this caption also is the source for the earlier claim that the protagonist makes about

Bastien-Lepage's Joan, who is described by the narrator as being "pulled into the future."[27] The *Challenger* disaster and Reagan's address are foundational to the understanding being developed in the novel of the relationship between history, memory, and representation, but it is significant that the reader is not provided at this stage with either the source of the quote from Reagan's speech or a fuller context for the inclusion of the photograph of McAuliffe. Unless the reader recognizes these words as lines from Reagan's speech from a context or source outside of the novel, it is not yet available to her as a quote, and she does not have the fuller context through which to interpret or understand either quote or photograph. Likewise, the photograph of McAuliffe serves merely as a visual reminder of the time-space being described, offering a set of visual markers to time and place (hairstyle, spacesuit, and shuttle interior), with no reference made to McAuliffe's own imminent future. That direct link is not provided until Lerner returns to the subject of the *Challenger* disaster some 100 pages later, and the various interrelations that Lerner is developing are fully developed.

In a speech that the narrator gives at Columbia University, he describes "the fiction about the origins of [his] writing," which he dates to hearing Reagan's televised speech in 1986. "Like most Americans who were alive at that time," the narrator begins, "I have a clear memory of watching the space shuttle *Challenger* disintegrate seventy-three seconds into flight." He then goes on to recall to his audience the general excitement about the *Challenger* mission, and then asks for a show of hands to see who in the audience remembers "watching the *Challenger* disaster live."[28] After the majority of the people in the room raise their hands, he goes on to explain that, while the shuttle's launch was broadcast live on a number of channels (including the nascent CNN) and shown in a number of school classrooms, all of the major networks cut away from live broadcast before disaster struck and that what people remember as the witnessing of an event unfolding "live" on television was actually in most cases a misremembering of something that they actually saw on replay, either minutes or hours later. What many people did watch live on television, the narrator points out, was Reagan's address to the nation broadcast live later that evening.

This engagement with the relationship of memory to event is evidence of one of the novel's key concerns: the shifting status of events in an era of live television broadcasting. As the narrator puts it, the *Challenger* disaster is "consistently noted as the dawning of our era of live disasters and simulcast wars: O.J. Simpson fleeing in the white Bronco, the towers collapsing, etc."[29] That so many of his peers remember, as he does, watching the events unfold live in front of their eyes, suggests a profound transformation in the status of witnessing. Not only are events "witnessed" on television rather than live, but they are also remembered retrospectively. "Unless you were watching CNN or were in one of the special classrooms," the narrator points out, "you didn't witness it in the present tense," but are the unwitting holder of what he refers to slightly later as the "false memory of a moving image."[30] In an era of live broadcasting (that might be anything but), the narrator suggests, memory is prone to temporal collapse. As such, the truth of an event is contingent and open to revision, not only in the face of the fallibility of memory but also in the transformed nature of the event itself, which no longer exists (if it ever did) in an unmediated status. Such questions of origin and authenticity also pertain to the speech's literary and linguistic qualities, which are shown to be equally powerful but just as tenuous.

In the subsequent discussion of Reagan's televised address to the nation that was broadcast that evening, the narrator devotes a great deal of attention, not only to the nature of subjective experience in an age of televised disasters, but also to the subject of plagiarism, which is a significant topic in the novel. It is the partial subject matter of "The Golden Vanity," the original short story from which the full-length novel was developed, and of the novel the protagonist has been contracted to write.[31] While the narrator suggests that this original subject gets dropped along the way, it is a strong theme throughout the novel. For example, it is a significant subject in the narrator's discussion of Reagan's address to the nation, which serves as his entry point into the possibilities of poetry as a literary genre. As the narrator puts it, "The speech was only four minutes long. And the ending—one of the most famous conclusions of any presidential speech—entered my body as much as my mind: *We will never forget them, nor the last time we saw them, this morning, as they prepared for the journey and waved goodbye and 'slipped the surly bonds of earth' to 'touch the face of God'*."[32] The narrator describes the effect of this bodily experience in the same terms with which he describes earlier both McAuliffe and Joan of Arc: "the sentence pulled me into the future" and awoke a sense of the capacity of "poetic language to integrate a terrible event and its image back into a framework of meaning."[33]

But the conclusion to the speech that so affects the narrator's younger self is not only an example of the power of poetry, but also an example of plagiarism. As the narrator explains, the final lines of the speech—"*'slipped the surly bonds of earth' to 'touch the face of God'*"—are neither Reagan's nor those of speechwriter Peggy Noonan, but are taken from a famous poem, "High Flight," written by John Gillespie Magee, a young American pilot who served in the Canadian Air Force during World War II and was killed in a mid-air collision shortly after writing the poem. For the narrator, that Magee's poem was used in Reagan's speech "showed poetry's power to circulate among bodies and temporalities, to transcend the contingencies of its authorship."[34] What comes to interest the protagonist most, however, is the fact that Magee's poem is heavily plagiarized from multiple other sources. That the poem turns out to be fraudulent is "beautiful" and "a kind of palimpsestic plagiarism that moves through bodies and time" circulating in the world untethered from any "single origin."[35] In this rendering, authorship becomes an obsolete category in which the power of poetic language itself is primary. The facts of any given poem's authorship are irrelevant in a world in which all information exists in a perpetual mode of revision and erasure. As such, authority—whether in the form of a speech that includes unattributed lines from an already plagiarized poem, of an event witnessed out of time, or of a Wikipedia entry with multiple anonymous authors—is placed under erasure in an era of contingency.

"Money Was a Kind of Poetry": Millennial Perceptions

"Weather is no longer a natural fact so much as a political-economic effect." Mark Fisher, *Capitalist Realism*

If the novel's engagement with visual forms of cultural representation, such as Baan's photograph and Bastien-Lepage's painting, stage an encounter between cultural artifacts and the referential world, it also signals one of the novel's other major preoccupations: the transformation of human perception and modes of cultural representation under millennial conditions. Throughout the novel, focal events such as superstorms and medical crises reveal the organizing structures of the neoliberal world as they render the perceived world as *"just a little different"* and human perception is transformed. One of the novel's primary engagements is with the question of what forms of culture are best able to represent contemporary conditions. Much is made in the novel of the ways in which contemporary lived experience requires new ways of seeing and representing the world. Mid-way through the novel's opening section, for example, the narrator describes the experience of shopping for emergency supplies at an upscale Brooklyn grocery store on the eve of Hurricane Irene. After describing the ways in which the coming storm appears to have produced a "common conversation" between all of the residents of the city, the narrator goes on to describe how the approaching storm made him "viscerally aware of both the miracle and insanity of the mundane economy."[36] Holding in his hand a jar of instant coffee he has just picked up from the now-almost-empty grocery store shelves, he states, "It was as if the social relations that produced the object in my hand began to glow within it as they were threatened, stirred inside their packaging, lending it a certain aura—the majesty and murderous stupidity of that organization of time and space and fuel and labor becoming visible in the commodity itself now that planes were grounded and the highways were starting to close."[37] Such descriptions abound in the novel and the relationship between limit events and human perception is absolutely central to it. What becomes "visible in the commodity itself" here are the social relations that are typically—and necessarily—hidden behind the surface structures of commodity exchange.

This relationship also is manifest in the novel's engagement with the September 11, 2001, terrorist attack on the World Trade Center, which—like the superstorm—is represented in the novel as a limit event. For example, in the passage described earlier, in which the narrator describes the scene of lower Manhattan plunged into darkness by the post-Hurricane Sandy power failure, a direct link is made between superstorm and terrorist attack: "A cab surprised us as we turned onto Park Place, the felt absence of the twin towers now difficult to distinguish from the invisible buildings. I had the sensation that if power were suddenly restored, the towers would be there, swaying a little."[38] Likewise, one hundred pages earlier, the narrator describes the "present absence of the towers" he feels while looking across the East River towards Manhattan from a bench in Brooklyn Bridge Park.[39] In each of these instances, the Twin Towers of the World Trade Center inhabit a position in which their absence exists as a felt presence. The "invisible buildings" of the first example render the Twin Towers "visible" by altering what is called elsewhere in the novel the "pictorial matrix";[40] the loss of electricity makes the fallen towers visible by rendering the surviving buildings in the skyline invisible, thereby producing a perceptual commensurability between them. The anticipation of the coming storm transforms the narrator's perspective on the world, in one example; the effects of the passing storm transform the skyline of lower Manhattan, in the other. In both cases, presence is produced by absence—either real or imagined—and perception is understood in relation not only to the subjective body, but also to ontological being. As with the example of Joan of Arc's hand, the material presence of objects in the world is manifest as a felt experience by the subjects moving through it.

Such ontological modes of perception are cited repeatedly in the novel as central facts of modern urban living in which the interconnections between advanced capital accumulation and the modes of perpetual and instantaneous contact enabled by contemporary communication technologies have altered the relationship of the subject to the world. As the narrator looks out over Manhattan from Brooklyn and describes the "thrill" he always experiences when he sees the city from afar, he claims, "It was a thrill that only built space produced in me, never the natural world, and only when there was an incommensurability of scale—the human dimension of the windows tiny from such distance combining but not dissolving into the larger architecture of the skyline that was the expression, the material signature, of a collective person who didn't exist yet, a still-uninhabited second-person plural to whom all the arts, even in their most intimate registers, were nevertheless addressed."[41] This sense of the city as a location that collapses the boundaries between the inside and the outside, between ontological and epistemological modes of being, is mirrored in an earlier description of the transformations produced in the city and its residents by the approach of Hurricane Irene. As the narrator states:

> From a million media, most of them handheld, awareness of the storm seeped into the city, entering the architecture and the stout-bodied passerines, inflecting traffic patterns and the "improved sycamores," so called because they're hybridized for urban living. I mean the city was becoming one organism, constituting itself in relation to a threat viewable from space, an aerial sea monster with a single eye around which tentacular rain bands swirled. There were myriad apps to track it, Doppler color-coded to indicate the intensity of precipitation, the same technology they'd utilized to measure the velocity of blood flowing through my arteries.[42]

In this passage, the novel's preoccupation with questions of millennial subjectivity are clearly visible. As modern technologies provide new knowledge of the body, they also transform its relationship to the external world, thereby collapsing such distinctions. Not only do modern technologies make visible the approaching storm, they also collapse the perceptual differences between the body and the world by rendering commensurate rain and blood. The similarities between the technologies that render the human body known in new ways also alter the subject's relationship to the larger patterns of the weather—what is manifest here is a difference in degree not in kind, a scalar transformation that collapses the distinction between the inside and the outside, the self and the environment, the self and the body.

This collapse is negotiated most fully in the novel's examination of contemporary culture's capacity to represent the present. As the millennial subject navigates a world transformed across all scales, new pressures are placed on the modes and genres of artistic and cultural expression through which such changes might be represented. In one such example, the narrator's sometimes girlfriend, Alena, who is an artist, cuts a deal with a major insurance company to stage an exhibition of damaged art that has been removed from the market because it has deemed beyond repair (or because the cost of restoration would be prohibitive), and which has become the property of the insurance company following settlement.[43] As the first visitor to the "Institute for Totaled Art," the narrator is struck by the ways in which a photograph by Henri Cartier-Bresson, "had transitioned from being a repository of immense financial value to being declared of zero value without undergoing what was to me any perceptible material transformation—it was the same only totally different."[44] This transformation has nothing to do with art, per se, and everything to do with commerce. The narrator describes how, while it is common to encounter "material things that seemed to have taken on a kind of magical power as a result of a monetizable signature [. . .] it was incredibly rare [. . .] to encounter an object liberated from that logic."[45] He continues, "I felt a fullness indistinguishable from being emptied as I held a work from which the exchange value had been abstracted, an object that was otherwise unchanged."[46] As with the jar of instant coffee described earlier (and mentioned here also in relation to this abstraction of exchange value—"I remembered the jar of instant coffee the night of the storm"), what is transformed is human perception.[47] Nothing perceptible has changed in the inherent qualities of the photograph, but its relationship to other objects, to the market, and therefore to the human subject, has been transformed.

As the link between the transformed art object and the jar of instant coffee makes clear, the subject of artistic representation is frequently tied to the risk and insecurity of millennial conditions in the novel. Alena's own art, for example, consists of the creation of paintings that she has "deftly aged" making them "appear like painting[s] from the past."[48] This process not only destabilizes temporal logics, it also produces a direct relationship between art and catastrophe. As the narrator states, while some of Alena's paintings "appeared compellingly unchanged, others seemed as if they'd been recovered from the rubble of MOMA after an attack or had been defrosted from a future ice age."[49] As elsewhere, acts of terrorism and "natural disasters" are linked through the subject of artistic representation and human perception. Likewise, the art on display in the Institute for Totaled Art evokes the relationship between art and catastrophe, and imagines a temporal shift in which it becomes the ideal representational form of a weather-related dystopic near future. "So many of the paintings had sustained water damage," the narrator states, "that I felt as though I'd been transported into a not-so-distant future where New York was largely submerged, where you could look down from an unkempt High Line and see these paintings floating down Tenth Avenue."[50] Later in the novel, the narrator states that, while in the aftermath of Hurricane Sandy "scores of Chelsea galleries had been inundated and soon the insurers would be welcoming the newly totaled art into their vast warehouses" (230), "Alena's work wasn't on a ground floor, I remembered; besides, she strategically damaged her paintings in advance; they were storm-proof."[51] By "storm-proof[ing]" her paintings, Alena places them in a different relationship to the logics of the market than those described above: already intentionally and perceptibly damaged, they are isolated from risk. Alena's weathered paintings are both representations of the ontological insecurities incurred by risk and, in their status as objects of commodity exchange, isolated from it. Already "damaged," they are insulated from the effects of further damage. As such, they are exemplary art objects for the millennial conditions of risk and insecurity that the novel describes.

Existing on the "very edge of fiction," *10:04* is both an attempt to think about what modes and genres of culture can best reflect the lived experience of the early years of the new millennium and an example of them. The novel uses its multiple references to other works of literature, to painting, to photography, and to cinema, as a way of working through the capacity of art to produce knowledge, on the one hand, and to situate the thinking subject in the world, on the other. In an era of profound anxiety, the novel suggests, culture is vital not only because it offers a retreat from the world, but also because it affords the subject the opportunity to think about the world. If, in Fredric Jameson's well-known formulations, modernism was "a kind of cancelled realism" and postmodernism the "cultural logic of late capitalism," novels such as *10:04* suggest a new cultural logic is beginning to take hold, one in which the extraordinary complexities of the neoliberal global financial order require the formal tools of postmodernism.[52] These tools are deployed, however, not to point out the futility of attempting to represent the real, but in order to allow an in-any-way-realistic fictional account of contemporary conditions. If, to quote from *Back to the Future*, the novel's favorite intertext, "where we're going, we don't need roads," we will certainly (*10:04* makes clear) need a culture attuned not only to its own representational limits, but also to those of a world transformed in both scale and time by the informational and communicational technologies that make contemporary neoliberal forms of global finance capital possible.

Notes

1. Ben Lerner, *10:04* (New York: Faber and Faber, 2014). The photograph was also used as the cover of *New York* magazine's commemorative issue. http://nymag.com/nymag/letters/hurricane-sandy-editors-letter-2012-11/.

2. The epigraph, parts of which are also cited repeatedly in the novel's narrative, where it is attributed to Walter Benjamin, contains the line "everything will be as it is now, just a little different." See, for example, 19, 21, 25, 133, and 156. It is significant, moreover, that the possible readings of the photograph that I discuss here become available only if the reader recognizes that the reversal has taken place (for it is something that can be

easily missed by the casual viewer). Which begs the question—and it is one that the novel repeatedly asks—has anyone noticed?

3. Lerner, *10:04*, 236–237.

4. Madhu Dubey, "Post-Postmodern Realism?" *Twentieth Century Literature* 57:3–4 (Fall/Winter 2011): 369.

5. Further examples of the cycle include Teju Cole, *Open City* (New York: Random House, 2011); Teddy Wayne, *Kapitoil* (New York: Harper Perennial, 2010); Joshua Ferris, *The Unnamed* (New York: Little, Brown and Company, 2010); John Haskell, *American Purgatorio* (New York, Picador, 2009); Benjamin Kunkel, *Indecision* (New York: Random House, 2005).

6. Mitchum Huehls, "The Post-Theory Theory Novel," *Contemporary Literature* 56:2 (Summer 2015): 283.

7. Huehls, "The Post-Theory Theory Novel," 283.

8. Huehls, "The Post-Theory Theory Novel," 285.

9. Mitchum Huehls, *After Critique: Twenty-First Century Literature in a Neoliberal Age* (Oxford and New York: 2016), 10.

10. For more on what has been called the post-postmodern turn in contemporary US fiction, see Jeffrey Nealon, *Post-Postmodernism: or, The Cultural Logic of Just-Time Capitalism* (Stanford, CA: Stanford University Press, 2012). See also the two special issues of *Twentieth Century Literature*: Andrew Hoberek, "Introduction: After Postmodernism," *Twentieth Century Literature* 53:3 (Fall 2007): 233–47; and Jason Gladstone and Daniel Worden, "Introduction: Postmodernism, Then," *Twentieth Century Literature* 57:3–4 (Fall/Winter 2011): 291–308.

11. Peter Fleming, likewise, makes the connection when he points out the frequency with which the financial crisis of 2007–2008 and the resulting global recession were likened in the media to a tsunami. He goes on to suggest that the two actual tsunami that bookend the crisis, in 2004 and 2011, grounded the metaphor with real-life and up-close footage recorded on mobile phones and other handheld devices (1).

12. I use the term millennial here not to name a generation, but to produce a rough periodization. While the conditions described in Lerner's novel can be traced back, as the leading theorists of neoliberalism do, to the 1970s, the post-9/11 decade—which has been marked by crises of various sorts—has produced particular cultural forms, of which *10:04* is a key example.

13. It is from *Back to the Future* that the novel gets its title; 10:04 is the time displayed on the stopped clock in the clock tower that Marty uses to return to the present in Zemeckis' film, a clip of which is included in Christian Marclay's art installation *The Clock* (2010), which is discussed in the film (50–4, 141).

14. Lerner, *10:04*, 8.
15. Lerner, *10:04*, 7.
16. Lerner, *10:04*, 9. My emphasis.
17. Lerner, *10:04*, 176.
18. Lerner, *10:04*, 175.
19. Lerner, *10:04*, 10.
20. Lerner, *10:04*, 11.
21. Lerner, *10:04*, 227.

22. In a further development that would seem to prove the point, a scientific paper published in 2015, the same year as Lerner's novel, argues for the accuracy of the name brontosaurus. See Charles Choi, "The *Brontosaurus* Is Back," *Scientific American* April 7, 2015. https://www.scientificamerican.com/article/the-brontosaurus-is-back1/.

23. Lerner, *10:04*, 17, 94, 213, 234.
24. Lerner, *10:04*, 15.
25. Lerner, *10:04*, 15–16.
26. Lerner, *10:04*, 16.
27. Lerner, *10:04*, 9.
28. Lerner, *10:04*, 110.
29. Lerner, *10:04*, 110.
30. Lerner, *10:04*, 111, 115.

31. "The Golden Vanity" was published originally in the *New Yorker* (June 18, 2012) and is included complete and largely unaltered as the second section of the novel. The single difference between the two versions is not textual but visual: it is the inclusion in the novel of a photograph of the surface of Mars, which resembles a human face, and which is used to illustrate the condition *pareidolia*, a phenomenon where "the brain arranges random stimuli into a significant image or sound" (69). The photograph is described in the text as "one of those standard textbook images used to illustrate" the phenomenon (69). While these words appear in the short story, the photograph does not.

32. Lerner, *10:04*, 112.
33. Lerner, *10:04*, 111.
34. Lerner, *10:04*, 113.
35. Lerner, *10:04*, 114.
36. Lerner, *10:04*, 17, 19.
37. Lerner, *10:04*, 19.
38. Lerner, *10:04*, 237.
39. Lerner, *10:04*, 108.
40. Lerner, *10:04*, 9.
41. Lerner, *10:04*, 108.
42. Lerner, *10:04*, 17.

43. Like much else in the novel that is drawn from real-world sources, the Institute for Totaled Art is modeled on a real-world corollary, the Salvage Art Institute set up by the Polish-born artist Elka Krajewska. Lerner discusses the SAI in "Damage Control: The Modern Art World's Tyranny of Price," in *Harper's Magazine* (December 2013). The discussion of the SAI is clearly the source for much of the description of the narrator's response to its fictional counterpart, which replicates some of its language. The article also contains the quote from Walter Benjamin that Lerner uses as the epigraph to *10:04* (see n2). See also http://salvageartinstitute.org/.

44. Lerner, *10:04*, 133.
45. Lerner, *10:04*, 133.
46. Lerner, *10:04*, 133–134.
47. Lerner, *10:04*, 133.
48. Lerner, *10:04*, 27.
49. Lerner, *10:04*, 27. The plot of Donna Tartt's novel *The Goldfinch* also turns on a fictional terrorist attack at an art gallery (the Metropolitan Museum of Art in New York).

For more on the relationship between art and terror see my "'Anticipating the Fall': Art, Memory, and Historical Reclamation in Colum McCann's, "Let the Great World Spin," in *9/11: Topics in Contemporary North American Literature*, ed. Catherine Morley, Bloomsbury Academic (2016) and "September 11 as Heist," *Journal of American Studies*, 44:4 (November 2011).

 50. Lerner, *10:04*, 132.
 51. Lerner, *10:04*, 230.
 52. Fredric Jameson, "Culture and Finance Capital." *Critical Inquiry* 24:1 (Autumn 1997): 261.

[6]

CHRISTIAN P. HAINES

FICTIONS OF HUMAN CAPITAL; OR, REDEMPTION IN
NEOLIBERAL TIMES

KAREN BENDER'S SHORT STORY "Refund" revolves around an irredeemable debt. Josh and Clarissa, two practicing artists, sublet their apartment in Tribeca in order to work as adjunct faculty at a university in Virginia. Their tenant, Kim, a tourist from Montréal, has the misfortune of visiting New York City during the terrorist attacks of September 11, 2001. Kim subsequently demands a refund for the entire amount of the rent: "I was on my way there. I wanted to go to the observation deck. I went the wrong way on the subway, or I would be dead."[1] This conditional death hangs over the story as a whole, an object of exchange whose value defies measure and, in doing so, defers the possibility of resolution. It is the central point of contention, defining not only the relations between characters, but also their respective values as persons. Kim and Clarissa debate the amount of the refund, Kim asserting her right to a full refund ("I want it all back"), Clarissa insisting that the refund should be partial, since Kim had occupied the apartment for a portion of time. As the debate continues, Kim amends the initial demand, charging interest on the basis of the event's psychological toll: "*I am requesting $3,000 plus $1,000 for every nightmare I have had since the attack, which currently totals twenty-four. You owe me U.S. $27,000, payable now*" (134). Josh and Clarissa cannot pay the initial amount, let alone the amount with interest added—indeed, the story opens with their insolvency: "They had been lonely, met, married, worked at their painting for years, presented their work to a world that was indifferent, floundered in debt, defaulted on student loans . . ." (120). For Kim, this insolvency amounts to a moral as much as a financial failure. "*My pet peeves are injustice and dishonesty,*" Kim writes to Clarissa, "*I know when I am being treated fairly*" (126). In this view, to live is to be exposed to and responsible for financial risks, including unpredictable ones, so that Josh and Clarissa's failure to pay up, to redeem their debt, constitutes a breach of an implicit social contract: financialization and neoliberalism, as I will explain, require the fundamental

Fictions of Human Capital; Or, Redemption in Neoliberal Times [115]

commensurability of every good, including not only tangible commodities, but also all of the qualities, skills, and capacities gathered under the rubric of "human capital." There is a moral economy to neoliberalism, a deontological framework that includes not only ethical imperatives—one *ought* to pay one's debts—but also procedures for evaluating an individual's character according to their fiscal history.

The story's climax interrupts this neoliberal moral economy, demonstrating that such financial commensurability can only assert itself as natural fact by operating as fiction: Clarissa writes a check for $263.75, an amount that is arbitrary except that it is the sum total of her savings. In response, Kim reiterates that she "want[s] it all" (plus interest), revealing to Clarissa that she was supposed to have met her friend Darla at the Towers:

> "I was talking to her on my cell phone," said Kim. "She was on the elevator to the observation deck." She paused. "She wanted to go to the Empire State Building, but I thought at the Towers we would get a better view."
>
> What did one owe for being alive? What was the right way to breathe, to taste a strawberry, to love?
>
> "Kim," said Clarissa, "I—"
>
> "Do you know how long I'm going to charge you?" Kim said, her voice rising.
>
> Clarissa closed her eyes.
>
> "Do you know?" said Kim. (140)

The story's conclusion cements the financial logic of the neoliberal era while at the same time highlighting its inconsistency: On the one hand, financialization depends on the convertibility of debt and guilt, that is, on the establishment of an uninterrupted circuit of exchange between personal and economic values, such that there's no gap between person and economic agent. For the Marxist critique of political economy, the person is the "bearer" (*Träger*) of economic relations, a conduit for the impersonal forces of capitalist accumulation. In contrast, for neoliberal market rationality, the personal and impersonal enter into a state of indistinction: to live is, in some fundamental sense, to incur debt, to shoulder the burden of one's material conditions, to engage in the Sisyphean task of making good on one's fundamental debt/guilt in respect to society. This indistinction is all too evident in the metonymic chain that Clarissa constructs between bare life ("What did one owe for being alive?"), the sensation of taste, and love. There is implicit in this existential lament a foundational debt from which all of creation hangs. On the other hand, this financial ordering of the world cannot help but be fictitious—contingent, fabricated, and, in a sense, made up— for value is a social matter and the ability to impute debt/guilt, to charge another ("Do you know how long I am going to charge you?"), hinges on the gap between value and activity, economy and person, exchange-value and use-value. My point here is not so much the structuralist insight regarding the arbitrariness of the sign, but rather the Marxist claim that capitalist exchange, occurring as it does on the basis of a general equivalent (money), conceals a history of violence—so-called primitive accumulation or accumulation by dispossession—which is its material condition of possibility.[2] In the failure of exchange between Kim and Clarissa, Darla and the Twin Towers function as a sacrifice to global capital, a material offering in the name of which the fiction of universal value sustains itself: the specter of Darla is the present absence through which the future remains indebted to the past—suspense, in this situation, an effect of pursuing an impossible restitution. The guilt/debt that is the basis of this financialized moral economy is infinite only so long as it materializes itself through sacrifice, only so long as it extracts interest payments in both a literal and figurative sense. In short, it is the ritual of repayment/atonement that not only signifies indebtedness, but also reestablishes it in an endless process of accountability.

"Refund" offers a paradigm for discussing contemporary fictions dealing with credit and debt. It suggests a way of discussing contemporary fiction as a ritual whose provenance is the political theology of debt, that is, the nexus of Judeo-Christian theology, financialized capitalism, and governance. Contemporary fictions of credit and debt enact rituals that either sustain or contest financialization, depending on how they deal with the logic of sacrifice built into financialized capitalism. In work by writers such as Bender, Don DeLillo, Gary Shteyngart, Thomas Pynchon, and David Foster Wallace, the fictitiousness of finance reveals itself in terms of what it costs—that is, in terms of the toll it exacts on groups of people. Their novels and short stories do not simply offer a realistic accounting of the social costs of finance, for they also reckon with the economic, existential, and ontological implications of financialization. They investigate the ways in which financialization erases easy distinctions between the abstract and the concrete, as well as between the immaterial and material.[3] Or, as Miranda Joseph has argued, they demonstrate "that injustice [the injustices involved in financialization or regimes of credit and debt] occurs not only through abstraction but in the inscription of particularities as well."[4] As I will argue, sacrifice is nothing less than the consecration of the abstract laws of finance through the violent articulation of social particularity.

Given that financial personhood is one of the central objects of this essay, it's worth pausing for a moment to reflect on the concept of personhood more generally. Personhood is the nexus where religious, juridical, and economic registers meet. In economics, the person is a fictive entity, one which includes

Fictions of Human Capital; Or, Redemption in Neoliberal Times [117]

corporations, as well as laborers, and which regulates activity through social technologies such as the wage, the credit score, and the stock price. It is also a juridical norm through which one is held responsible in respect to the law; it is the figure to which one attributes rights but also imputes guilt. Finally, the person is a religious artifact through which, in monotheistic (especially Christian) traditions, the planes of immanence and transcendence, earth and heavens, flesh and spirit, are articulated and administered. This three-dimensional figure of the person has been theorized in perhaps the most concerted manner by Roberto Esposito, who's argued persuasively that the person is one of the fundamental mechanisms governing social life in ancient and modern contexts, for personhood is what enables subjectivity and subjugation to coincide in a practical and theoretical manner.[5] Personhood produces a subjectivity whose status as legal, economic, and religious subject depends on submission to a sovereign (nation-state, corporation, etc.). As Esposito demonstrates, the politics of personhood hinges on degrees of inclusion and exclusion in respect to the shifting thresholds of what constitutes a person.

In this essay, I focus on the personhood of human capital, contending that financialization is a matter not only of shifting sources of profit—the shift of corporate revenue streams from productive capital to fictitious capital, or from commodity sales to speculation[6]—but also of a transformation in the mode of producing, regulating, and punishing social subjects. Michel Foucault makes this point in *The Birth of Biopolitics*, describing the neoliberal concept of human capital in terms of the governance of an entrepreneurial subject endowed with particular capacities to generate revenue. Human capital invests in itself by taking on risks that promise, without guaranteeing, certain profits, or by managing risk towards the end of appreciating self-value.[7] This neoliberal model of personhood has as its obverse side a regime of fiscal responsibility and discipline, which is to say a set of norms, institutions, and practices that ensure that the financial subject pays what she owes or suffers the consequences for failing to do so. As Maurizio Lazzarato argues, debt has become the universal apparatus ensuring the social reproduction of capitalism: "Neoliberalism governs through multiple power relations: creditor-debtor, capital-labor, welfare programs-user, consumer-business, etc. But debt is a universal power relation, since everyone is included within it. Even those too poor to have access to credit must pay interest to creditors through the reimbursement of public debt; even countries too poor for a Welfare State must repay their debts. [. . .] If in times past we are indebted to the community, to the gods, to our ancestors, we are henceforth indebted to the 'god' Capital."[8] Although "god" falls between quotation marks, the theological language in this passage is not incidental: Lazzarato suggests that the subjective correlate of capital's process of endless accumulation is an endless dialectic between guilt and penitence, between debt and obligatory repayment. As Friedrich Nietzsche—on whose work Lazzarato builds—puts it: "The conviction reigns that it is only through the sacrifices and accomplishments of the ancestors that the tribe *exists*—and that one has to pay them back with sacrifices and accomplishments: one thus recognizes a *debt* that constantly grows greater, since these forebears never cease, in their continued existence as powerful spirits, to accord the tribe new advantages and new strength."[9] The person qua human capital is therefore not only entrepreneurial agent, but also sacrificial figure, an indebted figure whose very existence depends on a never-ending process of making restitution to the abstract God of profit. Irredeemable debt becomes the social foundation of the economy. Although one can never pay off the principal, failure to pay the interest one owes transforms a person from agent of sacrifice—one able to sacrifice a piece of herself, the proverbial pound of flesh, while still remaining more or less intact—into object of sacrifice, the destruction of which sanctifies the neoliberal regime of fiscal responsibility. The apotheosis of this political theology of finance is the only seemingly strange overlap in contemporary US politics between an anger-fueled Christian fundamentalist rhetoric of salvation and damnation and a conservative fiscal ideology that divides society into "productive" or "responsible" members and "leeches" or "parasites."[10] Responsibilization, or the neoliberal system of imputing debt, entails an economy of sacrifice.

In what follows, I examine how two works of fiction, Gary Shteyngart's *Super Sad True Love Story* (2010) and Don DeLillo's *Zero K* (2016), negotiate this economy of sacrifice. In these fictions, debt—in the general sense of social obligation, as well as the specific sense of financial obligation[11]—constitutes the central problem and conflict around which the narrative revolves. Unsurprisingly, given the intimacy between debt and guilt established above, it is redemption that functions as the promise of resolution in these novels—"promise" and not "guarantee," however, because the critical value of these texts has less to do with successfully resolving such conflicts than with deferring, short-circuiting, or redirecting the desire for redemption. More specifically, Shteyngart and DeLillo diagnose contemporary capitalism as the pursuit of a secular version of immortality, an abstract yet material immunization of the self from economic and personal crises through speculation. Speculative practices are also rituals of sacrifice, borrowing against the profits of fictitious futures only so long as they appease the capitalist gods of fiscal responsibility through the collateral of subprime suffering. These novels suggest that the idea of redemption only intensifies the bond between social life and capitalist governance. To Clarissa's question, "What did one owe for being alive?" they seem to respond: "Everything"—at least from a neoliberal perspective.

Economy of Sacrifice

Gary Shteyngart's *Super Sad True Love Story* and Don DeLillo's *Zero K* could not be more different in regard to aesthetic form: DeLillo's sentences are short and choppy, structured more like fragments of code than imitations of natural language. They read like a strange blend of technical manual and philosophical treatise, instructions on wealth management merging seamlessly with analyses of art objects. Shteyngart's sentences, in contrast, alternate between two-to-three-word sentence fragments—frequently the punch-lines of jokes—and long sentences littered with technical jargon, proper nouns (geographic locations, fictional trademarks, etc.), and existential musings. If, as Annie McClanahan argues, Shteyngart oscillates between caricature and stereotype, or excess of descriptive detail and reductive social types, DeLillo favors an almost monotonous stream of theoretical abstractions, a flat plane of general equivalence in which characters are more ciphers for ideas than semblances of individual psychology.[12] There is no space for irony in *Zero K*, or, if there is, it is not irony in the comedic sense, but in the German Idealist manner of an endless series of reflections on reflections. *Super Sad True Love Story*, on the other hand, thrives on a self-deprecating humor sharing affinities with the films of Woody Allen and the novels of Nikolai Gogol. While both novels deal with the financialization of personhood, they would seem to do so in opposite ways.

At the same time, the two novels share an affinity not only because of their content—the late capitalist landscape of credit, debt, and speculation—but also because of the thematic and narratological structuring of this content in a dialectic between redemption and guilt, a dialectic driven by an aspiration for secular immortality. Not only do both novels fret over the ways in which impersonal financial abstractions such as credit scores and derivatives regulate social life. They both advance the same solution, namely, the pursuit of an immortality whose purview is not the afterlife, but the earthly realm; an extension of biological life beyond all finite limits through a practice of financial immunization, or the conversion of financial resources into technological means for insulating life from the accidents of living. The opening sentences of the novels signal this aspiration, so that the remainder of their narratives can be read as processes of working out the difficulties involved in financial immortality: DeLillo: "*Everybody wants to own the end of the world*"; Shteyngart: "Today I've made a major decision: *I'm never going to die.*"[13] I elaborate on the narrative motivations for these openings, below, but it's worth noting that the protagonist of *Super Sad* recruits clients for corporate life-extension services, while the plot of *Zero K* centers on a character's decision to enter a state of cryogenic stasis, rather than succumb to terminal illness. Each novel thus focuses on attempts to achieve sovereign mastery over death through financial means, and each introduces a pharmacological imaginary according to which it is only finance that can save us from the risks produced by finance.[14]

The strangeness of this pursuit of secular immortality dispels itself when one considers the political theological dimension of credit and debt. In general terms, secular immortality is the form that redemption takes when, instead of suspending the dialectic between guilt/debt and penitence/repayment, it immunizes a person from the consequences of the credit regime. This immunization doesn't erase the effects of debt, but instead transfers them on to others, which is to say that damnation—consignment to subprime status—isn't an accident of redemption, but its necessary condition. As Kiarina Kordela argues, the reproduction of contemporary capitalism requires the ideological support of fantasies of immortality, the corollary of which is a "bioracism" according to which dominant countries exorcise mortality by exporting it to others.[15] The underside of financialization is thus an economy of sacrifice through which the personhood of the "creditworthy" entails the symbolic and biological death of the subprime. What makes DeLillo and Shteyngart's fictions interesting in this context are the strategies they devise for short-circuiting this economy of sacrifice by conjuring up a return of the repressed (mortality) of financialized capitalism.

The economy of sacrifice can also be understood in terms of depersonalization, which is to say that financialization depends on stripping the personhood from particular social figures in an effort to justify killing them off. By sacrifice, however, I mean not only the taking of life in an absolute sense but also degradation of living conditions, imprisonment, detention, occupation, enslavement—in short, all of those practices through which one segment of society sustains its humanity or personhood by stripping it from another. In the context of financialized capitalism, this economy of sacrifice includes the practice of paying interest on loans, understood as a kind of tithe—a partial sacrifice, a tribute—through which one temporarily ensures one's personhood but, at the same time, sanctifies the power of the credit regime. In the financialized conditions of the present, it should be noted, interest payments have increased and multiplied because of the rise of consumer credit, the latter functioning not only as a means for capital to compensate for economic stagnation (by using financial profits to offset declines in profits from production) but also as a means for workers to compensate for declining wages.[16] Interest thus crystallizes a practical-symbolic circuit through which financialized capitalism sustains itself, not only as material mechanism for extracting profits, but also as ritual, as part of what Walter Benjamin (in the essay "Capitalism as Religion") terms a "system of guilt," in which atonement is impossible and in which "despair" and "destruction" are the "secret hope."[17]

According to this logic, human capital is not only, as the Foucauldian theorization of neoliberalism has it, a matter of entrepreneurial agents exposing themselves to risk in the pursuit of profits. It also entails an economy of sacrifice. This economy of sacrifice is immanent to human capital in the same manner in which credit-worthiness requires the subprime as its necessary point of reference. There are two bodies of human capital: a material body and an immaterial body. In the same way that sovereignty requires a split between body politic and natural body, human capital requires a division between the person qua bearer of immaterial value and the person qua living material substrate.[18] This dualism reduplicates the constitutive political division in the citizen between patriotic subject (citizen proper) and bare life (animal substrate), recoding it as a split between credit (speculative power) and debt (financial bondage).

In thinking financial risk in terms of personhood, I'm hoping to call into question the dominant discourse according to which financial matters belong to an autonomous sphere of social life. As McClanahan argues, social personhood mediates between the concrete social subject (indebted life) and abstract financial value (credit rating). *Pace* McClanahan, however, I would argue that the guilt associated with debt is not a "mask" covering over the impersonal character of the contemporary credit regime.[19] Instead, guilt, understood as an assemblage of affect, ritual, and morality, mediates between the personal and impersonal on capital's behalf. It should be understood, however, that *I* do not believe in my own guilt but rather *one* believes, which is to say that guilt is neither a matter of personal belief, nor an internalization of neoliberal morality. Instead, it is (in Lacanian parlance) belief in the Other's belief: motivation on the basis of the unconscious idea that there are others (benchmark persons, as it were) who truly believe that making good on one's financial obligations is a moral, as well as a legal and economic, imperative.[20] To paraphrase Louis Althusser's well-known formulation regarding ideology: one does not kneel because one believes, one believes because one kneels—it is the *ritual* of sacrifice that counts.[21] McClanahan is absolutely correct that guilt is not the efficient cause of debt, that "we are mostly in debt for more impersonal reasons, like the rising costs of health care and housing and education," but I would qualify this assessment by suggesting that guilt is the *formal* cause of debt, or the pattern through which debt organizes the psychic life of human capital.[22] A politics contesting financialized capital needs to grapple not only with impersonal economic conditions but also with the libidinal mechanisms that sustain attachments to these conditions.

Shteyngart's *Super Sad True Love Story* performs a parodic overturning of the credit regime's dialectic between guilt and penitence. The novel amplifies the contemporary credit regime by constructing a near-future setting in which credit evaluations are public ("credit poles" flash your credit score as you pass them by on the street) and the last vestiges of a distinction between social life and finance have disappeared. Lenny Abramov, the novel's protagonist and the dominant narrative voice, pursues secular immortality through a combination of romantic liaisons, financial practices, and personal habits. Lenny works as a "Life Lovers Outreach Coordinator (Grade G) of the Post-Human Services division of the Staatling-Wapachung Corporation," that is, as a salesman/analyst tasked with evaluating "High Net Worth Individual[s]" in terms of their ability to become clients of the company's life-extension services (5). He constructs a gradated continuum of personhood, one immediately bifurcated by wealth (high net-worth versus low net-worth, or those with manageable debts versus the subprime) and refined by considerations of physical and mental health, family history, spending habits, and affective disposition. Lenny's analytical perspective establishes a biopolitical continuity between these material and immaterial qualities, such that the character becomes a case in the medical sense—an object evaluated on the basis of norms of health, not least of all norms of financial health. In the final instance, however, each case comes down to an existential determination: a client not only needs to possess a living, material substrate capable of supporting the pursuit of immortality, she also needs to desire immortality. Thus, one potential client—a sculptor—gets diagnosed "ITP," or "Impossible to Preserve," as much because he is "swimming with the prevailing current toward his own nullification" as because he owes thirteen million dollars (18).

The credit regime, the novel suggests, is an apparatus that sorts life according to an imperative to take on the right kind of risks. The sculptor falls short not because he takes risks but because he indulges in *unprofitable* risks (drugs, sex, etc.). Randy Martin delineates the implications of risk-based assessments of subjectivity in sharp terms: "Risk is not simply a calculation that benefits will exceed costs, but a wager on accumulating beyond expected returns. When every cost and uncertainty can become an opportunity, the secure precincts of happiness are left behind for the dizzying heights of risk. Risk is not simply a construct that one abides but something somatized as a way of being."[23] It's this somatization of risk that makes contesting financialization so difficult, because historically contingent financial norms take on the appearance of both natural laws and providential signs, which is to say that they end up seeming not only eternal but also transcendent or otherworldly. Financial ideologies of risk draw on elements of Social Darwinism and religious fundamentalism to divide persons into the categories of "righteous agents of history" (the fit and savvy entrepreneurs who always come out on top) and history's "ashcan" (everyone who hasn't figured out how to adapt to financialized capitalism). One's lot in life comes to seem less like a consequence of determinate historical conditions than the predestined outcome of a financialized cosmos.[24]

The fundamental premise of *Super Sad* is not simply that Lenny ranks social subjects in terms of biological and financial fitness but also that he himself does not measure up, that because of his physical and mental health (overweight, depressive), financial resources (indebted without much in the way of liquid assets), family history (second-generation immigrant), and ethnicity (Russian-American Jew), he falls outside of the parameters of the proper client (the high net-worth individual capable of being preserved, the body that has been converted into a temple for the immortal financialized soul). In short, Lenny doesn't conform to a social type conventionally associated with taking the right kinds of risks or with entrepreneurial prowess. In this failure, however, Lenny is not alone, the novel making it clear that this falling short is a systemic, not an idiosyncratic, matter: "The truth is, we [Lenny alludes to his colleagues, as well as himself] may think of ourselves as the future, but we are not. We are servants and apprentices, not immortal clients. We hoard our yuan, we take our nutritionals, we prick ourselves and bleed and measure that dark-purple liquid a thousand different ways, we do everything but pray, but in the end we are still marked for death" (60). This passage develops a church of life-extension sustained by rituals that monitor and regulate the body for the purpose of rendering the afterlife immanent: living the good life means working on oneself in a manner that delivers one's material body over to an immaterial future. Such financial good works do not so much abstract from the body as convert the body into an abstraction—a scored object—from which potentiality can, in turn, be extracted. However, in a parodic repetition of the doctrine of predestination, good works can only function as signs, not precipitants, of capitalist salvation: "we" are but "servants" to the elect, to the high net-worth individuals, so that our activities can only constitute sacrifices in the name of their election. It's this contradiction between Lenny's aspiration for secular immortality and its foreclosure that fuels the text's critical stance: it exposes the providential vision of finance, with its fantasies of secular redemption, as no more than rituals of obedience, financial transactions disguised as prayers. That being said, these fantasies aren't purely imaginary, for they organize, in practical and symbolic terms, the extraction of vitality ("we prick ourselves and bleed and measure that dark-purple liquid a thousand different ways . . .") from indebted subjects. These financial rituals ward off the sacrifice of the subject only insofar as they reduce the subject to the material substrate of the financial elect, to the position of technical support for the speculative class. These subprime financial subjects are reduced to their mortal-material bodies (bodies without value, without the speculative dimension of immortality), and these bodies are, in turn, appropriated by high net-worth individuals as sacrificial offerings that enable the disavowal of mortality, as body doubles that absorb the material blows of risk. In short, Shteyngart narrates the class politics of financialized capitalism—the division of society into those for whom debt is a source of profit and those for whom it institutes bondage[25]—as a perverse communion in which, instead of a Christ figure that expiates guilt/abolishes debt, one finds the infinitely repeated sacrifice of financial and material vitality to the pockets of others.[26]

The overall narrative structure of *Super Sad* consists in the oscillation between, on the one hand, realizing the economy of sacrifice through apocalyptic revelation and, on the other, deferring apocalypse through the offering up of substitute sacrificial figures. Lenny's story revolves around his use of women as sacrificial objects, which sustain his investment in the capitalist fantasy of immortality. The novel represents Lenny's relationship with Eunice Park, a young Korean American woman, as yet another mode of transferring vitality: "I talked her out of her pants, cupped the twin, tiny globes of her ass with my palms, and pushed my lips right inside her soft, vital pussy. 'Oh, Lenny,' she said, a little sadly, for she must have sensed how much her youth and freshness meant to me, a man who lived in death's anteroom and could barely stand the light and heat of his brief sojourn on earth. I licked and licked, breathing in the slight odor of something authentic and human, and eventually must have fallen asleep with my face between her legs" (25). The qualities of prayer and revelation in this passage suggest a practice of worship, the implication of which would seem to be Lenny's subservience to Eunice, but, at the same time, Eunice constitutes a fountain of youth and an oracle: she is a well from which one draws pleasure, truth, and youth/vitality—a means for moving Lenny from "death's anteroom" to a restored humanity ("something authentic and human"). This image extends the previous financial equation—the reduction of the subprime to sacrificial bodies enabling the bourgeoisie's transcendence—by introducing a compensatory mechanism: the subprime sustain their own fantasies of immortality, their own fantasies of transcending conditions of exploitation, by transforming gendered and racialized figures into sacrificial proxies. The hierarchy implied in the economy of sacrifice moves beyond a simple binary structure, as the category subtending the ruling class of immortals bifurcates into the petty bourgeoisie (the intellectual-technical support staff of the bourgeoisie) and proletarianized subjects (including not only waged workers—so-called blue collar workers—but also the under- and unemployed, the subaltern, and a great deal of the service sector of late capitalism).

The hybrid of sentimentality and instrumentality in Lenny's romantic attachments takes on geopolitical dimensions in his articulation of the difference between Fabrizia, a former Italian lover, and Eunice: "Fabrizia. The softest woman I had ever touched. But maybe I no longer *needed* softness. Fabrizia. Her body conquered by small armies of hair, her curves fixed by carbohydrates, nothing but the Old World and its dying nonelectronic corporeality. And in front of me, Eunice Park. A nano-sized woman who had likely never known the tickle of her own pubic hair, who lacked both breast and scent, who existed as easily on an äppärät screen as on the street before me" (21). Love in the time of human capital recapitulates the Hegelian trajectory of world history, moving from "East" to "West," from Old World to New World, from material excess (fetishism as "primitive" religiosity, as subsumption of spirit in the sensuous object) to immaterial spirit (the Christian passion according to which sinful flesh gives way to a glorious, immaterial body).[27] In this geopolitical and sexual fantasy, Eunice constitutes the precise bare minimum of matter ("nano-sized") required for inclusion within secular existence, while at the same time being unloosed from mortal constraints, released into a reality in which there is no difference between screen and world, or avatar and material body. Although Eunice's Asian American identity might seem to break from the whiteness of the Hegelian world-historical telos, it does so only by transforming Eunice into an object of Lenny's fantasy, which is to say that the novel re-instantiates the racialization of history or, in dialectical terms, that Eunice occupies the position of the in-itself (sensuous raw material), Lenny the for-itself (self-consciousness, transcendence through the sublation of material conditions). In the context of financialization, the motor of history remains a slaughter bench, a constantly renewed ritual of sacrifice through which racialized and gendered (non-)persons sanctify the immortality of speculative agents through their social and biological deaths or through their reduction to raw material.

The novel attempts to preserve a critical stance in respect to this capitalist, misogynistic, and racist fantasy of immortality through ironic self-consciousness, polyphony, and narrative reversal. Not only does *Super Sad* repeatedly indicate the impossibility of transcendence or secular immortality by humorously commenting on Lenny's schlubiness, his inescapable material awkwardness, it also includes Eunice's voice by incorporating excerpts from her Globalteens account—a social media interface—providing another perspective on their romance and, in the process, calling into question Lenny's ideological investments. Finally, the novel's plot climaxes with a geopolitical reversal of fortunes, a US political and economic crisis (an historical conjuncture of social revolution and default on public debt) that forces the United States into a condition of peonage overseen by its lenders (China, in particular) and by global organizations including the International Monetary Fund (IMF) and the World Bank. One could elaborate on each of these aspects at length, but I want to focus on the way in which the novel's narration of crisis involves a return of the repressed mortality of finance. Following the consummation of the crisis, Lenny participates in the welcome party for a group of Chinese financial elite at which there is an art exhibition consisting of "extreme satellite zoom-ins of the deadly conditions in parts of the middle and the south of our country. [. . .] Dead is dead, we know where to file another person's extinction, but the artist purposely zoomed in on the living, or, to be more accurate, the forced-to-be-living and the soon-to-be-dead. Grainy close-ups of people using people in ways I had never openly considered, not because murder doesn't run through my veins, but because I grew up in an era where the baroque was safely held at bay" (318). The text articulates a zone of limbo in which life and death reach a point of indistinguishability, as life becomes consigned to a waiting for death ("soon-to-be-dead") secured by coercive force ("forced-to-be-living"). These hyphenated phrases register the truth of the capitalist world-system through the sheer banality of the deaths that the system engenders. "Murder," or the "baroque," is not extrinsic to capitalism, but rather its perverse underside, so that what distinguishes this post-crisis moment is not death as such, but rather the disappearance of viable immunitary mechanisms, or the extinction of means for practically and symbolically marking the division between the immortal soul of capitalist value and the material life sacrificed to it.

Shteyngart's *Super Sad True Love Story* is an analysis of petty bourgeois political theology. The novel charts the libidinal vicissitudes of the technical-intellectual support staff of the owners of the means of production, showing how the petty bourgeoisie invest themselves in fantasies of immortality and transcendence, in dreams of reaping the rewards of speculative capital without exposing themselves to its risks. At the same time, the self-consciousness of this class in regard to its own impotence entails the frantic pursuit of immunitary devices for warding off sacrifice, for protecting oneself from the vicissitudes of capitalist production. The force of this immunitary paradigm is not only to offer protection but also to enable the disavowal of redemption's impossibility. *Super Sad* interrupts this disavowal. It performs the affective labor of articulating redemption in class-specific terms, of demonstrating that transcendence over the dialectic between debt and repayment, guilt and penitence, is a luxury afforded only to the owners of the means of production (not least of all the owners of the means of issuing credit). Put differently, the novel indicates the insufficiency of sacrificial rituals, the impossibility of substitute objects filling up or overcoming the gap of class division. (It drives this point home, in plot terms, by having Eunice leave Lenny for his boss, Joshie Goldmann.) In doing so, *Super Sad* tracks the contemporary historical transition, described by Esposito, from sovereign debt to "debt sovereignty," "the transfer of sovereignty from the national government to global finance," a transition which means that "instead of talking about the end of political theology, we should be talking about its transformation into economic theology, one that is itself endowed with political attributes, including the supreme one of deciding on the possible survival of subjects."[28] Shteyngart's novel doesn't demystify financialization, instead it locates the theological niceties (as Marx puts it) that are constituent elements of financialized capitalism. In so doing, it offers not the hope of redemption, but rather a kind of apocalyptic frustration—a mode of revelation that supplements the economy of sacrifice with the practice of consolation: acknowledgement of mortality without pursuit of penitence, abandonment to one's own finitude without grace. Shteyngart writes a fiction of human capital only to do away with it by introducing another form of personhood, one in which dignity inheres in animality, in which value is not immortal but predicated on finitude. *Super Sad* does not therefore trace a horizon beyond financialized capitalism, but it does articulate the terms of a shared dissatisfaction with it.

A Final Shrine of Entitlement

The limit of *Super Sad True Love Story* lies in its consolatory vision: in allowing the pleasures of mortality to suffice, the novel holds redemption in reserve, implying that it is a real, if withheld, possibility. This is not to say that Shteyngart's novel doesn't criticize secular pursuits of immortality. *Super Sad* suggests that the pleasures of the speculative class are inauthentic, because they are not rooted in history. Indeed, its final pages identify authentic pleasure with literariness: the reader discovers that Lenny's diary—fictional excerpts of which compose the novel—has become "as Xiangbao [the literary critic] put it, 'a tribute to literature as it once *was* [emphasis mine]'" (327). Lenny's writing thus constitutes the final offering ("tribute") in the novel's economy of sacrifice, serving as an effigy of literature that encapsulates personhood (or humanity) in a protective shield. Literature, *Super Sad* proposes, testifies to human frailty and fallibility and, in doing so, it repeats the ritual of sacrifice, but in a manner that preserves dignity, that affords consolation. This is not the negation of human capital as an apparatus of control, but compensation for it. The novel cleaves out a third space beyond the dichotomy between person and sacrificial object, composing a fiction of human capital in which vulnerability coincides with non-monetary value. Echoing a well-known series of credit card commercials, one might describe this space as "priceless," noting that the term indicates not the negation of the capitalist value-form, but rather a playful suspension of it—its literary abeyance.

My analysis of DeLillo's *Zero K* will be brief, as my interest in it is specifically its foreclosure of the space of consolation articulated by *Super Sad*. *Zero K* narrates a financialized world from the perspective of the speculative class, so that the objects that circulate in the text are always already apprehended as assets subtending financial instruments. In this context, the concrete is not merely the condition of possibility of abstraction, but a set of disposable instruments for the sake of a specific genre of technical abstraction, namely, securitization, or the bundling of assets and the subsequent financial exchanges on the basis of this bundling.[29] In other words, the novel bypasses the question of whether or not there is a difference in kind between the abstract and the concrete by presupposing a world in which these ontological poles are always already convertible, if not simply identical. Identifying the perspective of the novel with the speculative class is not quite right, however, because the bulk of the narrative is presented through the son (Jeffrey Lockhart) of the entrepreneurial agent (Ross Lockhart, a "man shaped by money") (13). The text introduces a margin of difference, a perceptual gap as it were, through which the speculative class exhibits itself not so much against itself—though Oedipal conflict certainly informs the relationship between Jeff and Ross—but beside itself, in uneasy reflections on what it means to live in proximity to an agent of finance. If *Super Sad* provides insights into the credit regime by focusing on those affiliated with the speculative class (the technical-intellectual support staff), *Zero K*'s insights emerge by focusing on those *filiated* with the speculative class: those in and of, but not necessarily for, the credit regime.

This position "in and of, but not for" the speculative class enables a critique of financialized redemption, one which is not predicated on a distinction between authentic and inauthentic modes of existence but approaches finance as an arts of existence. The phrase "arts of existence" comes from Foucault, describing "those intentional and voluntary actions by which men not only set themselves rules of conduct, but also seek to transform themselves, to change themselves in their singular being, and to make their life into an *oeuvre* that carries certain aesthetic values and meets certain stylistic criteria."[30] From this perspective, financialized personhood and the aesthetic

Fictions of Human Capital; Or, Redemption in Neoliberal Times

domain should be understood as mutually imbricated, which is to say that novels such as *Super Sad True Love Story* and *Zero K* do not simply reflect finance, but participate in it. *Zero K* constitutes an extended meditation on this insight, for, as in much of DeLillo's recent fiction, it opens up a zone of interference between literary writing, philosophy, art criticism, and financial speculation. The novel develops a complex series of analogies between speculation and art, as well as between speculation and religious redemption. These analogies are not declared in an authoritative manner by the novel so much as posed as a series of questions: If the aesthetic tradition conventionally defines value as synonymous with immortality, then wouldn't the realization of a life in aesthetic terms coincide with its becoming immortal? If the aesthetic tradition sublimates the longing for redemption, then wouldn't a technics of immortality—a social assemblage of financial and biotechnological means for the preservation of human life—be the culmination of a secular arts of existence? Finally, if speculation is necessary not only to finance this technics of immortality but also to gain access to it, then what distinguishes the arts of existence from investment banking?

Zero K's critique depends on holding these questions open, on allowing them to interrupt both the valorization of financialized redemption and the romantic demystification of it. For every instance that the novel presents a seamless continuity between aesthetics, finance, and redemption—what might be called the aesthetic ideology of finance—Jeff's first-person narration introduces a tear into this continuity, as in the following passage:

> All pods [devices for cryogenic preservation] faced in the same direction, dozens, then hundreds, and our path took us through the middle of those structured ranks. The bodies were arranged across an enormous floor space, people of various skin color, uniformly positioned, eyes closed, arms crossed on chest, legs pressed tight, no sign of excess flesh.
>
> I recalled the three body pods that Ross and I had looked at on my earlier visit. Those were humans entrapped, enfeebled, individual lives stranded in some border region of a wishful future.
>
> Here, there were no lives to think about or imagine. This was pure spectacle, a single entity, the bodies regal in their cryonic bearing. It was a form of visionary art, it was body art with broad implications. (256)

Jeff draws a distinction between something like a realist art in which bodies and lives coincide in a quasi-organic fashion ("entrapped, enfeebled, individual lives stranded in some border region of a wishful future") and a "visionary art" in which the body achieves a spare perfection. The latter belongs to an ideology of late modernism, according to which the role of the work of art is to realize the potentiality of its medium, to achieve an identity between matter and form beyond the constraints of figuration.[31] The "structured ranks" of bodies suggest an efficiency of form in respect to function akin to the architecture (or at least the principles) of Le Corbusier. Of course, the corporeal form of the human body is the pinnacle of figuration, that which late modernism negates or disavows, but the constitutive tension of the pod qua modernist art object occurs between figuration as the overcoming of the merely mortal (the cultivation of "bodies regal in their cryonic bearing") and a post- or transhuman supersession of organic life ("no sign of excess flesh"). In other words, what intrigues Jeff in this presentation is the point of indistinguishability between figuration and sheer materiality—the point at which immortality transcends the human without leaving the material world behind. At the same time, however, this passage is situated in a novel that shifts back and forth between, on the one hand, a view of immortality technics as a subgenre of modernist aesthetics and, on the other, a demystifying view of it as a class-specific "final shrine of entitlement" (117). There's a kind of parallax effect according to which one and the same object—the cryogenic pods—can be viewed as the aesthetic negation of financial calculation and as the culmination of it.

Zero K derives its own aesthetic value from this back-and-forth between critique and consummation: while the aesthetic ideology of finance enables the text to engage in speculative flights—that is, to engage in a conceptual art of its own—the reflexivity regarding the material conditions of everyday life sustains a commitment to literature's power for social criticism. The implication of this fusion of critique and complicity is not only the general point that criticism is immanent, that it cannot help but be structured by its object. It is also the more specific one of a shared affinity between the speculative qualities of aesthetic practices and those of finance. This point is not novel—critics in the field of critical finance studies, as well as artists in a variety of mediums and genres, have been making it since at least the collapse of the dot-com bubble.[32] What is distinct, however, about *Zero K* is the way in which it links this affinity between conceptual art and finance to a theological vision of apocalypse and redemption. The novel suggests that the economy of sacrifice underpinning the mobility of speculative capital not only targets particular populations (the subprime), it also implies that the logical conclusion of this economy is nothing less than the annihilation of the entire world. The opening sentence of the novel—"*Everybody wants to own the end of the world*"—should be read in this light. The hypermodernity of the pod involves a suspension of worldliness, a rebirth or conversion of personhood consummated by the negation of history as such. As one of the ideologues of the immortality program puts it: "Your situation, those few of you on the verge of the journey toward rebirth. You are completely outside the narrative of what we refer to as history. There are no horizons here. We are pledged to an inwardness, a deep probing focus on who and where we are" (237). This suspension of worldliness characterizes not only the pods but also the compound that houses them: a labyrinth complex containing offices, art objects, apartments, and common dining areas, as well as the facilities for cryogenic preservation, and which exists in a zone of limbo beyond or between the borders of nation-states. It is, in other words, in the world but not of it, an aesthetic monad (in the Adornian sense) that incorporates the negativity of the social totality only insofar as it holds it at a distance, through its own negativity. However, whereas Theodor Adorno argues that the critical negativity of the work of art entails the guilt of luxury in a world in which humans still starve, the aesthetic ideology circulating in *Zero K* amounts to the sale of indulgences for a speculative elect.[33] Redemption becomes synonymous with economic privilege, the latter term having the precise meaning, in this context, of immunization from the material accidents that make up mortal life and of a kind of power over those condemned to creaturely existence. What Kordela describes as the secular fantasy of immortality and what Christopher Breu terms "avatar fetishism"—the exporting of mortality/materiality to so-called developing nations so that those in the core of the capitalist world-system can maintain the fantasy of immaterial value and immortal life—is inextricable from an apocalyptic vision of redemption. The "inwardness" to which the subjects of immortality pledge themselves entails an abandonment of the world—the world's consignment to the fateful drive of capital, as the latter exhausts the world's resources, including its people, in a never-ending pursuit of profit.

If I have touched very little on the plot of *Zero K*, it's because the novel does not attempt to resolve material contradictions, nor to provide consolation. It doesn't even sketch an itinerary of practical or theoretical opposition to the apocalyptic drive of high finance. Instead, its exceedingly bare plot tracks rituals of sacrifice and self-sacrifice insofar as they personalize the speculative class, that is, insofar as they mark the concrete dimension of the abstractions involved in belonging to the speculative class. The narrative begins with Artis (Ross's wife) surrendering herself to cryogenic preservation in order to avoid the conclusion of her terminal illness, but it then moves on to Ross's decision to do the same, despite being in good health. This self-sacrifice is, at one and the same time, a sentimental gesture (Ross would rather share non-life with Artis than live without her) and the ultimate symbolic consolidation of class power: to make even the suspension of one's life an element of an arts of existence not only requires wealth, but also consecrates wealth as the sign of true personhood.

There is much more one could say about *Zero K*, but I want to conclude by suggesting that in conjunction with *Super Sad True Love Story*, DeLillo's fiction of human capital indicates the political impossibility of redemption. There is no hope of recuperating redemption for the sake of opposing neoliberalism. Redemption itself is a financial instrument whose effect is the reproduction of the credit regime and its fiscal discipline. If *Super Sad* consoles readers by suggesting that the transcendence achieved by the speculative class is inauthentic, that its material pleasures imply spiritual bankruptcy, *Zero K* indicates that the very rhetoric of authenticity and inauthenticity is a symptom of financialized capitalism: it is the effect of a world so delivered over to speculation that existence itself comes to appear subprime and only "inwardness" (a speculative retreat into the soul) can save one from exposure to risk. In such a world, redemption can only ever constitute an alibi in support of dominant class power or a fantasy of escape. Instead of turning to redemption as a possible answer to finance, we would do better to turn to profanation, understood as a way of working through the political theology of debt. Giorgio Agamben has described profanation as a process of "deactivat[ing] the apparatuses of power and return[ing] to common use the spaces that power had seized."[34] In Esposito's terms, profanation implies an exodus from the apparatus of personhood, a suspension of the economy of sacrifice for the sake of an unqualified generosity, an impersonal yet singular gift of existence. In other words, it involves the production and reproduction of social life in terms other than human capital. This third space beyond the personhood of human capital and the economy of sacrifice, which is to say beyond neoliberalism, would not involve another kind of redemption but rather (to borrow from Hollis Phelps) an "unredeemable" manner of living. It is only then that one could respond to Bender's question in "Refund," "What did one owe for being alive?" with the only politically adequate answer: "Nothing."

Notes

1. Karen Bender, "Refund," *Refund* (Berkeley: Counterpoint Press, 2015), 126. Further citations indicated in the body of the essay parenthetically.

2. On the violence of so-called primitive accumulation in capitalism, see Marx, *Capital: A Critique of Political Economy*, Vol. 1, trans. (New York: Penguin, 1990), Chapter 26; David Harvey, *The New Imperialism* (Oxford: Oxford University Press, 2003), Chapter 4; Silvia Federici, *Caliban and the Witch: Women, the Body, and Primitive Accumulation* (New York: Autonomedia, 2004).

3. On the critical, social, and political implications of the distinction between the abstract and the concrete, in the context of finance, see Leigh Claire La Berge, "The Rules of Abstraction: Methods and Discourses of Finance," *Radical History Review* 118 (2014): 93–112.

Fictions of Human Capital; Or, Redemption in Neoliberal Times [133]

4. Miranda Joseph, *Debt to Society: Accounting for Life under Capitalism* (Minneapolis: University of Minnesota Press, 2014), 55.

5. See Roberto Esposito, *Two: The Machine of Political Theology and the Place of Thought*, trans. Zakiya Hanafi (New York: Fordham University Press, 2015); *Persons and Things: From the Body's Point of View*, trans. Zakiya Hanafi (London: Polity, 2015); *The Third Person*, trans. Zakiya Hanafi (London: Polity, 2012).

6. On financialization in terms of a political economic shift in revenue streams, see especially Greta Krippner, "The Financialization of the American Economy," *Socio-Economic Review* (2005) 3:173–208. On financialization as a transformation of the politics of everyday life, see especially Randy Martin, *The Financialization of Daily Life* (Philadelphia: Temple University Press, 2002) and *An Empire of Indifference: American War and the Financial Logic of Risk Management* (Durham, NC: Duke University Press, 2007); Wendy Brown, *Undoing the Demos: Neoliberalism's Stealth Revolution* (Brooklyn: Zone Books, 2015), 70–72.

7. See Michel Foucault, *The Birth of Biopolitics: Lectures at the Collège de France, 1978-1979*, ed. Michel Senellart, trans. Graham Burchell (Basingstoke, UK: Palgrave Macmillan, 2008), 215–266; Michel Feher, "Self-Appreciation; or, the Aspirations of Human Capital." *Public Culture* 21.1 (2009): 21–41.

8. Maurizio Lazzarato, *The Making of Indebted Man*, trans. Joshua David Jordan (Cambridge: Semiotext(e), 2012), 32.

9. Friedrich Nietzsche, *On the Genealogy of Morals and Ecce Homo*, trans. Walter Kaufmann. (New York: Vintage Books, 1989), 88–89.

10. Melinda Cooper has written incisively on the specific confluence of Christian fundamentalism, financialization, and neoliberal politics. See especially Melinda Cooper, *Life as Surplus: Biotechnology & Capitalism in the Neoliberal Era* (Seattle: University of Washington Press, 2008), Chapter 6; *Family Values: Between Neoliberalism and the New Social Conservativism* (New York: Zone Books, 2017), Chapter 7.

11. On debt as the fundamental paradigm of the social bond, see Richard Dienst, *The Bonds of Debt: Borrowing Against the Common Good* (New York: Verso, 2011), especially Introduction and Chapter 7. Dienst distinguishes between debt, understood as a framework for social belonging constituted by the memory of obligation, and credit understood as the extraction of profit from debt.

12. Annie McClanahan, *Dead Pledges: Debt, Crisis, and Twenty-First Century Culture* (Stanford: Stanford University Press, 2016), 55–75.

13. Don DeLillo, *Zero K* (New York: Charles Scribner's Sons, 2016), 3; Gary Shteyngart, *Super Sad True Love Story* (New York: Random House, 2010), 3. Further citations of the respective texts indicated in the body of the essay parenthetically.

14. On the pharmakon, see Jacques Derrida, *Dissemination*, trans. Barbara Johnson (Chicago: University of Chicago Press, 1983); and Bernard Stiegler, *What Makes Life Worth Living: On Pharmacology*, trans. Daniel Ross (Cambridge: Polity, 2013).

15. Kiarina Kordela, *Being, Time, Bios: Capitalism and Ontology* (State University of New York Press, 2013), 139–52. Kordela's critique of the secular fantasy of immortality accords with Christopher Breu's critique of avatar fetishism. See Christopher Breu, *Insistence of the Material: Literature in the Age of Biopolitics* (Minneapolis: University of Minnesota Press, 2014), 22–23.

16. On financialization as a compensatory mechanism in respect to the stagnation of

productive capital, see Giovanni Arrighi, *The Long Twentieth Century: Money, Power, and the Origins of Our Times* (New York: Verso, 2010); and Greta Krippner, "The Financialization of the American Economy," *Socio-Economic Review* 3 (February 29, 2008): 173–208.

17. Walter Benjamin, "Capitalism as Religion," *Selected Writings*, Vol. 1: 1913–1926, eds. Marcus Bullock and Michael W. Jennings (Cambridge, MA: Harvard University Press, 2004), 289.

18. This argument regarding the two bodies of human capital builds on the theories of sovereignty articulated by Esposito, Giorgio Agamben, and Eric Santner (which, in turn, build on Ernst Kantorowicz's *The King's Two Bodies: A Study in Medieval Political Theology*). In addition to Esposito's *Two*, see Giorgio Agamben, *Homo Sacer: Sovereign Power and Bare Life*, trans. Daniel Heller-Roazen (Stanford: Stanford University Press, 1998), 91–94; Eric Santner, *The Royal Remains: The People's Two Bodies and the Endgames of Sovereignty* (Chicago: University of Chicago Press, 2011).

19. Annie McClanahan, *Dead Pledges*, 94–95.

20. See Slavoj Zizek, *How to Read Lacan* (New York: W.W. Norton, 2006), 29; and Jodi Dean, *Crowds and Party* (New York: Verso, 2016), 185–190.

21. Louis Althusser, "Ideology and Ideological State Apparatus (Notes Towards an Investigation)," *Lenin and Philosophy and Other Essays*, trans. Ben Brewster (New York: Monthly Review, 2001), 114.

22. McClanahan, *Dead Pledges*, 95.

23. Randy Martin, *An Empire of Indifference*, 21.

24. Randy Martin, *An Empire of Indifference*, 21.

25. Ivan Ascher articulates this financialized mode of class struggle in terms of the extraction of credibility; that is, he argues that just as capitalism depends on the management of labor-power and control over the means of production, it also depends on the management of lines of credit and the means of prediction (credit evaluation). See Ivan Ascher, *Portfolio Society: On the Capitalist Mode of Prediction* (Brooklyn: Zone Books, 2016), 78–81.

26. On the tendency of Christian theological tropes to re-inscribe debt, even as they appear to abolish it, see Hollis Phelps, "Overcoming Redemption: Neoliberalism, Atonement, and the Logic of Debt," *Political Theology* 17.3 (May 2016): 264–282.

27. See G.W.F. Hegel, *Introduction to the Philosophy of History: with Selections from the Philosophy of Right*, trans. Leo Rauch (Indianapolis: Hackett Classics, 1988).

28. Roberto Esposito, *Two*, 204.

29. On the subject of securitization, see Li Puma and Lee, *Financial Derivatives and the Globalization of Risk* (Durham, NC: Duke University Press, 2004); Dick Bryan, Randy Martin, and Mike Rafferty, "Financialization and Marx: Giving Labor and Capital a Financial Makeover." *Radical Political Economics* 41:4: 458–472.

30. Michel Foucault, *History of Sexuality*, Vol. 2, trans. Robert Hurley (New York: Vintage Books, 1990), 11–12.

31. See Fredric Jameson, *A Singular Modernity: Essay on Ontology of the Present* (New York: Verso, 2002), Part II.

32. On the affinity between finance and aesthetics in the contemporary period, see especially Fredric Jameson, "Culture and Finance Capital," *The Cultural Turn: Selected Writings on the Postmodern, 1983–1998* (New York: Verso, 1998); "The Aesthetics of Singularity," *New Left Review* 92 (March/April 2015): 101–132; Joshua Clover, "Autumn

of the System: Poetry and Financial Capital," *Journal of Narrative Theory* 41.1 (Spring 2011): 34–52; and Leigh Claire La Berge, "Wages Against Artwork: The Social Practice of Decommodification," *South Atlantic Quarterly* 114.3 (2015): 571–593.

33. On the critical negativity of the work of art, see especially Theodor Adorno, *Aesthetic Theory*, trans. Robert Hullot-Kentor (Minneapolis: University of Minnesota Press, 1998); and "On Lyric Poetry and Society," *Notes to Literature*, Vol. 1 (New York: Columbia University Press, 1991), 37–54. Elsewhere, I've attempted to update Adorno's insights on lyric poetry and critique in response to financialization. See Christian Haines, "Financialisation," *The Routledge Companion to Literature and Economics*, eds. Michelle Chihara and Matt Seybold (Abingdon: Routledge, 2018), 240–251.

34. Giorgio Agamben, "In Praise of Profanation," *Profanations*, trans. Jeff Fort (New York: Zone Books, 2007), 77.

[7]

DONALD E. PEASE

THE UNCANNY RE-WORLDING OF THE POST-9/11 AMERICAN NOVEL, JOSEPH O'NEILL'S *NETHERLAND*; OR, THE CULTURAL FANTASY WORK OF NEOLIBERALISM

FROM THE DAY OF its release in 2008, literary scholars welcomed Joseph O'Neill's *Netherland* as the long-awaited post-9/11 novel that had lived up to their expectations. Its publication also marked the occasion for academic journals to publish critical assessment of the scores of novels about the events that took place on September 11, 2001. In an *American Literary History (ALH)* essay written in the wake of the 2008 financial collapse titled "Open Doors, Closed Minds: American Prose Writing at a Time of Crisis," Richard Gray criticizes an assortment of post-9/11 novels for their domestic focus and their tendency to reduce what he calls a "turning point in national and international history" to the dimensions of an "insular domestic dispute."[1] To correct this tendency, Gray enjoins American writers to renounce their nationalist proclivities by reframing post-9/11 United States culture as itself a transcultural space—a setting for the interaction and transformation of conflicting national and transcultural constituencies. The value of such a 'deterritorializing' process, Gray argues, lies in the fact that 'whether they know it or not—and as it happens, many of them do—Americans find themselves living in an interstitial space, a locus of interaction between contending national and cultural constituencies." (134)

As his title suggests, Gray is not interested in offering an objective description of the norms inhering in the rules of a new literary subgenre. Gray instead makes clear his intention to elevate the criteria he invokes to distinguish strong from weak examples of the post-9/11 US novels into the basis for the demand that US novelists act upon what he calls the "obligation" to write novels that "world" America differently after 9/11.[2] Michael Rothberg published a response to Gray in the same issue of *ALH* that correlates US novelists' retreat into the domestic sphere with a species of xenophobic nationalism whose overcoming requires a change in orientation: "what we need from 9/11 novels are cognitive maps that imagine how US citizenship looks and feels beyond the boundaries of the nation-state, both for Americans and for others."³

Two years later ALH featured essays by Elizabeth Anker and Caren Irr that, when read together, track a salutary change in the "worlding" prospects of post-9/11 US fiction. For her part, Anker diagnosed the forces that impeded such a change by offering a psycho-social rationale for US male novelists' retreat into domesticity. According to Anker, post-9/11 US fiction includes an assemblage of elements—allegories of "falling" men; middle-class, middle-aged masculinity in crisis; retreat into the domestic and domesticity under attack; the "divorce plot"; the "menace to paternity"; "conspiracy subplots"; amnesic connections to the past—out of which US novelists composed plots in which their male protagonists feel compelled to correlate the decline of American economic and military dominance to their own waning sexual prowess and to imagine the 9/11 attacks as a threat to the patrilineal bond at the core of their masculinity.⁴

Anker's provision of this psycho-social rationale for post-9/11 male novelists' retreat into domesticity seemingly foreclosed the possibility of their carrying out what Gray and Rothberg called their "worlding" obligations. However, Irr contributed an essay to this same issue proposing that several recently published fictions written by and about expatriates relocating to the United States had introduced salutary revisions to the norms of post-9/11 US fiction capable of liberating the genre from its nationalizing proclivities. Irr's essay, tellingly entitled "Toward the World Novel: Genre Shifts in Twenty-First-Century Expatriate Fiction," readily acknowledges the psychic impasses Anker finds embedded in versions of this genre written by US novelists.⁵ However, Irr goes on to argue that expatriates in the United States alone are capable of installing the transcultural spaces that could transform US readers' geopolitical orientations. Fictions of expatriation are uniquely empowered to carry out the "worlding" imperatives of the post-9/11 novel because expatriates in the United States are capable of representing what took place within the American scene without "universalizing its timespace." (660)⁶ The expatriate novels under Irr's description decisively reshape the national novel by "incorporat[ing] politically charged elements of the global scene that foster sensitivity to the augmented presence of migrants and refugees" and awareness of the "increased interpenetration of global markets" across US culture. (660)

Gray and Rothberg, and Anker might disagree about the generic rules and norms at work in Irr's account of the post-9/11 novel, but the four critics are unanimous in their designation of Joseph O'Neill's *Netherland* as the gold standard for defining what post–9/11 fiction should and should not do. Gray describes *Netherland* as a new fiction of "immigrant encounter" that fosters American "deterritorialization." Gray goes on to celebrate the kind of fiction typified by *Netherland* that explores difference and hybrid identity within a multi-racial post 9/11 New York where the idea of a Cricket Club promises to "start a whole new chapter in US history." (141) As counterpoint to Gray's "centripetal" demand for a globalized vision of domestic America, Rothberg underscores the novel's "centrifugal" features that offer "a fiction of international relations and extraterritorial citizenship." Hailing it as one of "the finest novels of the post-9/11 condition thus far" (156), Rothberg describes *Netherland*'s "deterritorialized recharting" of the "altered geographies" of a transcultural urban pastoral "in a fully globalized terrain" (156) as the much-awaited exception to Gray's rule of domestic retreat. Anker singles out *Netherland* for bringing marginal urban cultures that rarely find a voice in mainstream American literature to the attention of readers. Irr describes *Netherland* as exemplary for its salient display of the elements within the post-9/11 expatriate novel—multi-stranded narration, broad geographical reach, a cosmopolitan form of ethics, and, most of all, a desire for a sense of community—that are unassimilable to the conventions of the national novel.

Literary scholars have cited *Netherland*'s deterritorialization of established narratives of nationhood, its break from unilateral accounts of national trauma, its repositioning of the American nation toward the world, its movement of post-9/11 fiction past an insular focus while maintaining a multicultural, postcolonial framing of global interests and identities, its promotion of a "cosmopolitan" disposition capable of binding in unprecedented ways the world's peoples, traditions, and aesthetic practices, and numerous related examples of the novel's "worldliness" to justify the academy's enthusiastic embrace of Joseph O'Neill's *Netherland*.[7] *Netherland* was greeted with comparably extravagant praise within the popular press.

Writing in the *New Yorker*, James Wood called it "one of the most remarkable post-colonial books I have ever read ... O'Neill finds in cricket a beautiful controlling metaphor; it comes to stand variously for upward aspiration; for camaraderie; for innocence; for fragile, ridiculous, sublime democracy—for all the things Hans feels he lost in the fall of 2001."[8] In his review for the *New York Times*, Michiko Kakutani exalted O'Neill's novel as "the wittiest, angriest, most exacting and most desolate work of fiction we've yet had about life in New York and London after the World Trade Center fell."[9] Arguing that Hans van den Broek, the novel's protagonist, displaced Gatsby's unappeasable need for Daisy onto Khamraj (Chuck) Ramkissoon's unrealizable dream of resurrecting Americans' archaic passion for cricket, Declan Hughes described *Netherland* as a candidate for the Great American Novel that intentionally brings to mind and mood F. Scott

Fitzgerald's *The Great Gatsby*.[10] "It's the post–September 11 novel we hoped for," Zadie Smith remarks in her November 2008 *New York Review of Books* review, "Two Paths for the Novel," "It's as if, by an act of collective prayer, we have willed it into existence."[11] These critics believe that the friendship between Chuck and Hans in *Netherland* is not based on business, but on a post-racial, post-national vision for which the cricket field creates a cosmopolitan fold.[12] Barack Obama added immeasurably to the novel's cultural and literary capital when he added it to the top of his list as the one book to which he preferred to turn when he sought respite from the accumulating pile of briefs and policy papers. Christian Moraru affords the ethical imperatives threading their way through these enthusiastic popular and academic responses of the novel with a suitably magisterial formulation:

> *Netherland* is a concrete, athletically embodied modality of presentifying or updating an America that, in the September 2001 aftermath, must re-constellate itself *qua* community so as to work through the meanings of not only the World Trade Center tragedy but also of the planetarization without which the traumatic event would remain meaningless. A community driven to the limit by the violently worlding world, the United States cannot afford *not* to use its new, liminal position in the world to think through its communal, cultural-ethical limits and spatio-temporal limitations.[13]

These are productive ways of reading the novel. No matter whether they frame it as an example of cosmopolitan precarity, an insurgent postcolonial imaginary, an example of the transnational /diaspora complex, or as an emergent planetary imaginary, these commentators have elevated *Netherland* to the status of a classic work of American world literature. In doing so, the reviewers and critics responsible for *Netherland*'s spectacular hypercanonization have drawn on a pre-existing fund of democratizing values they have projected onto the cricket dream at the center of the novel. However, the critics who have assigned *Netherland* these quasi-utopian purposes, have attributed desires and aims to the narrator, Hans van den Broek, that bear scant resemblance to Hans's account of his interactions with Chuck. Hans is not connected to Chuck by way of storied memories. Indeed, there is no lasting bond between them: "A story that's what I need," Hans informs his readers at the beginning of his narrative. "Not so Chuck he died without a story. Chuck is on memory weighty, but what is the meaning of this weight, what am I to do with it? . . . . Chuck was a clandestine man who followed his own instincts and influences and would rarely be influenced by advice—not my advice that's for sure . . . I was capable of a Samaritan urge to save him. But I had troubles of my own and Chuck's companionship functioned as a shelter—this taking of shelter."[14] In the remarks that follow, I want to propose a different interpretive frame by re-describing the novel's canonizing values—cosmopolitan planetarism, transnational democracy, egalitarian justice, non-identitarian resistance—as evidence of the neo-liberal fantasy work of *Netherland* whose purpose is to establish an imaginary relationship with the financialized-military complex Hans depends upon for his livelihood. Chuck Ramkissoon draws upon the key terms of this fantasy in the slogan—"Think fantastic!"—animating his tireless promotion of Chuck Cricket Inc.

> "Cricket is instructive, Hans, it has a moral angle ... Americans cannot really see the world. They think they can, but they can't. I don't need to tell you that. Look at the problems we're having. It's a mess, and it's going to get worse. I say, we want to have something in common with the Hindus and Muslims? Chuck Ramkissoon is going to make it happen. With the New York Cricket Club we could start a whole new chapter in US history. Why not? Why not say so if it's true? Why hold back? I'm going to open our eyes ... Anyhow that's what I'm doing here Hans. That's why I'm ready to do whatever it takes to make this happen." ...
>
> Hans said, "Chuck *get real*. People don't operate on that level. They're going to find it very hard to respond to that way of thinking." "We'll see," he said, laughing and looking at his watch. "I believe they will." (211–212)

The opening lines of this dialogue articulate Chuck Ramkissoon's final sales pitch in his novel-long effort to persuade the Dutch financier Johannus van den Broek to provide the mezzanine financing needed to subsidize the New York Cricket Club, the prime speculative venture in the Chuck Cricket Inc. portfolio. Rather than signing on to this project, Hans says that people don't respond to that way of thinking. Whereas Chuck's motto is to "Think fantastic!" Hans, who is an analyst in the large cap oils and gas futures market, is not predisposed to exaggerate the value of a property. Hans's job is to express reliable opinions about the current and future valuation of certain oil and gas stocks. At the time he offered Chuck this assessment, London's prestigious *International Investor* ranked Hans number four among the world's equities analysts. Indeed he was so good at evaluating the difference between non-risky investments and sure things that traders on the stock exchange floor sought out his assessment before closing their deals. It did not take long for the catchphrases—"Dutch" and "Double Dutch"—that Hans used to distinguish an ordinary recommendation from a strong recommendation to enter the popular idiom of the industry. "So what are you saying Dutch or Double Dutch?" (52) Millions of dollars could be made or lost at Hans's response to this question.

But who does Hans presuppose as the referent for the people who would refuse to acknowledge social uplift, democracy, hospitality, mutual responsibility, intimate closeness as apt criteria for adding their names to Chuck's list of investors? It is Hans's refusal to identify with the people Chuck presupposes as the audience for his bid that sets him apart from *Netherland*'s reviewers and critics. These reviewers differ from Hans in that they have taken up the position of Chuck's addressees—apparently ready to do and say whatever it takes to turn his dream into reality. The cultural and political values that critics have attributed to *Netherland* are saturated with the liberal multi-culturalist tropes—the social justice of cricket, its transnational and post-national participation, the multicultural legacy—that Chuck himself deploys to persuade Hans to proffer the mezzanine financing his scheme requires. In taking up this position of Chuck's implicit addressees, readers and reviewers acquire the subject positions of membership in a fully-achieved post-national, post-racial, multi-cultural democracy that the neoliberal economic order wants them to want.[15]

These critics and readers might be described as contributing the symbolic capital to Chuck's financial instrument—and to the novel that O'Neill initially intended to call the *Brooklyn Dream Machine*—that Hans van den Broek does not. In buttressing the market rationality of the neoliberal state, their collectively shared cricket fantasy does not merely distract readers from questions of economic inequality, this fantasy aggressively legitimates social and economic inequality.[16] Here is a representative instance of the fantasy production Chuck's Cricket Inc. motivates in Chuck's intended addressees:

> Cricket, like every sport, is an activity and the dream of an activity. Cricket in this novel is much more than these associations: it is an immigrant's imagined community, a game that unites, in a Brooklyn park, Pakistanis, Sri Lankans, Indians, West Indians, and so on, even as the game's un-Americanness accentuates their singularity. Most poignantly, for Chuck, cricket is an American dream, or perhaps a dream of America; this man is convinced that, as he claims, cricket is not an immigrant sport at all but "the first modern team sport in America . . . a bona fide American pastime," played in New York since the sixteen-seventies.[17]

Chuck's cricket field, as this quotation attests, is a symbolic fiction that supplies these interpreters with master signifiers seemingly capable of converting the losses of 9/11 into the gain of a "cosmopolitan" imaginary.

In the course of his narration, Hans van den Broek mentions the Enron scandal, the Bush administration's invasion of Iraq and Afghanistan, suicide bombings, the Iraq oil bonanza, the CIA's use of renditions, and related workings of the terror-security complex taking place contemporaneously. Although these calamitous matters incite his investors' desire for his cricket scheme as a quasi-utopian alternative, Chuck's over-idealization of the game is designed in part to deflect attention from them. He nonetheless connects the rationale of Cricket Inc. to the US security apparatus when he proclaims the sport's ability to render rowdy 3rd World cricketers from the Global South docile US subjects: "'But cricket more than any other sport, is, I want to say,' Chuck played for effect—'a lesson in democracy.' 'What this means is that we have an extra responsibility to play the game right . . . You want to know what it feels like to be a black man in America. Put on the white clothes of a cricketeer. Put on white to feel black'" (16).

The space opened up between the events—9/11, the death of Hans's mother, the declaration of war in Iraq, the break-up of Hans's marriage, the endless series of financial scandals, Chuck Ramkissoon's murder—and the retroactive causes the narrator assigns responsibility for bringing them about gets filled in and emptied out by the cricket field. Chuck turns his cricket dream into an affective mechanism to try and instruct Hans in how to want Chuck's speculative, financial schemes. But Hans does not invest either his capital or his credibility in the culturally transformative values Chuck has imputed to cricket. The critics who have assigned *Netherland* this quasi-utopian purpose have attributed desires and aims to Hans that bear little resemblance to the motives Hans explicitly expresses for befriending Chuck.

> My instinct was to keep him at a distance, at that distance certainly between ourselves and those we suspect of neediness. I was wondering when he was going to ask me for money for his cricket scheme . . . I've never been open to the fantastical side of business. I'm an analyst, a bystander. It's the incompleteness of reveries that brings trouble—and that brought Ramkissoon the worst trouble. His head wasn't sufficiently in the clouds, he had a clear enough view of the gap between where he was and where he wanted to be, and he was determined to find a way across. (102)

Unlike the book's reviewers, Hans never takes up the symbolic identity—a Caucasian male who wants to "put on white to feel black"—to which Chuck attempts to interpellate him. Hans does not base his interactions with Chuck Ramkissoon on a shared post-racial vision. Hans's perception of the cricket field is itself a racial formation. Indeed, from the first day they met to the day of their final leave-taking, Hans's view of the game and field they share is the outcome of the workings of racial constraints that turns Hans's teammates and opponents into a racialized, and potentially terrorist assemblage:[18] "The day I met Chuck . . . We, Staten Islanders, were playing a bunch of guys from St. Kitts . . . My own teammates variously originated from Trinidad, Guyana, Jamaica, India, Pakistan and Sri Lanka. That summer of 2002, when out of loneliness I played after years of not playing, and in the summer that followed, I was the only white man I saw in the cricket fields of New York" (10–11). When a Kittian onlooker threatens to settle a dispute over a call on the field with a gun he brought with him, Hans's teammates back away in a panic. But Hans tightens the grip on his Gunn and Moore Maestro bat, ready to resolve the dispute after the manner of his Dutch settler ancestors, which is the symbolic identity Hans will learn how to re-acquire through his relationship with Chuck Ramkissoon, and which, as I will demonstrate shortly, affords the actual basis for Hans's desire for this relationship.

Netherland is organized around two separate narrative tracks. One track concerns the changes in the psycho-geographical coordinates of Hans van den Broek, who lost his bearings after he was confronted with three unpredictable, and *uninsurable* losses—the death of his mother, the destruction of the Twin Towers, and the break-up of his marriage. That narrative is organized around movements back and forth from Hans's memories of his childhood years in Holland where, following the death of his father when Hans was two, his mother raised him as a single parent—to memories of his life with Rachel and his son, Jacob, in 1998, 2001, 2002, 2003. It terminates in 2006 when Hans, happily reunited with Rachel and Jake at their home in the upscale Highbury neighborhood of London, receives a phone call from a *New York Times* reporter with the news that the remains of Khamraj Ramkissoon's ("Chuck Ramkissoon" Hans corrects her) had been found in the Gowanus Canal. "There were handcuffs around his wrists and evidently he was the victim of a murder." (5)

Netherland travels backward and forward in time, arranging events by an affective, rather than chronological, order—and, in the process, creates the need for a space of emotional shelter that the cricket field fills in. *Netherland*, which starts as a murder mystery, becomes a post-9/11 novel about the mending of a marriage fallen apart. Although it is in the thrall of the disorderly comings and goings of Hans's involuntary memories and free associations, this narrative possesses the coherence of a *Bildungsroman* as Hans undergoes a shift in his disposition *from* the abject misery brought about by Rachel's announcement that she has decided to leave him shortly after 9/11 ("I felt shame that life was beyond mending, that love was loss, that nothing worth saying was sayable, that dullness was general, that disintegration was irresistible" [30]) *to* the more happily placed "idiomatic man who can take her or leave her."

The second narrative track consists of a chronicle of vignettes in which Chuck Ramkissoon plays multiple parts. Chuck's repeated failure to persuade Hans to invest in Chuck Cricket Inc. is offset by his success at guiding Hans through Brooklyn's hinterlands; by his success at persuading Hans to become his chauffeur as Chuck made drop offs and pick-ups at his kosher-sushi restaurants, at sundry gambling rackets and real estate deals; and by his success at teaching Hans how to bat cricket the American way. As Hans travels through Queens and Brooklyn with Chuck Ramkissoon, cricket brings the uneven development of New York's post-colonial cityscape into visibility.[19]

Chuck befriends Hans to gain access to the financial elite. Hans's narrative relation to Chuck is structured in finance capital's relationship to the class that it exploits and expropriates. Rachel and Hans are members of the transnational financial class. Before he took up residence in the Chelsea hotel, Hans sold the loft in Tribeca for 1 million dollars with another 2 million in a joint banking account, and since the market "was making me nervous," another 200,000 in various accounts. Unlike commentators on his narrative, Hans does not attribute his desire to work with Chuck to any planetarily progressive motives. Hans met Chuck after Rachel left him. Their meeting coincides with the US invasion of Iraq as well as a series of scandals—Enron, World Com, AIG—(Hans mentions the Jack Grubman and Henry Blogett cases) in the financial sector. Hans's decision to latch onto Chuck is in part informed by his need to understand why Rachel, who never before expressed the desire to take up the cause of the socially oppressed, should have, upon her return to London, taken up work in a non-governmental organization (NGO) protecting the rights of asylum seekers.

Rachel is, like Hans, a member of the transnational financial elite. A corporate litigator who defended CEOs accused of financial fraud before 9/11, Rachel became "radicalized only in the service of her client without the smallest bone to pick about money and its doings." (96) But the events that took place on September 11 triggered political anxieties and paranoid fantasies in Rachel that scholars in settler colonial studies claim originated in Anglo-America's white colonial settler past.[20]

Hans's association with Chuck began shortly before the US invasions of Iraq and Afghanistan when the Homeland Security Act regressed the population to a minority condition of dependency upon the state for its biopolitical welfare. But the state thereafter correlated this regression in political standing with the reenactment of a formerly suppressed historical event. After the people were regressed to the condition of a political minority, the state produced a series of lurid spectacles which returned the population to the historical moment in which colonial settlers had deployed the illicit use of force against native populations. As witnesses to the state's colonization of Afghanistan and Iraq, the US spectatorial publics were returned to the prehistoric time of the colonial settlers who had formerly spoliated Indian homelands. By way of "Operation Infinite Justice" and "Operation Iraqi Freedom" the Homeland Security State restaged the colonial settlers' conquest of indigenous peoples and the acquisition of their homelands. Both spectacles invited their audiences to take scopic pleasure in the return of the traumatic memory of the unprovoked aggression that the colonial settlers had previously exerted against native populations.[21]

Chuck figures as the means through whom Hans gets in touch with the iteration of the person Rachel says she now wants to be. The turning point in Hans's relationship with Chuck took place at the moment he discovered the linkage between Rachel's paranoid behavior and the collective political mania that Chuck Ramkissoon aspired to exploit in the wake of 9/11. When Hans heard Chuck's story about the public's reaction to the New York Humane Society's transport to Pier 40 of hundreds of household pets abandoned or lost after 9/11—Chuck considers it a wonderful venture, but not because of what the American public did for the creatures. Chuck was impressed instead with how many Americans needed to identify with the image of themselves as good shepherds dedicated to caring for the welfare of creatures rendered helpless by the 9/11 attacks. Hans observed that "[t]he catastrophe had instilled in many—*though not in me*—a state of elation." (77) It is at this moment that Hans associates the manic change in Rachel's political disposition as a symptom of this pathology: "I'd suspected that, beneath all the tears and the misery, Rachel's leaving had basically been a function of euphoria." (78) Rachel wanted to replace all of the confusion that resulted from the destruction of the Twin Towers with an ethical and political standpoint that would liberate her from the logics of retribution that motivated her colonial-settler fears. Hans experienced the disappearance of his *need* to play cricket in the wake of this revelation.

As we have seen, Chuck serves as the psycho-social vehicle through whom Hans works through the death of his mother and the break-up of his marriage.[22] After Hans converts Chuck into a stand-in for these experiential losses, Chuck Ramkissoon disappears into an ungrievable memory. Chuck's deferred death becomes the precondition for the securitization and valorization of the life of another population—Hans van den Broek, his wife Rachel and their son Jacob—that triumphs in its shadows.

The key to understanding the difference between Hans and the readers who eagerly identify with the values Chuck attributes to Cricket become discernible in Hans's account of what at first sight would appear the confession of a corrigible lapse in character. The admission takes place at the conclusion of what reads like a litany of remediable shortcomings in his moral development.

> I could take a guess at the oil capacity of an American-occupied Iraq. But I found myself unable to contribute to conversations about international law or

the feasibility of producing a dirty bomb, or the constitutional rights of imprisoned enemies or the efficiency of duct tape as a window sealant or the merits of vaccinating the American masses against small pox or the weaponizing of deadly bacteria. In this ever-shifting, all enveloping discussion, my orientation was poor. I could not tell where I stood. If pressed to state a position, I would confess that I had not succeeded in arriving at a position . . . I had no idea, and to be truthful, and to touch on the real difficulty, I had little interest. I didn't really care. In short I was a political-ethical idiot. (100)

When Hans describes himself a moral and political idiot, he also embraces the attitude that enabled him to keep his number four ranking as Double Dutch. If Hans were to present any position on the war in Iraq, other than his prediction of its effect on the rise and fall of world oil prices, he would likely lose his number four ranking. It is Hans's moral and political idiocy that positions him apart from the people Chuck would tether to the fantasy work of neo-colonialism. Hans does not examine the causes of the war for the same reason that he does not search for the causes of Chuck's death.

But if Hans's *Bildungsroman* does not entail the transformation of Hans's moral and political idiocy who or what does he become when he says he could take his marriage to Rachel or leave her? I shall let my attempt at a brief response to this question serve as a conclusion. In *Netherland* the memory work of a financial analyst turns a prototypical post-9/11 neoliberal fantasy (the cricket field imagined within the global enterprise Chuck Cricket Inc. as a post-racial, post-national utopia) into the technology for the accumulation of an emotional and psychic surplus—"I can take her or leave her"—through dispossession. But the figure who performs this taking or leaving is not the same person who felt that he could not lose Rachel without losing himself; it was, as Hans makes clear in the following observation, a third person: "Rachel saw our reunion as a continuation, I felt differently: that she and I had gone our separate ways and subsequently had fallen for third parties to whom, fortuitously, we were already married" (229). Hans first takes up the position of this third person when he bats the American way on Chuck's cricket field. When Hans identifies with this position on Chuck Ramkissoon's cricket field, however, he undergoes regression to the subject position of a Dutch settler in Breukelen colony of the new Netherland. In an early moment of intimate male bonding, Chuck tells Hans that putting on the whites of the twenty-first century cricket player is one sure way for a white man to "feel black." Contrary to Chuck's instruction, however, when Hans puts on the whites, he does so as a seventeenth century Dutch settler who turns his batting position into the colonial instrument that facilitates his dis-identification from Chuck. After batting in American style, Hans says that he feels *naturalized* as an American. But the America to which he refers is the colonial America his Dutch ancestors inhabited as settler colonists. Chuck's cricket field performs its most efficacious cultural work by enabling Hans to once again become a Double Dutch American in this unsettled state.

When Hans thereafter put Chuck to the affective labor of working through his separation from Rachel, Hans time-travels to the hinterland of the New Netherland in pre-Modern America where his Dutch colonial ancestors in Breukelen built tobacco plantations next to the Gowanus creek where Khamraj Ramkissoon's Trinidadian ancestors worked as slaves and indentured servants. Like Chuck, some of those ancestors preceded him in the watery grave of the Gowanus canal.

An interviewer recently asked Joseph O'Neill "Why is there such a need to return to the colonial origins of the nation ... to superimpose regressive images of Netherlanders and Indians on the landscape," O'Neill answered: "Hans is Dutch for a reason ... Once he is Dutch, then there are consequences of him being Dutch. Nick Carraway is not Dutch. So he just briefly mentions the Dutch right at the very end. But Hans van den Broek is the original colonial eye revisiting New York. And I suppose his whole friendship with Chuck wakes up the Dutch colonial settler from the Netherland of Hans's memory."[23] Hans reawakens these old colonial eyes on a holiday in India to record what he saw when he looked in on a column of poor workers by the side of the road. "They were small and thin and poor and dark-skinned, with thin arms and thin legs. They were men walking in the forest and the darkness." For some reason, Hans tells us, he keeps on seeing these men. "I do not think of Chuck as one of them, even though, with his very dark skin, he could have been one of them. I think of Chuck as the Chuck I saw. But whenever I see these men I always end up seeing Chuck." Hans's career as a cricket player assumes two distinct phases enacted by two different personae. When he recalls his years playing for the exclusive cricket club in his native Holland, he feels under his mother's approving eye. But when he remembers his time on Chuck Ramkissoon's bush league cricket field, he retroactively solicits Rachel's worried gaze. The latter regression transports Hans from the memory of his childhood in metropolitan Holland to the more archaic memory of the Dutch settler colonies of Hendrick Hudson's New Netherland. Hans's oscillation between these noncomparable cricket fields renders visible the third person interconnecting the Dutch colony in the New Netherland to the twenty-first century world capitalist system. Hans recognizes the third person he has become when he opens his colonial eye to the indirect part he played—as a descendant of the Dutch settler-colonists dating back to Henrick Hudson—in Chuck Ramkissoon's death. This colonial eye illuminates the material linkages between the Dutch colonial settlers' accumulation by dispossession in the America of the seventeenth century and the global financial military establishment's accumulation by dispossession in the Iraq of the twenty-first century.

At novel's end, Hans takes Rachel's reaction to the news of Chuck's death as a sign that she had recovered her old self. Rachel does not now construe Chuck a member of the Global South in need of asylum or protection or collaboration. She now considers him a gangster and a terrorist threat to Hans's status as number four in the *Institutional Investors* ranking of oil equities analysts.

The difference between Hans van den Broek's colonial settler's relationship to Chuck Ramkissoon's cricket enterprise and the cultural fantasy work that post-9/11 critics have projected onto this narrative reveals what I find truly uncanny in *Netherlands* re-worlding of the American novel.[24]

Notes

1. Richard Gray "Open Doors, Closed Minds: American Prose Writing at a Time of Crisis," *American Literary History* 21 (2009): 134. Pages from this essay are hereafter cited in parentheses in the body of the essay.

2. This call for the worlding of United States literary works began two decades earlier when numerous American studies scholars published works—*Cultures of United States Imperialism*, ed. Amy Kaplan and Donald Pease (Durham, NC: Duke University Press, 1993), 3–21; Carolyn Porter, "What We Know That We Don't Know: Remapping American Literary Studies," *American Literary History* 6 (1994): 467–526; Gregory S. Jay, "The End of American Literature," *College English* 53 (1991): 264–281; Jane C. Desmond and Virginia R. Dominguez, "Resituating American Studies in a Critical Internationalism," *American Quarterly* 48 (1996): 475–490—that generated a post-national geopolitical imaginary emerging at the critical juncture between American Studies and postcolonial theory, comparative literature, and the study of globalization. The fact that the demand for the worlding of American literature increased exponentially after 9/11 discloses the increased urgency of this pre-existing desire.

3. Michael Rothberg "A Failure of the Imagination: Diagnosing the Post-9/11 Novel: A Response to Richard Gray," *American Literary History* 21 (2009): 152–158. Pages from this essay are hereafter cited in parentheses in the body of the essay.

4. Elizabeth Anker, "Allegories of Falling and the 9/11 Novel," *American Literary History* 23 (2011): 463–482. Pages from this essay are hereafter cited in parentheses in the body of the essay.

5. Caren Irr, "Toward the World Novel: Genre Shifts in Twenty-First Century Expatriate Fiction," *American Literary History* 23 (2011): 660–679. Pages from this essay are hereafter cited in parentheses in the body of the essay.

6. Irr constructed her account of expatriate fiction in part as a response to Bruce Robbins's complaint that US novelists had endowed what took place on 9/11 with its "own unique local surround, a restricted time/space that replaces and cancels out any abstract

planetary coordinates." See Bruce Robbins, "The Worlding of the American Novel," in *The Cambridge History of The American Novel*, ed. Leonard Cassuto (Cambridge: Cambridge University Press, 2011), 1096.

7. Numerous essays and essay collections, and monographs have been published on "post-9/11 literature" over the last decade. Notable studies include *Literature After 9/11*, ed. Anne Keniston and Jeanne Follansbee Quinn (New York and London: Routledge, 2008); Kristiaan Versluys, *Out of the Blue: September 11 and the Novel* (New York: Columbia University Press, 2009); Martin Randall, *9/11 and the Literature of Terror* (Edinburgh: Edinburgh University Press, 2011); Richard Gray's *After the Fall: American Literature Since 9/11* (Oxford: Wiley-Blackwell, 2011).

8. James Wood "Beyond a Boundary." *New Yorker* (May 26, 2008) http://www.newyorker.com/arts/critics/books/2008/05/26/080526crbo_books_wood.

9. Michiko Kutani, "Post 9/11, a New York of Gatsby-Size Dreams and Loss," *Books of The Times*, May 16, 2008 http://www.nytimes.com/2008/05/16/books/16book.html.

10. Katherine V. Snyder elaborates on O'Neill's re-accentuation of Fitzgerald's novel in "Gastby's Ghost: Post-Traumatic Memory and National Literary Tradition in Joseph O'Neill's *Netherland*," *Contemporary Literature* 54 (2013): 459–490.

11. Zadie Smith, "Two Paths for the Novel," *New York Review of Books* 55 (18), November 20, 2008 http://www.nybooks.com/articles/2008/11/20/two-paths-for-the-novel/ Smith is also quite critical in her assessment of *Netherland*. She takes them to task for seeming so "perfectly done," at an historical moment when demonstrations of stylistic felicity are incompatible with political right-mindedness: "*Netherland* is only superficially about September 11 or immigrants or cricket as a symbol of good citizenship. Its worries are formal and revolve obsessively around the question of authenticity . . . It is absolutely a post-catastrophe novel but the catastrophe isn't terror, it's Realism."

12. In "Cricket's Field of Dreams: Queer Racial Identifications in Joseph O'Neill's *Netherland*," *Critique: Studies in Contemporary Fiction* 55 (2014): 341–357, John Duvall contends that the inter-ethnic, homosocial relationship Hans and Chuck forge in the cricket field moves the post 9/11 novel beyond narratives of traumatized males in mid-life crisis and encourages readers to re-examine the notion of national community from the standpoint of the limits and exclusions this formation produces.

13. Christian Moraru, *Reading for the Planet: Toward a Geomethodology* (Ann Arbor: University of Michigan Press, 2015), 168.

14. Joseph O'Neill, *Netherland* (New York: Pantheon, 2008), 71, 132. Pages from the novel are hereafter cited in parentheses in the body of the essay.

15. The geopolitical imaginary of post-national American literature that these critics have projected onto *Netherland* remains dependent on these liberal multicultural beliefs, values and assumptions that also regulate their interpretations of the novel. In harnessing their observations about the post-9/11 novel to liberal multicultural and cosmopolitan values, these critics simply ignore the tensions neoliberalism creates between market and state and between capital and territory in clear view throughout *Netherland*.

16. This interpretation of the critics' hyper canonization of *Netherland* as symptomatic of the encompassing fantasy-work of neoliberalism draws on Jodi Dean's account of neoliberalism as an ideological formation that produces imaginary rather than symbolic identities and that deploys multiculturalist, post-nationalist, and anti-racist sloganeering to mask real economic inequalities. See Jodi Dean, *Democracy and Other Neoliberal*

Fantasies: Communicative Capitalism and Left Politics (Durham, NC: Duke University Press, 2009).

17. Wood "Beyond a Boundary."

18. For an excellent discussion of the positioning of terrorist assemblages within the financial-military apparatus, see Jasbir Puar, *Terrorist Assemblages: Homonationalism in Queer Times* (Durham, NC: Duke University Press, 2007), 1–37.

19. In "Cricket and the World-System, or Continuity, 'Riskless Risk' and Cyclicality in Joseph O'Neill's *Netherland*," *Journal of Postcolonial Writing* (2016), Claire Westall shows how Hans's trips through the enclaves of his cricket partners uncovers the uneven economic development of Brooklyn's urban geography. http://dx.doi.org/10.1080/17449855.2016.1203102.

20. For contextualization of post-9/11 political anxieties within the broader histories of the colonies of white settlement see essays gathered in *Settler Colonial Studies*, 3:1; especially Penelope Edmonds and Jane Carey "A New Beginning for *Settler Colonial Studies*," 2–5.

21. For a discussion of the mode of cultural production see, "From Virgin Land to Ground Zero: The Mythological Foundations of the National Security State" in Donald Pease, *The New American Exceptionalism* (Minneapolis: The University of Minnesota Press, 2009), 153–180.

22. For different interpretations of the part Chuck plays in Hans's psycho-history, see Katherine V. Snyder's "Gastby's Ghost: Post-Traumatic Memory and National Literary Tradition in Joseph O'Neill's *Netherland*." *Contemporary Literature* 54 (2013): 459–490, and John N. Duvall's "Cricket's Field of Dreams: Queer Racial Identifications in Joseph O'Neill's *Netherland*." *Critique: Studies in Contemporary Fiction* 55 (2014): 341–357.

23. Nathalie Cochoy and Olivier Gaudin, "An Interview with Joseph O'Neill," *Transatlantica*, http://transatlantica.revues.org/6393.

24. As the extension of American Literature on a global scale, the "worlding" of post-9/11 American literature also gets facilitated through the world market's global reach, which is a literary equivalent to Chuck's Cricket Inc. The worlding of American literature refers to its imbrication in this market via the commercial culture of rapid and pervasive translation. As an exemplary instance of this phenomenon, *Netherland* renders emergent geo-economic conditions of the capitalist world system—accelerated migration, increased interpenetration of global markets, combined and uneven development—increasingly legible to readers. See Donald E. Pease, "Introduction" in *Re-Mapping the Transnational Turn" in Re-Framing the Transnational Turn in American Studies*, ed. Winfried Fluck, Donald Pease, and John Carlos Rowe (Hanover, NH: Dartmouth College Press, 2011).

[8]

LIAM KENNEDY

DESERT STORIES: LIBERAL ANXIETIES AND THE
NEOLIBERAL NOVEL

WHAT CAN AMERICAN LITERATURE tell us about the role of the United States in a neoliberal global order in which American hegemony is both maintained and undermined by flows of unfettered capital? As is widely documented, the inexorable spread of free-market capitalism in the wake of the endings of the Cold War has led to an increasingly complex interdependence—of markets, nations, and technologies—and accelerated movements of people, capital, and information. There have emerged new geographies of economic connectivity and power, new divisions of labor, and new landscapes of work and waste. The representation of these changes has been a challenge for literary fiction (and many other forms of cultural production), in part due to the speed and scale of the processes of change and the barely legible nature of some of these processes. Benjamin Kunkel, writing of the protagonist in Joseph O'Neill's *Netherland*, observes: "Many of us live . . . this kind of far-flung life, globalized in all its localities, international even on a molecular scale, but contemporary fiction has struggled to keep pace with the aggressive contemporaneity of this way of living."[1] But the challenge for contemporary fiction surely goes deeper than this, to produce narratives commensurate to the shifting coordinates—economic, political, and representational—of the neoliberal global order and, concomitant to this, to reimagine the value of literature (including that of a national literature) in relation to these coordinates. This is a tricky balancing act and in the work of American writers who take up this challenge we often find that residual liberal anxieties come up hard against regnant neoliberal realities. I will consider two recent examples in the work of Dave Eggers and Joseph O'Neill.

There is some evidence of an emergent geopolitical imaginary in American literary production as a growing number of writers seek ways to narrativize America's global engagements and map shifting contours of American power and identity in global terms. Bruce Robbins, in his essay "The Worlding of the American Novel," notes that American writers are becoming more "worldly," trying to connect global and domestic spheres and also remap American literary identity, yet he argues that this is restrained due to the continued focus on self-discovery and inability to work out the degree or kind of harm America does in the world.[2] More recently, Caren Irr, in her book *Toward the Geopolitical Novel: US Fiction in the Twenty-First Century*, has argued that American writers are productively exploring global matters and that there is an emerging geopolitical consciousness that is "proto-political" in recognition of formative effects on global inequalities.[3] Yet, she too points up limitations and constraints on this emergent consciousness.

I think both critics are right to be cautious about the claims for a "worlding" of contemporary American literature, even as they identify and map new energies in this regard. At its best this literature explores new forms of relationality and illuminates some of those coordinates of a neoliberal global order referred to above. Yet, the emergent geopolitical imaginary of contemporary American literature remains conditional on national beliefs, values and assumptions, not least in its difficulties in representing the "obscene underside" of the neoliberal world order.[4] It tends to gloss the tensions neoliberalism creates between market and state and between capital and territory, whilst registering anxieties about American self- and national identity. This is most evident in literature that either mandates or assumes the critical facility of a liberal imagination or the adequacy of realist form in responding to a market-saturated socio-political world. The novels under review here not only signify the limits of a liberal imagination, they also refer us to (in)capacities of literary fiction to realize or realistically depict the dreamwork of neoliberal capital.

Dave Eggers' *A Hologram for the King* (2012) and Joseph O'Neill's *The Dog* (2014) might be described as "worldly" in that they dramatize America's economic and spiritual declensions in the context of its faltering global hegemony. Both writers create narratives that explicitly address excesses and contradictions of neoliberal capitalism. Notably, both employ desert settings in expatriate narratives that take their protagonists to the Middle East, to Saudi Arabia in Eggers case, and to Dubai for O'Neill. In this they follow on the heels of a growing cadre of Western journalists and scholars who have visited Middle Eastern sites of urban development to which international flows of speculative finance have been drawn. Most commonly, Dubai is the focus of analysis, though several other cities in the Arab Gulf states are also cited.[5] Dubai first caught global attention with its spectacular credit-fuelled growth in the post-Cold War period, as it built on abundant amounts of debt to create a global hub for banking, tourism, and transportation, all attractive to neoliberal capital investment—and all with the tacit approval of the US, which has sold the UAE its military hardware and software, secured shipping lanes, and can rely on it as a regional base. Dubai's perceived success in transforming itself into a "city as corporation" has encouraged a trend of entrepreneurial urbanism and master-planned cities on the Arabian Peninsula and the Gulf, including the "economic cities" emerging out of the deserts of Saudi Arabia and Qatar as these states prepare for a post-oil era.[6] These cities provide special regulatory frameworks that facilitate modes of "flexible citizenship," which allow the "proficient class" to flourish while sustaining more disposable workforces, many of whom became heavily indebted in order to obtain employment.[7] The urban social orders that result reveal specific contradictions of neoliberal capitalism, notably in the ways that their elites seek to manage social progress in relation to economic liberalism.[8] Western commentators, and especially media reports, have generally observed these developments with apprehension, though with limited focus on nuances of local structures and contexts, rather focusing on these "cities of the future" as portents of a dystopian global urbanism. To be sure, narratives about hyper-exploitation of workers are common, and many of these commentators note the stark inequalities and prohibition on political freedoms and citizenship rights, contrasting with the expansion and celebration of consumer freedoms and private accumulation. Mike Davis and Daniel Bertrand Monk refer to these sites of excessive speculation and privatization as "evil paradises," "dreamworlds of consumption, property and power," and ask: "Toward what kind of future are we being led by savage, fanatical capitalism?"[9]

It seems likely Eggers and O'Neill have been reading some of these narratives. Each novelist has researched their locales in some detail and has something to say about these settings as symbolic or allegorical sites of neoliberal capital. In an interview, O'Neill remarks: "Dubai markets itself as an outlier ... and 'we' seize on this in order to view Dubai's horrors and drawbacks as a special case ... and in no way reflective of 'us.'"[10] At the same time, as he notes in another interview, "A lot of the humanist ideas we are attached to are put in question by Dubai. I think this makes Dubai less an outlier than a forerunner to the West."[11] While cognizant of economic realities, each author represents their Middle Eastern settings as shimmering mirages, projections of Western fantasies. This is to say that even as they utilize sociological perspectives to depict socio-economic realities of these urban developments, they also romanticize them as projections of individual angst and ennui. In both novels, harsh realities and legacies of neoliberal financialization are explored through the consciousness of hapless middle-aged white male protagonists whose singular woes are universalized and imaginatively mapped onto a broad canvas of globalization, readily conflating national and self-diminishment. Their protagonists attempt, often humorously, sometimes poignantly, to hold onto outmoded or devalued values, struggling to find a language to express their subjectivities—symbolic inefficiency is writ dramatically large in their sense of victimization and diminished expectations.[12] There is a note of the absurd in both novels, as the protagonists find themselves in worlds that appear to be abstracted beyond common reference points of language or human interaction. The absurd atmosphere heightens tensions between the authors' aims to tell us something about the inequities and human costs of neoliberalization and their difficulties in representing this something.

Made in America

Alan Clay, the protagonist of Eggers' *A Hologram for the King*, is a not unfamiliar figure, a successful salesman in his youth he is now an unsuccessful consultant in middle age. More than a few critics have referred to him as the Willy Loman of the post-industrial age and viewed the novel as "a kind of 'Death of a Globalized Salesman.'"[13] Eggers tells us that Alan was "born into manufacturing and somewhere later got lost in worlds tangential to the making of things."[14] His skills have become irrelevant, "Now he was fifty-four years old and was as intriguing to corporate America as an airplane built from mud. He could not find work, could not sign clients" (14). In the present of the novel we find him in Saudi Arabia in the surreal setting of The King Abdullah Economic City (KAEC), a spectacularly ambitious urban initiative to build a city north of Jeddah that will compete with Dubai.[15] Alan has been hired by the American IT giant Reliant to sell holographic communications technology to the King, with a view to picking up further contracts for the KAEC development. He desperately hopes this job will enable him to literally and figuratively salvage himself—"Alan's commission, in the mid-six figures, would fix everything that ailed him" (36)—reflecting a belief in the dreamwork of capital that he cannot let go off. And so he waits, futilely, for hours and then days for the King to come. It comes as no surprise to the reader at the end of the novel that the contract he seeks is awarded to a Chinese company that "could deliver the IT far quicker and at less than half the cost" (330).

As Alan waits in the desert, the author takes us into his backstory. We learn that he has played a role in the demise of American industry that he now laments and sees himself as a victim of, for he was involved in the outsourcing of manufacturing at American firms he worked for, most notably the bicycle firm Schwinn. As Eggers details this story we cannot avoid the more didactic and diagrammatic elements of the novel: Alan's fate is clearly intended to parallel America's in the age of globalized capital, the loss of a

Desert Stories: Liberal Anxieties and the Neoliberal Novel

meaningful "place in the world's economy" (14). Underlining this, Alan's father is presented as a symbolic foil to his son, a virile World War II veteran who was a foreman in a shoe factory and now retired on a healthy union pension on a farm in New Hampshire. In a phone call, his father inveighs:

> I'm watching this thing about how a gigantic new bridge in Oakland, California, is being made in China. Can you imagine? Now they're making our goddamned bridges, Alan. I got to say, I saw everything else coming. When they closed down Stride Rite, I saw it coming. When you start shopping out the bikes over there in Taiwan, I saw it coming. I saw the rest of it coming—toys, electronics, furniture. Makes sense if you're some shitass bloodthirsty executive hellbent on hollowing out the economy for his own gain. All that makes sense. Nature of the beast. But the bridges I did not see coming. By God, we're having other people make our bridges. And now you're in Saudi Arabia, selling a hologram for the pharaohs! That takes the Cake! (87)

Even the hologram points out Alan's (America's) diminishment: having been a man who sold real things made in America to real people who lived in America he now tries to sell a simulacrum to an invisible king.

A Hologram for the King presents an oddly skewed narrative of progress and decline, one that all but ignores historical and environmental contexts of the building of KAEC. At one point Alan reflects, "The work of man is done behind the back of the natural world. When nature notices, and can muster the energy, it wipes the slate clean again" (117). Such observations mystify the relations between state, market, and environment, and all but ignore the biopolitics of neoliberal capital's accumulation by dispossession. To be sure, there are references to the uneven conditions of labor and capital relations in the building of KAEC and flashes of insight about labor exploitation and curtailments of civil rights, but they are mostly just that, isolated flashes of commentary that rarely entail as either analysis or documentation. Eggers is deft at sketching incongruities. For example, as Alan and his driver leave his hotel "they drove past a desert-colored Humvee, a machine gun mounted on top. A Saudi soldier was sitting next to it, in a beach chair, his feet soaking in an inflatable pool" (24–25). But such sketches tell us little or nothing about the structural conditions of governance in Saudi Arabia. One of the most common motifs of literary (and visual) representation of globalization is to depict incongruities formed by the juxtapositions occasioned by uneven development or the contact points of different cultures. This can make for a somewhat lazy way of signifying globalization, making it visible via the frisson of incongruity and indulging the reader in what are often passive pleasures of irony or parody.

At times, Eggers extends this technique to provide fuller narrative detail on the excesses and contradictions surrounding his narrator at KAEC. Visiting a condominium development, Alan comes across the sleeping quarters of migrant laborers: "Alan opened the fire door and a roar of echoes flooded through. He was in a large raw space full of men, some in their underclothes, some in red jumpsuits, all yelling. It looked like pictures he'd seen of prison gyms converted to dormitories. There were fifty bunks, clothes hanging on lines between them" (221). Alan is forced to flee this space of squalid otherness when his efforts to adjudicate in a fight between the men ends in dismal failure and he makes his way to a luxury apartment a few floors above the migrant quarters: "It occupied the full width of the building, panoramic window to panoramic window. The décor was sophisticated, with gleaming hardwood floors, custom rugs, a mix of low-slung mid-century couches and tables, the occasional antique flourish . . . Over the mantle, a quartet of drawings by someone who was either Degas or drew dancers precisely as he did" (226). While moving beyond clichés of incongruity Eggers stops short of documenting or analyzing underlying structural or systemic elements of global forces and their impacts on human subjects. The realities of the laborers lives are neither explained nor explored, rather they exist to dramatize Alan's failure to take responsibility, to engage or connect.

In some part, Egger's focus on Alan's failings, the indignities, humiliations, and shame he experiences, registers the author's care to paint his protagonist as limited in self-understanding, placing an ironic distance between the reader and protagonist. Alan is not analytic for the most part, rather he is given to indulgent reflections and nostalgic reverie, but this creates an odd tension in the novel, between the belated worldview of the protagonist and the ironic omniscience of the author, exacerbated by the battened-down prose style. If the aim is that we comprehend the limitations of Alan's worldview, by looking over his shoulder, as it were, the results are unsatisfying, though perhaps deliberately so. It may be that Eggers sees this as a means to represent the affectless condition of Alan's stasis and so he glosses the socio-economic realities of KAEC's development to underscore the dreamwork of neoliberal capital. On this reading, Alan's wait for the King is a record of the finacialization of time and Alan's thralldom to speculation, to a hypothetical outcome, the paralysis of which is represented in the style of the prose.

In some sense, this is a logical outcome of Alan's interpellation of economic thinking from his early career days as a door-to-door salesman selling household products. We are told: "Alan became a good salesman, and quickly. He needed the money to move out of his parents' house, which he did a month later. Six months after that he had a new car and more cash than he could spend. Money, Romance, Self-Preservation, Recognition: he'd applied the categories to everything" (83). As his career develops, he learns that "he had to act like he was selling happiness, security, possibility"—this selling of emotions and values is of course the basis of commodity fetishism.[16] Later, when he worked as an executive at Schwinn bicycles in Chicago, he successfully puts these lessons into practice. Alan has rosy memories of his early days at Schwinn:

> In the morning he'd be at the West Side factory, watching the bikes, hundreds of them, loaded onto trucks, gleaming in the sun in a dozen ice-cream colours. He'd get in his car, head down state, and in the afternoon he could be in Mattoon or Rantoul or Alton, checking on a dealership. He'd see a family walk in, Mom and Dad getting their ten-year-old daughter a World Sport, the kid touching the bike like it was some holy thing. Alan knew, and the retailer knew, and the family knew, that that bike had been made by hand a few hundred miles north, by a dizzying array of workers, most of them immigrants . . . and that bike would last more or less forever. (50)

This nostalgic vision links the economics of production and consumption to an idealized American scene, of family and nation, reproduction and futurity, all held together by the fetishized bicycle: "the kid touching the bicycle like it was some holy thing."

Alan is unable to become a dutiful citizen-subject of a neoliberal order, for he lacks the capacity for self-care, the moral autonomy demanded of the neoliberal subject. This is only most evident in his refusal to take responsibility for his role in outsourcing American industry. Yet, this disavowal remains stubbornly inarticulate in the narrative. At the end of the scene Alan remembers of the family buying Schwinn bicycles the rhythmic reverie stumbles as he wonders "Why did this matter? Why did it matter that they had been made just up Highway 57? It was hard to say" (50). Unable to articulate his predicament, Alan holds onto an illusion and we learn that following his departure from Schwinn, he sank his savings into developing a bicycle of his own design. The initiative collapsed of course, but Alan still dreams: "He could still do this. He thought of his silver bike, the prototype he'd had made. It was so beautiful. Everything was silver and chrome, even the gears, even the seat. Had anyone ever made a more beautiful object? You could see it from space it was so bright and shone so defiantly" (75). Alan knows manufacturing the bike is not possible, yet is guided by fetishistic illusion, a disavowal that both sustains an ideological fantasy of an America that never existed and allows him to continue to invest in the dream of neoliberal speculation.

Alan remains trapped within an American worldview that is troubled by, but unwilling or unable to confront, the obscene underside of global capitalism. Perhaps the most telling moment of his disavowal occurs when wandering around the site of KAEC he comes across a large pit, seemingly a foundation for a building, and descends into it. At the bottom he sits and remembers a business deal a friend had recounted to him about a US glass manufacturer that had gotten the contract for the first twenty floors of the World Trade Center building, but were usurped at the last moment by a Chinese company using the very patent the US company had developed. Alan grows angry as he remembers this and is distressed that the New York Port Authority "would go abroad for such a thing, would knowingly lead PPG on—millions in equipment upgrades and retooling to enable them to build the glass—my God, the whole thing was underhanded and it was cowardly and lacking in all principle. It was dishonour. And at Ground Zero. Alan was pacing, his hands in fists. The dishonour! At Ground Zero! Amid the ashes! The dishonour! Amid the ashes! The dishonour! The dishonour! The dishonour!" (136) In this scene of trauma the references to dishonor seem tritely or comically discordant in relation to the feelings and facts of what the narrator is describing, and yet this is precisely the language Alan would use, for he experiences this as an issue of national shame, contiguous with his own humiliations and shame in the present moment in Saudi Arabia. The linkage of Ground Zero and the attacks on 9/11 to Saudi Arabia is a suggestive one of course, and not just in terms of the networking of terror, but also that of global finance capital, but this glimpse of the Real is elided by the focus on Alan's conflation of personal and national traumas. Here, as throughout the novel, Eggers seems uncertain about how to narrativize the realities of neoliberal capitalism beyond ironic references to his narrator's delusions. At the end of the novel, Alan decides to remain at KAEC, "Otherwise who would be here when the King came again?" (331).

Given the use of irony to create distances between author, narrator, and reader, it can be difficult to delineate Egger's own investment in this narrative of American decline. Yet, the very style of the narration bespeaks a commitment to literary form that reflects this author's sense of value in the act of writing and in certain forms of writing. In a 2011 interview, where he is talking about McSweeney's magazine, he observes: "There was a time when we looked first and foremost for successful or at least interesting experiments in form. Now we're really looking for plain old good writing. After living for a while, and knowing things do happen in this world, I look for novels and short stories to reflect that."[17] This paean to "plain old good writing" bespeaks a fetishization of craft that oddly echoes the nostalgia for industrial production that Alan Clay expresses in *A Hologram for the King*. In the lengthy Acknowledgements section at the end of the book, Eggers thanks the "entire staff" at "Thompson-Shore printers in Dexter, Michigan," a shout out that hints at his passionate investment in the design and production of

Desert Stories: Liberal Anxieties and the Neoliberal Novel [159]

his books. In an interview, Eggers describes visiting the firm and meeting workers: "I went to visit them and found it was a relatively small plant in the middle of homes and farms. They did exceedingly high quality work and had an archival bindery, too, and so I just was really taken with the whole enterprise."[18] The embossed hardback version of *A Hologram for the King*, designed by Jessica Hische, drew much appreciative comment from reviewers and readers:

> I was loathe to even crack the spine for fear of upending its sensual, aesthetic gestalt . . . The book's packaging seems to reference a bygone time (early 20th century? the Victorian age? early Gutenberg era? all three?) when books were rarer specimens—sacred tomes of knowledge and wisdom.[19]

> Even the book cover is hipster-cool . . . it has the updated-antique aesthetic coveted by people who home brew and buy moustache wax.[20]

The designer Hische says: "I couldn't be happier with how it turned out, it's really a beautiful object to hold in your hands."[21] This sounds a lot like: ". . . the kid touching the bike like it was some holy thing." The very book functions as a fetishistic disavowal of the anxieties it narrates; like the story it tells, it is made in America.

"It's Not My Forte"

Joseph O'Neill embraces what he terms his "elective statelessness" and has stated he is "interested in putting characters in places where the world order is changing, and changing in a particular way."[22] In his novel *Netherland*, an Anglo-Dutch Wall Street financial analyst, estranged from his wife, connects the worlds of old and new immigrants in New York. In *The Dog*, the narrator is another depressed and rootless individual, an attorney who leaves his unhappy life in New York, escaping the painful aftermath of a failed relationship to take up an ill-defined position in Dubai as a legal-financial "majordomo" for a very wealthy and profligate Lebanese family.[23] O'Neill milks humor from the high-end self-fashioning of his narrator's class of wealthy expatriates in Dubai. An example is the association of buildings with status: the narrator lives in a neighborhood called Privilege Bay in a luxury highrise called the Situation inhabited by the Uncompromising Few (according to the building's website); it is one of a triad of luxury high rises called the Privileged Three, the other two are called the Statement and the Aspiration. He frets at the reputation and value of his apartment building, and comments ironically on the affectless world of very rich expatriates, people who, he dryly observes, "prioritize their own future prestige or devote themselves to producing deathless *objets* for their meuseological self-representation in posterity" (23).

The narrator is an unnamed everyman and, in certain respects, resembles Alan Clay, at least in his belated masculinity and bouts of humiliation and shame. However, O'Neill's narrator-protagonist is a much more analytical character, given to ironic scrutiny of his role: "Mine is the inevitable fate of the overwhelmed fiduciary: inextinguishable boredom and fear of liability" (41). Mostly, his job consists of rubber-stamping documents he doesn't understand. As O'Neill comments in interview, "He's not even sure he really knows what his job *is*, beyond its humiliations and shame."[24] If Alan Clay is a twenty-first century Willy Loman, the narrator of *The Dog* is Bartleby the Scrivener in neoliberal drag.

The Dog is a very knowing "comedy of ethics."[25] The narrator tries to hold on to and articulate ideas and arguments that have little value in the neoliberal present, and there is comedy in the absurdity of his efforts to reason in the face of a world that does not conform to his outmoded liberal sensibility. He is adrift in a world devoid of responsibilities and obligations, with no sense of shared purpose or common assumptions. He mentally composes emails he never sends and muses on many subjects, all are ethical minefields: "There's no such thing as 'to get' something," he thinks to himself. "The inevitable consequence of resolving knotty unknown A is the creation of knotty unknown B" (109). Like Bartleby, he takes us into a dark web of bureaucratic complexity that produces ever greater confusion and dysfunction. Stylistically, the novel represents this complexity via baroque passages in which the narrator's efforts to reason produce endlessly digressive "and tortuous disclaimers" (144) and serial use of parentheticals. The narrator's mordant observations on the diminishment of values are darkly echoed in the environs of Dubai, which is depicted as "the capital of an absurd transactional culture" in which "foreigners are allowed in to do work, in exchange for certain liberties."[26] It is a city where citizenship is interminably suspended and responsibility is always deferred; it is a nightmare state of neoliberal governance where suspensions of political freedoms are consequent on endless expansions of consumer freedoms. As an allegory of neoliberal governmentality, *The Dog* provides a sharply satirical take on the *lack* of responsibility at the heart of a system that requires individuals to self-responsibilize. The paradox of such a requirement, as Mark Fisher notes, is that when everyone is responsible then no one is; the required subject—a collective subject— does not exist.[27]

It is no accident that O'Neill has chosen Dubai as the setting for this allegory. He describes the city as an "abracadabropolis" (67), a space of spectacular self-invention. As noted above, he recognizes its symbolic status as "a forerunner to the West." Clearly, O'Neill did his research on Dubai and intends to represent it as a dystopian manifestation of the logic of neoliberal capitalism. Not that he makes such direct points about socio-economic realities in the novel, where these tend to be refracted through an oblique narrative voice. In his more direct commentary on the economic order, the narrator focuses on the ways in which Dubai represents a neoliberal fantasy of mobility and choice. This is most obviously symbolized by the Dubai International Finance Centre, which is a satellite jurisdiction of Dubai and is described by the narrator as "a zone of win-win-win flows of money and ideas and humans" that promises a "future community of cooperative productivity, that financial nationhood, of which all of us here more or less unconsciously dream" (106). He uses similar terms to describe Dubai International Airport as a "dream-like world" of transience and consumer choice: "Dubai's undeclared mission is to make itself indistinguishable from its airport" (57).

In this dream world, markers of ethnicity are erased or air-brushed into near invisibility. Espying members of the Emirates air crew in his building, the narrator muses: "How clearly I remember my first exposure to this superior polyglot race, which is how these ethnically elusive women with smiling creaseless faces first struck me. They seemed indigenous to the skies" (133). At the same time, he is confronted with race and class markers of immigrant labor, including the service crew in the hotels and apartment blocks and the men building new hotels and blocks. He learns about the indeterminate status of his assistant, Ali: "He is a 'bidoon' (Arabic for 'without', apparently), i.e., a stateless person, i.e., a person who is everywhere illegally present . . . Neither *jus sanguinis* nor *jus soli* avails bidoons. They are, as things stand, fucked" (30). These socio-economic observations draw attention to the contingencies of "freedom" in Dubai and to ways in which these are abrogated. In interview, O'Neill observes: "The problem [the narrator] faces is that to be in Dubai is to become complicit in a very naïve sense. The wrongdoing of the government is transparent . . . In Dubai you cannot ignore what is happening."[28] But the narrator does ignore what is happening, or at least he tries to. He attempts to reason his distance from service personnel and migrant laborers, constructing elaborate disclaimers. He remarks that "I'm not blind to the jobsite labourers" (77) and goes on:

> I have taken steps to inform myself about the oppressive and predicamental working conditions, not to say near-enslavement, to which many of them are subject from day one . . . I also know enough not to give weight to the emotion of solidarity by which I experience, from inside my chilled apartment, a one-sided connection to these men, who are in the blazing hot outdoors. I'll

simply say this: I have run the numbers, and I am satisfied that I have given the situation of the foreign labour corps, and my relation to it, an appropriate measure of consideration and action. (78)

Yet, the presence of this sub-class is most pointedly narrativized as a source of ethical anxiety for the narrator who wants to "figure out how to do the right thing" (80) but winds himself ever further into a paralytic web of his own inactions and over-reasoned reflections.

For all his freedom of movement and choice the narrator is thoroughly disconnected from human interaction and this is at one with his highly financialized sense of the world around him, constantly working out the monetary value of his actions and relationships. He regularly hires Eastern European prostitutes with whom he has minimal conversation and tells us that "often, after she has left, I will Google the place a given girl says she's from and I will learn a little about the world. My investigations are mainly photographic. I have contemplated the smokestacks of Magnitogorsk and the poplars of Gharm. A gas station in burned grassland ... a window among thousands in a sovietiv housing complex—these are the icons of personal desolation with which I have come to associate the women I pay to have sex with" (83). This perverse effort to connect with emotional lives of the women through this virtual imaging of deindustrialized Soviet wastelands presents a striking biopolitical metaphor that maps the geopolitics of capital accumulation and dispossession onto financialized sexual relations. Like so much in the novel, it is an oddly skewed yet suggestive perspective on the networks of global relationships that undergird unequal exchanges at local levels. It is also of course a metaphorization of the narrator's extreme self-alienation, a commentary on the dialectics of distance and intimacy that channel his desires and disavowals.

This distancing also feeds into his musings on national identity and his status as an expatriate. He reflects on "loyalties of country" (109): "I might add that I feel more cleanly American than ever. Leaving the USA has resulted in a purification of nationality. By this I mean that my relationship to the US Constitution is no longer subject to distortion by residence and I am more appreciative than ever of the great ideals that make the United States special. I pay my federal taxes to the last dime, and, without in any way devaluing citizenship to a business of cash registers, I can assert that I am well in the black with my country" (109). The irony is thickly layered here. In parsing national identity in terms of political and economic registers of citizenship the narrator calls attention both to the precarious nature of this identity, the contingent freedoms it signifies, and the contradictory logics of capital and territory. Towards the end of the novel he further reflects on his deterritorialized identity as he looks at his passport and has a "sudden insight that American nationhood is part of a worldwide protection racket and that it should be possible, surely, to live without a state's say-so. I set to one side all theories and systems" (235). This rhetorical sloughing off of national identity seems deliberate as he prepares to be apprehended for financial mismanagement (though it is not clear what the crime is or even if a crime was committed) and refuses to flee, as many advise. And yet there is considerable ambiguity in this expressed desire to "live without a state's say so." After all, in many respects he already lives in a state of statelessness and this expressed desire along with the novel's ambiguous closure speaks to the confused ethical and political dimensions of the narrator's refusal (and his deeper disavowals of responsibility).

The novel ends with an act of self-negation as the narrator awaits a knock at the door signaling the arrival of authorities to arrest and charge him, a reminder of the European literary antecedents of O'Neill's narrative—Dostoyevsky, Kafka, and Beckett all loom large. However, it is Melville's Bartleby, a very American antecedent, who is the more relevant reference point both at the end of the novel and throughout. There is much that requires more careful analysis to detail the parallels with Melville's story. For example, the ways in which each writer plays off the relationship between preferences and principles in articulating human relationality in societies increasingly saturated with market values. Bartleby sums up his refusal with "I would prefer not to" while the narrator of *The Dog*, seeking for a phrase to avoid accountability in response to mails and documents he receives takes to writing on them "It's not my forte" (98), a rather droll mimicking of Bartleby.[29]

In borrowing some of Melville's clothes, however, the narrator only underlines confused distinctions in the novel between the market and the state. What is O'Neill's narrator resisting? The knock on the door, if it comes, will surely be that of the market not the state, for neoliberalism, as Michel Foucault avers, envisions "a state under the supervision of the market rather than a market supervised by the state."[30] But will it come? Surely that knock would represent a centralized authority that the novel otherwise posits does not exist. The narrator's anticipation of it signifies what Fisher calls "the negative atheology proper to Capital: the centre is missing, but we cannot stop searching for it or positing it. It is not that there is nothing there—it is that what *is* there is not capable of exercising responsibility."[31] We might say that the narrator's refusal is an ontological refusal and that as such, it has a formal power as a means of establishing critical distance from a normative, if absurd, social order. But it would seem that his refusal is essentially private, he is unable to articulate any political principles that might displace or revalue market preferences.

O'Neill is not alone in invoking Bartleby as a figure of resistance in neoliberal times. Theorists such as Giorgio Agamben, Michael Hardt and Antonio Negri, and Slavoj Zizek have all invoked Bartleby as a symbolic figure for a radical politics—he was even something of a mascot for the Occupy Wall Street movement. Notwithstanding the debates about the efficacy of such invocations by the theorists, I find O'Neill's invocation unsatisfying and confusing, but also telling in that it signifies some of the underlying anxieties in the novel. The narrator's refusal is at one with the narrative's refusal of meaning, registered in in its parenthetical digressions and baroque styling, and it is as much its formal refusal as its narrative content that marks out the anxieties in this shaggy dog story.

In this respect I am reminded of Zadie Smith's comment on O'Neill's *Netherland*, describing it as "an anxious novel, unusually so," a book that "wants you to know that it knows you know it knows."[32] In her essay "Two Paths for the Novel" Smith writes: "But *Netherland* is only superficially about September 11 or immigrants or cricket as a symbol of good citizenship. It certainly is about anxiety, but its worries are formal and revolve obsessively around the question of authenticity. *Netherland* sits at an anxiety crossroads where a community in recent crisis—the Anglo-American liberal middle class—meets a literary form in long-term crisis, the nineteenth-century lyrical Realism of Balzac and Flaubert."[33] While I think Smith's essay is an overdetermined polemic on the subject of "establishment literary fiction," I think she is right about the existence of an anxiety crossroads and I think O'Neill is still at that crossroads with *The Dog*, anxious about how to express either his literary or political credentials. In interview, he is acerbic in commenting on what he terms the "chattiness" of contemporary discourses, referring to a "banal and treacherous lucidity that's underpinned by a bogus, consumeristic egalitarianism, which cannot tolerate the idea that good writing might not instantly and cost-effectively yield its full significance, and might in fact make one feel in some sense *beneath* the work."[34] What "good writing" means here in some part is writing that is "writerly," that withholds ready meaning, and O'Neill clearly ascribes this as in itself a value. At the same time, and notwithstanding the stylistic differences between *Netherland* and *The Dog*, in each novel O'Neill fetishizes his own prose style as an oblique commentary on the way we live now.

I do not think O'Neill is alone at what Smith calls the "anxiety crossroads" and Dave Eggers can be seen loitering there too. Both *A Hologram for the King* and *The Dog* evoke a sense of a transitional moment, an interregnum, reflecting rearrangements of the circuits of global economic power and the emergence of a liquid global order that exacerbates the tensions between capital and territory. The tropes of waiting and stasis are to the fore in each, signifying that the protagonists are caught between the powers of state and market but believe in neither; they are unable to satisfactorily self-govern and so conform to neoliberal norms, yet they can neither imagine nor commit to any symbolic identity outside of these. Their precarity is pronounced but not grounded, it is privatized in their expressions of desire and loss and their disavowals of responsibility. Matters of freedom, justice, and inequality hover in the narratives, though rarely come into view as structural conditions of the socio-economic contexts—the obscene underside of the neoliberal world order remains obscure.

These novels reflect an American unease about the legitimacy of liberal democracy under global conditions of neoliberal capitalist hegemony. In this they also represent the "worlding" of the American novel as an apprehensive charting of new relations between the national and the global, wherein learned habits and values are losing their meaning and utility. This is not only an ideological unease, it is also a matter of formal uncertainty about the capacity of literary fiction to express the realities of a post-American world. Both writers stretch conventional features of literary realism to near abstraction—minimalist in Eggers' case, baroque in O'Neill's—while retaining belief in the value of literary form as a hard-earned aesthetic freedom. Such consolations of form yet beg the question if American literary realism is commensurate with neoliberal reality.

Notes

1. Benjamin Kunkel, "Men in White," *London Review of Books* (July 17, 2008): 21.
2. Bruce Robbins, "The Worlding of the American Novel," *The Cambridge History of the American Novel*, ed. Leonard Cassuto (Cambridge: Cambridge University Press, 2011), 1096–1106.
3. Caren Irr, *Toward the Geopolitical Novel: US Fiction in the Twenty-First Century* (New York: Columbia University Press, 2014), 194.
4. Slavoj Zizek, *The Desert of the Real* (London: Verso, 2002), 32.
5. See Brid Aine Parnell, "The Mega Cities of the Middle East," ThinkProgress (November 28, 2017), Accessed August 6, 2018. http://www.think-progress.com/ae/mobility/the-mega-cities-of-the-middle-east/.
6. On Dubai, see Ahmed Kanna, *The City as Corporation* (Minneapolis: University of Minnesota Press, 2011). On "economic cities" in Saudi Arabia, see Sarah Algethami, "Saudi Arabia Builds Cities in the Sand to Move Beyond Oil," *Bloomberg* (August 6, 2017), Accessed August 6, 2018. https://www.bloomberg.com/news/articles/2017-08-06/saudi-arabia-builds-cities-in-the-sand-to-take-economy-past-oil.
7. On the "proficient class," see Guy Standing, *The Precariat: The New Dangerous Class* (London: Bloomsbury, 2011).
8. Kanna focuses on such contradictions in his anthropological study of Dubai. Kanna, *The City as Corporation*.

9. Mike Davis and Daniel Bertrand Monk, "Introduction," *Evil Paradises*, eds. Mike Davis and Daniel Bertrand Monk (New York: New Press, 2007): v–xix. While Davis and Monk frame this question as part of a critical inquiry on global examples of such developments, there is a strain of hyperbole in some of this Western commentary on Middle Eastern urbanism that reflects a neocolonial sense of moral superiority. This is particularly evident in the "Dubai bashing" articles that appeared in the wake of the global economic recession that began in 2008. See Todd Reisz and Rory Hyde, "Abandoned Cars and Memories of a Bashing," *Huffington Post* (July 19, 2010), Accessed January 14, 2018. https://www.huffingtonpost.com/todd-reisz/abandoned-cars-and-memori_b_651448.html).

10. Nico Israel and Matthew Hart, "Even the Toothbrush Has More than Two Paths: An Interview with Joseph O'Neill," *Los Angeles Review of Books* (September 11, 2014), Accessed January 4, 2018. https://lareviewofbooks.org/article/even-toothbrush-two-paths-interview-joseph-oneill/#!.

11. Duncan White, "Joseph O'Neill: Dubai is Where the West is Heading," *Telegraph* (August 17, 2014), Accessed January 4, 2018. https://www.telegraph.co.uk/culture/books/11034985/Joseph-ONeill-Dubai-is-where-the-West-is-heading.html.

12. In Jodi Dean's terms, neoliberalism "does not provide symbolic identities, sites from which we can see ourselves," rather, it offers imaginary ideals, promoting the cultivation of our individuality, our self-fashioning. This decline in symbolic efficiency has become a staple motif of contemporary American literature. Jodi Dean, *Democracy and Other Neoliberal Fantasies: Communicative Capitalism and Left Politics* (Durham, NC: Duke University Press, 2009): 66.

13. Pico Iyer, "Desert Pitch," *New York Times* (July 19, 2012), Accessed January 6, 2018. http://www.nytimes.com/2012/07/22/books/review/a-hologram-for-the-king-by-dave-eggers.html.

14. Dave Eggers, *A Hologram for the King* (New York: Vintage, 2012), 13. Pages from this novel are hereafter cited in parentheses in the body of the essay.

15. This development is not a fiction though is still under construction. Built by Emaar Properties, the real estate company owned by Dubai's Maktoum dynasty, it is on the coast of the Red Sea approximately 65 miles north of Jeddah. See Sylvia Smith, "Saudi Arabia's New Desert Megacity," *BBC News* (March 20, 2015), Accessed August 6, 2018. https://www.bbc.com/news/world-middle-east-31867727.

16. Stephen Elliott, "The Rumpus Interview with Dave Eggers where Dave Announces his New Book, *A Hologram for the King*," *The Rumpus* (June 4, 2012), Accessed January 4, 2018. http://therumpus.net/2012/06/the-rumpus-interview-with-dave-eggers.

17. Sophie Elmhirst, "Putting on the Clown Suit," *New Statesman* (April 21, 2011), Accessed January 14, 2018. https://www.newstatesman.com/books/2011/04/eggers-book-writing-fiction.

18. Devin Leonard, "Dave Eggers on his New Novel and Globalization," *Bloomberg Businessweek* (August 9, 2012), Accessed January 14, 2018. https://www.bloomberg.com/news/articles/2012-08-09/dave-eggers-on-his-new-novel-and-globalization.

19. Eric Heiman, "*A Hologram for the King* Book Packaging: McSweeney's," *Design Envy* (May 21, 2013), Accessed January 14, 2018. http://designenvy.aiga.org/a-hologram-for-the-king-book-packaging-mcsweeney's.

20. Miya Tokumitsu, "First World Problems: Dave Eggers's *A Hologram for the King*

and John Lanchester's *Capital*," *Slant* (May 7, 2013), Accessed January 10, 2018. https://www.slantmagazine.com/house/article/first-world-problems-dave-eggerss-a-hologram-for-the-king-and-john-lanchesters-capital

21. Jessica Hische, quoted in Heiman, "*A Hologram for the King*."

22. Jonathan Lee, "Nothing Happened: An Interview with Joseph O'Neill," *The Paris Review* (October 3, 2014), Accessed January 14, 2018. https://www.theparisreview.org/blog/2014/10/03/nothing-happened-an-interview-with-joseph-oneill.

23. Joseph O'Neill, *The Dog* (London: Fourth Estate, 2014), 5. Pages from this novel are hereafter cited in parentheses in the body of the essay.

24. Lee, "Nothing Happened."

25. Lee, "Nothing Happened."

26. John Freeman, "*The Dog* by Joseph O'Neill," *Boston Globe* (September 17, 2015), Accessed February 14, 2018. https://www.bostonglobe.com/arts/books/2014/09/17/book-review-the-dog-joseph-neill/19Q8hQPlTRWNM8NgNz8kXJ/story.html.

27. Mark Fisher, *Capitalist Realism: Is There No Alternative?* (Winchester: O Books, 2009), 66.

28. White, "Joseph O'Neill."

29. Indeed, there are some clear references to Bartleby in the closing pages of *The Dog* as the narrator looks forward to going to prison, a site he associates with "surface[ing] from illusion" of being "in the clear" and marking "a limit of culpability" (241). In Melville's story, the imprisoned Bartleby tells a lawyer "I know where I am." Herman Melville, "Bartleby, The Scrivener: A Story of Wall Street," *Billy Budd, Sailor: And Other Stories* (New York: Penguin Books, 1986), 44.

30. Michel Foucault, *The Birth of Biopolitics*, translated by Graham Burchell (Basingstoke: Palgrave, 2008): 116.

31. Fisher, *Capitalist Realism*: 65.

32. Zadie Smith, "Two Paths for the Novel," *New York Review of Books* (November 20, 2008), Accessed January 3, 2018. http://www.nybooks.com/articles/2008/11/20/two-paths-for-the-novel.

33. Smith, "Two Paths."

34. Lee, "Nothing Happened."

[9]

CAREN IRR

BEYOND PRECARITY: IDEOLOGIES OF LABOR IN
ANTI-TRAFFICKING CRIME FICTION

WRITING IN 1960, THE patron saint of neoliberal economics, Friedrich Hayek warned that "the whole basis of our free society is gravely threatened by the powers arrogated by the unions."[1] Describing unions as coercive because they "make the market system ineffective" and exert a "constant upward pressure on the level of money wages," Hayek argues that projects purporting to advance the interests of the working classes actually divide, control, and damage them (237). This assertion reinforces Hayek's earlier and broader claim that "the Road to Freedom was in fact the High Road to Servitude."[2] Condemning collective economic action as servitude or serfdom, Hayek identified genuine freedom with individuals who align their projects with market concerns with minimal mediation by the state or other bodies. This idealized portrait of free labor as radical economic individualism lies at the heart of neoliberal ideology.

Inspired by Hayek, programmatic neoliberals have assaulted social security—from unemployment insurance and food and housing supplements to on-the-job protections, union rights, and even full-time employment. "Deregulation, privatization, and withdrawal of the state from many areas of social provision" become policy priorities.[3] Critics of neoliberal projects often describe these efforts as the acceleration of precarity. They point out that neoliberal precarity concentrates capital's control over labor power while simultaneously allowing capitalists to disavow responsibility for the laborer. To clarify this effect, Guy Standing names the collective subject of neoliberal labor practices the precariat.[4]

Accounts of precarious labor have often pointed to the rise of short-term contracts as well as the loss of benefits, job security, pension, and the stability of a career. Temporary office workers, Uber drivers, and Airbnb hosts emblematize this increasingly prevalent form of precarity. Once these concerns became well established, though, some labor analysts began to point out the geographical and industrial limitations to "gig work" as a figure for precarity. In his introduction to *Industrial Labor on the Margins of Capitalism*, for instance, Jonathan Parry asserts that the shift from contractual to casual labor is less significant than it might seem, because "the 'standard employment contract' was only ever of major significance in the most affluent Western countries and possibly Japan."[5] From a global perspective, Parry and his contributors argue, labor precarity has been a much more long-standing and varied form than US-centered discussions have suggested.

Parry's broader perspective suggests a need to tell the story of precarity in a more rigorous manner. We can begin by noting that precarity does not only characterize the excessive and scandalous freedom of gig work, but also forms of labor that appear to be gig work's opposite, such as forced labor. We can then learn to see slavery in the form of human trafficking as being at least as characteristic of neoliberal regimes as the provisional forms of employment more commonly associated with precarity. In Hayek's terms, we can recognize the literal servitude of trafficked persons as a by-product of neoliberal freedom.

Several forces have converged to intensify modern slavery. Geopolitical changes, such as the implosion of the Soviet bloc and the rise of China, are "push" factors, while deregulated labor markets and digital communications in advanced capitalist economies have increased the "pull" and eased the transmission of trafficked bodies, as well as images of those bodies. A grey-market remittance economy also heightens the appeal of trafficking by simplifying the international transfer of payment.

State shrinkage is, in short, only part of the trafficking puzzle. Bureaucratic surveillance, data collection, and policing also arguably call into being the neoliberal object they observe. Anti-trafficking organizations range from official state bodies to non-governmental organizations (NGOs) such Human Rights Watch, the International Labor Organization, and the Polaris Project. These groups collect data to the extent this is possible for an illicit activity and publish documents such as the US State Department's annual Trafficking in Persons report, a document evaluating every nation on its adoption of anti-trafficking legislation and efforts on behalf of victims. Similar bureaucratic measures enable surveillance by border agents and immigration officials, and all these efforts share a common master narrative.[6] Anti-trafficking documents articulate an ideological program that advances a broader neoliberal agenda.

The social criticism offered by anti-trafficking narratives assumes the virtue of market freedom and US hegemony. Some might describe anti-trafficking discourse as "left neoliberalism"—that is, as a project that mistakes itself for opposition to an economic system whose logic it shares.[7] The left neoliberal position arguably traces its origins to the free labor program of the mid-nineteenth century. Opposing chattel slavery to the autonomy of workers selling their labor, antebellum free labor ideology embraced markets while criticizing the commodification of labor.[8] Some of the same contradictions inform criticism of twenty-first-century slavery, as the immanent critique of anti-trafficking narratives that follows will demonstrate. In these narratives, we find a left neoliberal affirmation of the labor market, an account largely unable to explain or contest the persistence of slavery in a capitalist economy.

The Master Narrative of Anti-Trafficking Discourse

In 2000, the United Nations' so-called Palermo protocol defined trafficking as

> the recruitment, transportation, transfer, harbouring or receipt of persons, by means of the threat or use of force or other forms of coercion, of abduction, of fraud, of deception, of the abuse of power or of a position of vulnerability or of the giving or receiving of payments or benefits to achieve the consent of a person having control over another person, for the purpose of exploitation. Exploitation shall include, at a minimum, the exploitation of the prostitution of others or other forms of sexual exploitation, forced labour or services, slavery or practices similar to slavery, servitude or the removal of organs.[9]

This laundry list links sexual exploitation with nonsexual forced labor. It defines exploitation independent of consent, and it makes a distinction between human smuggling and coercive enslavement difficult to sustain, while also linking practices involving partial and indirect payment of wages to outright slavery.

Despite the breadth of the protocol's definition, activist depictions of human trafficking consistently narrow the scope of activities representative of trafficking and restrict the range of possible responses. The anthropologist Edward Snajdr isolates three features of activist rhetoric: 1) asserting that "trafficking-in-persons exists on a massive and ever-increasing scale"; 2) blaming trafficking on "a set of legal shortcomings on the part of other states"; 3) endeavoring to "to strengthen laws and law enforcement . . . and to encourage the non-profit sector to assist with helping victims" (231). Snajdr points out the use of questionable statistics, simplified maps, and emotionally manipulative images; he also notes the preoccupation with women and children coerced into prostitution. These innocent victims make antitrafficking narratives feel "oddly similar to urban legends or modern-day myths," Snajdr argues (239). He concludes that these myths exist to justify interventionist rescues and transformations of the legal regions of developing nations.

Other observers also note the prevalence of salvation plots that begin and end with the victims' legibility to state authority.[10] The sociologist Wendy Hesford explains how trafficking narratives depend on spectacle, infantilization, and ethnocentric representations of supposedly backwards cultures.[11] Anti-trafficking discourse reminds some observers of Victorian-era moral panics and others of the evangelical activism of the first Bush presidency.[12] This discourse also relies on well-established American oppositions between supposedly shameful enslavement and self-respecting waged labor.[13] Commentators agree that by framing the story of trafficking as a rescue plot orchestrated by police, these activist narratives implicitly endorse both the state's monopoly over violence and the rectitude of a supposedly free labor market in which the formerly trafficked person will presumably thrive. Anti-trafficking narratives envision the freed slave as necessarily benefiting from entry into a laissez-faire market in labor, a market defined by precarious autonomy.

The function of this master narrative of labor, as Paul Willis reminds us, is to "confirm those aspects and resolutions of cultural processes which are most partial to the current organization of interests and production and dislocate . . . those which retain a degree of critical penetration of that system."[14] In other words, whether by design or not, anti-trafficking activist narratives in effect endorse reigning neoliberal ideologies about the ideal form and relations of labor.

Narrative confirmation of dominant ideologies, however, tends to be incomplete. For instance, rescued victims may not consider the conditions they have experienced to be trafficking; they may have given consent to their servitude, or they may view rehabilitation facilities as inadequate care or even as form of imprisonment.[15] Apparent victims may also exercise agency by framing their stories (sometimes for profit) for willing auditors with well-known narrative expectations.[16] Some organizations representing sex workers object to the one-dimensional portraits of trafficked persons and suggest depicting them instead as "capable individuals navigating extreme, unjust, and complicated circumstances."[17] In short, various actors disrupt the artificial clarity imagined by anti-trafficking activists.

Efforts to contain potential ideological irritants can stimulate the literary imagination. This is evident in contemporary crime fiction published by reputable commercial presses since the Palermo protocol entered into force in 2003. Corban Addison's *A Walk Across the Sun*, James Lee Burke's *Feast Day of Fools*, Linda Fairstein's *Hell Gate*, M. C. Grant's *Beauty with a Bomb*, Brandon W. Jones' *All Woman and Springtime*, Ed Lin's *Snakes Can't Run*, Ridley Pearson's *Choke Point*, and Joseph Wambaugh's *Harbor Nocturne* all employ the dominant anti-trafficking ideology of labor.[18] While affirming nineteenth-century oppositions between freedom and slavery, these novels also introduce disruptive elements in their depictions of contemporary conditions. Analyzing the resulting tensions in this fiction thus fosters recognition not only of the narratological expression of neoliberal ideologies of labor, but also of their fault lines.

Depicting the Victim

All of the anti-trafficking fictions examined here envision the same passive victim described by activists; often the victim is an orphan.[19] Addison's *A Walk Across the Sun*, for instance, begins with two Hindu sisters whose parents die suddenly in a tsunami. A middle-class upbringing and multilingual convent education do not protect the heroines from being sold into a Mumbai brothel. Jones's *All Woman and Springtime* starts with two teens in North Korea. Their dreary routine in an orphanage and factory makes the girls susceptible to a slick smuggler who transports them to South Korea, where they are sold into sexual slavery. Orphaning the victims allows these narratives to sidestep any more complex explanation for the supply of trafficking victims. Sentimental conventions make the extreme vulnerability of poor orphans so ideologically redundant that no other motive or reason feels necessary.

Even when the trafficking victim is not technically an orphan, her isolation from a family of origin is crucial. Of the novels considered, only one provides a scene depicting the hero's encounter with a trafficked child's family. Pearson's *Choke Point* is set in Amsterdam, and it follows the fortunes of child laborers in a "knot shop" producing hand-tied carpets. Investigators interview the mother of one of these laborers, a "plain-looking Slavic woman" named Yasmina (175). When they ask how and why the family deals with the traffickers, she responds "I do not expect you to understand . . . I do not want your sympathy. Maja is an important part of this household. She helps us all" (178). As the questioning escalates, the mother mutters "without her . . . we starve" (181). This self-consciously stereotypical scene is framed by hostile judgement; wondering how much the grandmother's cigarettes cost, a photographer shoots a silhouetted image of the matriarch. Similarly stripped of detail, the truncated and unsympathetic back story flattens the account of the family's motives.

Simplification is not clarity, though. In *Hell Gate*, Manhattan District Attorney and sex crime expert Linda Fairstein injects some perplexing context into an interview with a Ukrainian survivor who washed up on a New York City beach: "Olena described life in her small town and her dreams of escaping it. The fall of the Soviet Union caused many of the small satellites

Beyond Precarity: Ideologies of Labor in Anti-Trafficking Crime Fiction [173]

formerly in its grasp to suffer economic collapse. I knew that its borders had become porous, and that human rights activists estimated that as many as 10 percent of the female population of countries like Ukraine had been sold into prostitution" (173). As in *Choke Point*, Olena's story is immediately rendered generic and supposedly representative of the "10 percent of the female population of countries like Ukraine." This confusing pseudo-statistic (which countries are "like Ukraine"? What is 10% of an unknown quantity?) behaves as if it were knowledge, and the victim's subsequent story of being smuggled, married off, sold, abused, and trapped is thus positioned not as a personal confession, but rather as an allegorical one. Olena is a type, and she disappears from the novel as soon as the witnessing investigator transports her to a safe house. In such narratives, trafficking victims are statistics, legible to others but not to themselves. They are feminized, passive, and largely inarticulate; they exist to be rescued and deposited in the arms of the state.

Only two of the novels considered take men as their trafficking victims, and both concern nonsexual labor. Ed Lin's *Snakes Can't Run* explores restaurant labor in Manhattan's Chinatown, and James Lee Burke's complex borderlands novel, *Feast Day of Fools*, introduces trafficking into an espionage plot when Russian gangsters capture and try to sell an MIT weapons expert to al-Qaeda. Even these exceptions incorporate prostitution in subplots, however, feeding the genre's preoccupation with debasement. Pearson's *Choke Point* also quickly migrates from the knot shop to prostitution; the novel's title refers to a key transition when pubescent girls age out of manual labor and are sold into the sex trade. This motif reproduces a dominant ideological association between forced labor, moral humiliation, and sexual shame.

Prostitution stories dominate the trafficking genre even though researchers agree that forced sexual exploitation may account for as little as 22 percent of human trafficking.[20] While unrepresentative, the prostitution motif is ideologically useful because it makes exploitation involuntary, stressing menacing violence, physical deprivation, and melodramatically dependent victims. Often these scenes are mediated through a described image—usually an internet site or a photo. Unlike literary fiction (such as Joseph O'Neill's *Netherland*), these crime novels do not directly invite sadistic titillation or an erotic response to the voluntary renunciation of consent. They attempt to distance readers from the spectacle of the slave's debasement. In *All Woman and Springtime*, for instance, the North Korean heroines are tutored by a more experienced prostitute: "everything in this business is about pleasing men," their tutor asserts. "Once you understand men, then you can be in control of the situation. Mr. Choy will still be the boss, of course. There isn't anything you can do about that. But what I mean is, men are not really all that complicated. They like tits, they like ass, they like pussy, and they like a pretty face" (195). The world-weary speaker creates moral horror by naturalizing and neutralizing the dynamics of sexual exploitation. In the same mood, she describes an experiment with male turkeys: "They discovered that male turkeys will try to mate with a stuffed, dead female turkey just as readily as they would a live one ... Men are just like turkeys—it doesn't matter how artificial we are, they will still behave the same way" (195–196).[21] Similarly, in Addison's *A Walk Across the Sun*, an experienced federal agent explains that "trafficking will stop when men stop buying women. Until that happens, the best we can do is win one battle at a time" (312–313). Both speakers locate male sexual demand outside the marketplace and ground trafficking in a laissez-faire attitude, one that naturalizes the connection between sexual desire and commodification and makes self-marketing in an irrational environment the only plausible form of female agency. Acceptance of normative misogyny is thus not an inadvertent side-effect of these narratives, requiring a demystifying exposé; it is an explicitly acknowledged ideological ground.

The account of labor presented as a hard-hitting truth in these novels relies, in short, on a confirmation of the conditions of alienation, not its refusal. Accepting one's status as "a stuffed, dead female turkey" and learning to exploit this position is the distasteful path to personal dignity outlined in these novels. Other routes are depicted as implausible. In particular, plans for escape consistently fail, because forced labor is assumed to damage the capacity for autonomy. Even the climax of Grant's girl-power-inflected *Beauty with a Bomb* repeats the required clichés about pathetic, cowering, undignified slaves. "The woman's eyes grow wide in panic as the other women clutch at each other and start weeping again," their would-be rescuer observes (185). Together with chained ankles, saucer-eyed passivity provides an iconographic shorthand for the trafficking victim. This image reinforces the idea that spectacular and alienating male desire drives trafficking by making the least powerful women into paralyzed observers of their own humiliation. To watch is to participate, and the trafficked women witness their own debasement, thus confirming the power of a system that defines them as its prey. The victims' passivity, in other words, is the moral inverse and necessary complement to the active, rebellious but always failed escape narrative. The rare individual who attempts escape necessarily abandons a more numerous group of trafficked women, because they create the negative ground of passivity against which she defines herself. The autonomous free laborer is the exceptional fantasy that sustains conditions governed by neoliberal enslavement.

Beyond Precarity: Ideologies of Labor in Anti-Trafficking Crime Fiction

These two facets of the ideology of trafficked labor—the naturalization of predatory alienation and a moralistic but impossible standard of personal agency—cohere in a cynical worldview that confirms existing relations of production. In this worldview, dignity reduces to the necessary effort to escape as an individual from collective conditions created by nature. Even though this task appears to be impossible, the enslaved are indelibly tainted. Their lost virginity is thus simultaneously sexual and ideological, and they must undergo ritualized cleansing and rehabilitation before re-entry into social life is permitted. These processes are not depicted directly in anti-trafficking fiction, but they appear in supplementary fantasy spaces such as the aristocratic manors converted into safe houses in Addison, Fairstein, and Jones's novels. These frankly utopian refuges are required to convert the morally contaminated former slave into run-of-the-mill embodiments of free labor eligible for full citizenship. As part of this magical transformation, former victims either die or are tearfully reunited with their siblings—or, as in *All Woman and Springtime*, they magically discover a hidden talent (e.g., mathematical genius) that ensures their instantaneous success in a post-trafficking economy. They are reborn as self-sufficient individuals, the mythic heroines of neoliberalism.

Of the novels considered here, Ed Lin's *Snakes Can't Run* does the most to interfere with this fairy tale of labor—mainly by eroding the barriers between the victims, investigators, and operators of trafficking networks. Lin's title refers to snakeheads, Chinatown slang for human smugglers who lead strings of illegal migrants (or snakes) across borders. The immobile snake in question in this novel is both the trafficker under investigation and the investigator's father. Although family lore attributed the crankiness of Robert Chow's deceased parent to his efforts to pay off debts to traffickers, an old ledger reveals that Robert's father was actually part of the trafficking organization and scarred by his deception: "the sour man who was left was beyond redemption. He was already pickled by the poisonous choices he'd made in life. My father was a snakehead who couldn't handle his own bite," Robert concludes (284).

Paternal sourness here replaces sexual shame as the affective hangover from enslavement, but the trafficked subject is still defined by the failure to rebel individually—that is, freely. The trafficked person is still disparaged for his presumed passivity in Lin's narrative. However, the novel also directs attention to the cycle of entrapment and attempts to modulate an absolute distinction between victims and criminals. The snakehead himself is also trapped, bitten, and pickled in this novel, and he is already dead. Lin also historicizes trafficking through the metaphor of the parent-child bond. This generational figure allows a fleeting recognition of the fact that labor relations entangle all parties and (in the old Hegelian motif) damage the master as well as the slave, although certainly not to equal degrees.

In Lin's novel, the opposition between free and slave labor shifts to the question of debt. To envision the conditions of labor as continuous indebtedness alters the neoliberal matrix of anti-trafficking discourse somewhat. The debt motif removes the moral imperative for liberation from the isolated subject and focuses attention on more clearly calculated, social, and negotiable forms of social exchange.[22] Debt also shifts the definition of free labor from an exertion of individual agency over desire to a skillful and shared manipulation of symbols in an information economy. Cracking open the trafficking narrative, in other words, allows moralistic scenes of victimization to give way to investigative interpretation.

The Investigator's Eye: Police Labor

If the victims in contemporary anti-trafficking crime fiction recall the pliant heroines of sentimental romance, the investigators typically derive from mid-twentieth-century hard-boiled fiction. They work in or around law enforcement—as journalists on the crime beat, employees of private security firms, sheriffs, lawyers, or beat cops—and despite the novels' rescue plots, they are more likely to be cynical critics of the powers that be than heroic defenders of justice. Regardless of the investigators' professional affiliation, in other words, they express the occupational ideology of the police.

Positioned between the working class and local elites, urban police officers in English-speaking nations have well documented workplace ideologies that encode their unusual situation. In her study of gender in the Canadian police force, Marilyn Corsianos describes the "occupational themes that dominate police culture" as including "conformity and/or solidarity, loyalty, secrecy, autonomy, authority, uncertainty, danger, suspicion, 'us versus them' mentality (i.e., the police versus the public), administration and being distinct from other occupational cultures."[23] Similarly, historian Sam Mitrani identifies a "deeply pessimistic view of human nature" with the core ideology of the Chicago police.[24] Charged with executing the laws that protect an economic elite of which they are generally not members, police serve as indirect regulators of working-class life as well as providers of informal social services such as youth counseling. Officers are thus split off from the working-class milieu to which they often belong by virtue of origin and/or racial or ethnic affiliation, and their repeated exposure to criminal behaviors in those milieu tends to calcify into an "us versus them" mentality. This sense of distinctness is bolstered by the police force's paramilitary structure and monopoly over legitimate forms of violence directed at the urban proletariat. British scholar

Michael Brogden concludes that through policing "the working-class problematic becomes incorporated, through the mediation of state functionaries, within the problematic of the dominant class, rendered harmless and a unity knot tied between the classes."[25] On this analysis, the police articulate an occupationally specific ideology that justifies their own social function as mediators and symbolic resolvers of social contradictions.

The occupational ideology required for this "unity knot" loosens somewhat, though, where it connects to free-labor thinking. From the perspective of free labor, the worker's fullest autonomy is realized in the acquisition of his own land or shop and thus his independence from employers and official networks of social support; this is obviously not a route open to public employees, such as the police.[26] Perhaps for this reason, vigilantism or "going rogue" is heroized. The idealized maverick or on-the-job vigilante ideologically compensates for the officer's incorporation into the bureaucratic police force. As public employees protected by powerful unions but valorizing Wild West individualism, American police developed a particular hard-boiled sensibility that encodes their unique and contradictory position within free-labor (or perhaps more properly laissez-faire) ideologies. Operating at the periphery of the free market in labor but serving as regulators of that market in the interests of local elites and in transparent contradiction to their ideologically valorized roles, police have developed a distinctive cynicism about state, freedom and "human nature."

This multilayered occupational ideology receives regular scrutiny in noir-influenced police procedural fiction. The genre is commonly understood as confirming the existing social order by introducing criminal disruptions that investigators rationally explain and defeat. Sharply delineated social differences are thus crucial to the genre: "a legitimate 'us' is defined in relation to a deviant 'them,'" one genre analyst observes.[27] Transferring an occupational sense of uniqueness into a generic distinction, procedurals use a clear narrative formula or "frame" that Fredric Jameson and Slavoj Zizek argue in essays on Raymond Chandler and Henning Mankell, respectively, stimulates close observation of the criminal (i.e., social) scene.[28] Zizek in particular is interested in the way that Mankell's commitment to generic formulas creates a parallax view of geopolitical contradictions arising in the zone between a Swedish social democracy in crisis and Mozambiquan condition of deprivation. Understood in this spirit, the investigator's conventional eye in anti-trafficking crime fiction offers both a transfer into narrative form of the occupational ideology of police and a moment of reflection on the conflicted global economy that it observes.

These moments of insight into the global economy do not necessarily occur in the places in anti-trafficking fiction where the investigator presents his (or, less often her) hackneyed account of criminality. As already noted, anti-trafficking fiction generally focuses on sex crimes and attributes these crimes to a naturalized male desire for female debasement—i.e., the "dead turkey" theory of trafficking. Transparently ideological, these explanations tend to confirm rather than disrupt dominant ideologies of prostitution and involuntary labor; they easily coexist with misogynistic accounts of masculine courage and autonomy presumed to be requisite for policing itself.[29]

Turning from scenes of explanation to novelistic action—especially scenes of police labor—introduces a different issue: the shift from face-to-face street-level policing to technologically mediated information management. Comic treatment of this theme appears in *Beauty with a Bomb* when the police-affiliated investigator grudgingly accepts an iPhone from her employer—eventually finding it useful during the final rescue operation. In *Choke Point*, the shift is even more literal; it features two investigators: an old-school ex-military WASP and a younger, ethnically Chinese forensic accountant. At one point, the latter literally leaps up into the information hardware stowed in a false ceiling, evading capture and facilitating victory over traffickers because of her familiarity with computer systems. Ideological closure insists that street-level and informational styles of policing complement one another this way, but the tensions created by transitioning between forms of police labor are not always easily contained.

After all, expertise in digital networking belongs mainly to the traffickers in these narratives. Forcing girls to participate in internet porn ventures features prominently in *A Walk Across the Sun, All Woman and Sunshine*, and *Choke Point*. Consequently, not only the digital tools, but also the decentralized labor involved in nerdier forms of police work are often depicted as ethically compromised or insufficiently macho in this fiction. Increasing entanglement with digital information flows also threatens the historical arrangement of the police force into hierarchical paramilitary structures. When police work starts to resemble the activities of white-collar workers and criminals, the process of social mediation falters a bit—potentially dislodging the us/them opposition that supposedly justifies the sacrificial labor performed by the police on behalf of an oligarchic social order. Perhaps for this reason, we discover an excessive exertion of physicality and moral rectitude in the more digitally mediated trafficking narratives. The cult of the hyper-physical maverick officer intensifies in anti-trafficking fiction in direct proportion to the digitization of police labor.

This ideological disturbance also pulls anti-trafficking narratives into climactic chase scenes. During these set pieces, the distinctive humor of Raymond Chandler's hard-boiled repartee gives way to an ideologically necessary shoot-out. After escalating tension in scenes of techno-surveillance, these novels redirect tool use into a fantasy of hyper-aggressive hand-to-hand combat. A heavily armed multinational team assembles, for instance, at the climax of *A Walk Across the Sun*, in order to rescue a handful of traumatized girls from a suburban Atlanta brothel. Information management gives way to militaristic invasion.

Perhaps paradoxically, these scenes of weaponized physicality seem to disrupt the reigning neoliberal orthodoxy most fully when the would-be maverick officer colludes with official state military functions, as in James Lee Burke's *Feast Day of Fools*. This novel layers its treatment of policing in the US/Mexico borderlands with religious reflection and parallels to wartime conflict. The investigating sheriff in Burke's novel teams up with a female war refugee, and the pair atone for their misdeeds in Korea by pursuing traffickers. Sacrificial physical encounters allow former combatants to expiate some of the sins of their wartime pasts.

Where Burke's novel puts historical and geopolitical wrongs at the center, others make more indirect reference to their position in a post-Cold War global economy. They use the investigators' labor to represent the informatization of American violence in a decentralizing world system. While still displacing and disavowing elite control over working populations, this post-hegemonic police labor spawns new investigative heroes—private security agents, border-crossing vigilantes, renegade journalists, love-struck lawyers, and the like. The bureaucratic entanglements of the neoliberal police affiliates them slightly with the trafficking victims' enslavement; both are objects of empathy in these novels. The police themselves are usually exemplary figures of tolerance—often involved in partnerships that cross racial, ethnic, or age barriers. But, these mournful statist liberals[30] are also snared in a digital web that threatens them with obsolescence and restricts their physical movements. Melancholic, ineffective freedom within the labor market characterizes the investigator's condition, and these figures often acquire a tragic moral authority by observing the abusive power exercised by a ruling class that they serve but do not respect. The police retain their ties to an old order displaced by neoliberalism, because they rely on, without advocating for, a public sphere. The investigators serve, in short, as the vanishing mediators of a neoliberal social logic.

The ideological error of these novels, then, is not that they involve rescue plots that overstate the power and authority of these tragic police liberals vis-a-vis their presumed objects. That too-common empowerment story hopes to shatter an imagined monopoly of agency, believing that the investigator pulls all potential for action into his own orbit, and less socially privileged (and female) actors' access to action is presumed to be uplifting and ideologically disruptive. By contrast, this analysis argues that labor and action—not characterization—confirm the neoliberal status quo in trafficking narratives. In the context of neoliberal deregulation of the labor market, the failures of a cynical state operative when faced with market-based enslavement spiral back to figure the irrelevance of state actors themselves—even when these narratives heroize the investigator's sacrifices and see the world through his eye. Like the trafficking victim, the investigator also experiences limited agency as a laborer, and this is one of the ways in which the investigative narration reproduces (although with some small degrees of friction) neoliberal ideologies about the confusion of freedom with servitude.

What Kind of Labor Is Trafficking?

Shifting attention from the victim/rescue motif to the ideology of labor in anti-trafficking narratives brings the figure of the trafficker and his (almost always his) relation to the investigators to the foreground. As the previous section argued, in this fiction investigators commonly signal a weakening of state authority and mourn the displacement of their function as moral regulators by the responsibility to operate systems of techno-surveillance. From this vantage point, the trafficker makes a difficult villain, since he simultaneously triggers a moral scandal, an administrative and technological threat, and an aspirational ideal in his capacity for confidently wielding violence and exerting authority on the global stage. The task of anti-trafficking crime fiction is to contain this disruptive figure and redirect its appeal toward goals endorsed by the neoliberal status quo. This necessarily incomplete task requires multiple variations on the genre formula. Anti-trafficking narratives innovate in order to find newly effective ways to neutralize the ideological incoherence triggered by the trafficker.

This fiction usually begins by depicting the trafficker as a tediously perfect neoliberal subject. He rigorously applies free market logic to capitalize on local resources, extract profit, and concentrate resources within the organization, regardless of state regulations and obsolete moral or cultural limitations. The trafficker's mentality and practices are quite nakedly those of neoliberal entrepreneurship. In *All Woman and Springtime*, for instance, the narrator reports that the Korean trafficker "Mr. Choy finished his degree [in Seattle], a business major with a minor in computer science—not with honors, as he had hoped, but well enough ... He had a million bright ideas and boundless energy"; on graduation, he expected that "one of the large corporations was bound to snap him up and make him a star" (177). His ideals and self-image are continuous with those of American business, as are those of smaller-scale traffickers such as Hector in *Harbor Nocturne*.

Hector reflects that there are many "options for a smart white man around the harbor if he took the time to check things out. The Armenians from Hollywood had made a bundle when they'd shipped in imported vodka in fifty-five-gallon drums labeled 'window-washing fluid.' They knew that the LAPD didn't investigate international smuggling, and that at worst it would be a tariff violation that nobody would really bother with" (245). The rhetoric of callous entrepreneurial self-interest is also crucial in the dialogue given to Mr. Ng, a trafficker in *Snakes Can't Run*. "'They make more money now than they ever would have in China.' He switched to Mandarin so some of the men could understand. 'Yes, these people have suffered, but in the long run they will be much better off than if they had stayed in China. They will remember me for helping them'" (271). These novels describe traffickers, their opportunities, and their relations to others in the language of legitimate free-market business. There is nothing especially eccentric or ideologically corrupt about the traffickers' labor. They simply mobilize the inexplicable and naturalized misogynistic desires of their target market. "'I abhor child pornography, the kiddie sex trade,'" a trafficker insists in *Choke Point*; his girls are sold to "Asian buyers" for purely pragmatic reasons—because "the hormones and the mess are bad for business" once they begin to menstruate (378). Traffickers simply capitalize on existing physical and social conditions in this fiction.

The trafficker's turn toward crime rather than legitimate business is regularly attributed to local or historical irregularities within the capitalist system. Racist exclusions meant that "for an unknown, unconnected Korean kid the gates to success seemed closed" to Mr. Choy in *All Woman and Springtime* (177). Class snobbery and secret social clubs underlie the Manhattan trafficking ring described in *Hell Gate*; "'Those rich boys didn't want me anywhere near their dinner parties,'" the ringleader sneers (360). These confessions insist that it is not moral failure but rather irrational social exclusions limit access to capitalist goods and thereby produce as perversely unanticipated effects the illegal activities of traffickers.

Once excluded, the traffickers rely on own historical and cultural solidarities to facilitate their criminality. Ed Lin's traffickers, for instance, insist they are patriotic in supporting their "fellow Chinese" (271), while in the ethnically divisive LA of *Harbor Nocturne*, a faux-Russian crime boss reveals his Serbian roots and irrational old-world habits: "'Croats,' Markov said, and his lip curled slightly" (272). Residual racism and ethnic hostility as well as patriotic pride are original sins in the neoliberal universe of these novels, and they mark those who articulate these sentiments as historical residues of a territorially differentiated globe fading into obscurity. Old-fashioned ethnic and racial solidarities create secret organizations from the *tontine* of elite Manhattanites in *Hell Gate* to the *tong* system in *Snakes Can't Run*.

In fact, any clan-like ethnic or familial network has the potential to convert itself into a criminal organization in anti-trafficking fiction. The contradictions of this racist anti-racism are efficiently presented in an explanatory speech in *Harbor Nocturne*: "'What you have to understand about these organized crime foreign nationals from former Eastern bloc countries,'" the jaded detective Bino Villasenor professes, "'and I'll lump the Koreans in there with them, is that they don't do business like our OC types. They're basically cold war hoodlums. No matter what kind of show they put on with big cars, and tailor-made suits, and houses on Mount Olympus, they're still thugs. Which makes them unpredictable'" (203–4). In the guise of distancing criminal thugs from legitimate capitalists, in other words, the detective invents the bizarre category of cold war hoodlums by lumping together the products of struggling post-Soviet and rising Asian economies—i.e., old and new threats to US hegemony. In the familiar logic of American political alterity, all those on the margins of the dominant merge into a generic other. All traffickers are arguably "cold war hoodlums" in this fiction because they fill the place of the monstrous totalitarian villain that was vacated with the fall of the USSR; they menace freedom and the market by too perfectly embodying their principles until or unless they face limits created by their embeddedness in a nondominant culture and history. In anti-trafficking crime fiction, the trafficker excludes himself from the legitimate neoliberal projects he himself ardently desires by allowing himself to remain marked by race, ethnicity, culture, and history. He becomes criminal by exposing the limits of a supposedly culture-free neoliberal market.

That said, a full erasure of difference is not the aim of anti-trafficking fiction. Quite the opposite. These novels are not written from the point of view of a right-wing neoliberalism that endorses a total capitalist evacuation of culture. Instead, the figure of the ethnically marked trafficker in these crime novels is simultaneously villainous and admirable; he becomes a utopian alter ego hovering on the perimeter of what is permissible to the investigator. In the recurring confrontation scenes that appear essential to this genre, the investigator's task with respect to the trafficker turns out to be, first, interpreting his motives back to him and, secondly, exacting extra-legal vigilante justice. The investigator recodes the trafficker's business logic into explicitly moral terms relative to his identity group and then eliminates him. "'It's very patriotic to exploit your fellow Chinese, isn't it, Ng?,'" Robert Chow sarcastically inquires a moment before firing at the man who insulted his father (271). Similarly, "'that's horseshit,'" the security agent Knox asserts at the climax of the trafficker's police station confession in *Choke Point*, and "'The

Beyond Precarity: Ideologies of Labor in Anti-Trafficking Crime Fiction [183]

saddest part . . . is if you actually believe that'" (378). This combination of judgement and execution closes down the investigator's pursuit of the trafficker. The investigator must expose the trafficker's motives in order to claim his initiative (but not his identity) for himself. "'Young girls, high prices, fancy settings,'" the DA summarizes in *Hell Gate* just before she pushes the bad guy down a stairwell (360).

Because identification with the criminal is scandalous to the somewhat nostalgic investigator, this moment of judgment must culminate in the investigator's extra-legal brutality. The DA is shocked but successful in her shove; Robert Chow shoots his interlocutor, and many other traffickers die in similar turning point battles. The exemplar of a weak and compromised state thus activates the police function not by turning over the ultimate neoliberal subjects to legal prosecution (and thus reinforcing the juridical authority of the state), but rather by seizing the traffickers' own propensity for coercion and turning it back on the perpetrator. The investigator's violence supplements the weak state with righteous violence on behalf of a version of left neoliberalism that is visibly American in its articulation and practice.

The dead traffickers in anti-trafficking fiction serve, in other words, a perversely utopian function for American readers. They legitimate an apparently on-going need for direct expressions of US state power in a global economy that actively erodes the basis for ethnic, cultural, and, by extension, national solidarity. In *The New Imperialism*, David Harvey describes this arrangement as a neoliberal force countered by neoconservative territorial power. "The fundamental point is to see the territorial and the capitalist logics of power as distinct from each other," he asserts (29). Strongly associated with neoliberal business practice, the traffickers represent that ideology's distinctive fusion of brutally embodied and digitally immaterial labor; their deaths then fulfill a presumed desire (on the part of the nostalgic reader) for a state capable of dominating and stabilizing global relations. As unpredictable thugs and "cold war hoodlums" living on, zombie-like, in the present and exploiting inexplicably persistent desires for sexual predation in particular, the traffickers trigger a hypothetical and nostalgic public longing for an American-dominated global order.

Given the open acknowledgement of historical traumas (war, exploitation, inequality) in this fiction, this desire appears contradictory, and this in turn suggests refinements to Harvey's clean distinction between neoconservative territorialism and neoliberal globalism may be necessary. Here we can turn to Giovanni Arrighi, who contests Harvey's conclusion that neoliberal globalization amounts to a new imperialism organized on behalf of an overextended American hegemony. Arrighi asserts that the United States' cultural and moral authority as a hegemon moved into a visible crisis phase during the post-9/11 invasion and destruction of Iraq.[31] He describes the subsequent situation as "domination without hegemony" and points to the transfer of ownership over US debt as a major sign of a shift in economic and cultural authority to East Asia (especially China).

Arrighi's scenario most closely approximates the geopolitical imaginary of anti-trafficking fiction. In these novels, human trafficking exemplifies a neoliberal practice associated with moral panic; it invokes a need for police functions enacted on a global scale—practices enacted by subjects aware of the futility of their efforts to constrain their ideologically authoritative opponents. Anti-trafficking narratives use the trafficker as a pretext for supergluing US domination into a central place in the global distribution of power, even though the ideology of free labor and laissez-faire autonomy that the United States supposedly upholds is clearly not well regulated if trafficking is a major global industry.

In other words, this fiction shores up the fantasy space of a waning hegemon, not through appeals to regressive territorialism, as Harvey would have it, but through the creation of zones of delirious moral free space—a neoliberal utopia—in which domination without hegemony works, and free labor is preserved by unfree, borderline obsolete, and paramilitary means. By vanishing into the mobile trafficker's universe, anti-trafficking police carve out a role for free-floating domination. The investigator rescues himself, on Arrighi's analysis, by absorbing some of the trafficker's functions and redirecting them toward the vacant position known as the victim. The trafficker serves as the utopian ideal not only for neoliberal business logic, then, but also, when severed from his residual prejudices, for the weakened state operative to the extent that he employs the tools of domination without the constraints of legitimation. The grimly compelling story of trafficking thus exposes a range of tensions, disruptions, and containments that illuminate neoliberal concerns about free labor. Furthermore, these assessments of contemporary slavery deepen our understanding of the horrific paradoxes of global precarity. They teach us not only to recognize trafficking as an exemplary form of precarity but also to grapple with the profound ideological difficulties surrounding its eradication.

Notes

1. Friedrich Hayek, *The Constitution of Liberty* (Chicago: University of Chicago Press, 1960), 234.
2. Friedrich Hayek, *The Road to Serfdom* (Chicago: University of Chicago Press, 1943), 27.
3. David Harvey, *A Brief History of Neoliberalism* (Oxford 2007), 3.
4. Guy Standing, *The Precariat*. (London: Bloomsbury, 2011).

5. Jonathan Parry, "Introduction," *Industrial Labor on the Margins of Capitalism* (London: Oxford University Press, 2018), 3.

6. Sharon Pickering and Julie Ham. "Hot Pants at the Border: Sorting Sex Work from Trafficking," *British Journal of Criminology* 54 (2014): 2–19; Edward Snajdr, "Beneath the Master Narrative: Human Trafficking, Myths of Sexual Slavery and Ethnographic Realities," *Dialectical Anthropology* 37:2 (2013): 229–256; further citations in text.

7. Walter Benn Michaels develops the concept of left neoliberalism in several places, including "Let Them Eat Diversity," an interview published in the first issue of *The Jacobin*. https://www.jacobinmag.com/2011/01/let-them-eat-diversity.

8. Eric Foner, *Free Soil, Free Labor, Free Men: The Ideology of the Republican Party Before the Civil War* (Oxford: Oxford University Press, 1970).

9. United Nations Convention Against Transnational Organized Crime and the Protocol to Prevent, Suppress, and Punish Trafficking in Persons, Especially Women and Children, Article 3, section (a). http://www.unodc.org/documents/treaties/UNTOC/Publications/TOC%20Convention/TOCebook-e.pdf.

10. Crystal DeBoise, "Human Trafficking and Sex Work: Foundational Social-Work Principles," *Meridians* 12:1 (2014): 227–233; Julietta Hua, "Telling Stories of Trafficking: The Politics of Legibility," *Meridians* 12:1 (2014): 201–227.

11. Wendy Hesford, *Spectacular Rhetorics: Human Rights Visions, Recognitions, Feminisms* (Durham, NC: Duke University Press, 2011).

12. See Viviene Cree, Gary Clapton, and Mark Smith. "The Presentation of Child Trafficking in the UK: An Old and New Moral Panic?" *British Journal of Social Work* 44:2 (March 2014): 418–433 and Denise Brennan, *Life Interrupted: Trafficking into Forced Labor in the United States* (Durham, NC: Duke University Press 2014).

13. The shame motif appears in Eric Foner, "Free Labor and Nineteenth-Century Political Ideology" in *The Market Revolution in America: Social, Political and Religious Expressions, 1800–1880*, eds. Melvyn Stokes and Stephen Conway. (Charlottesville: University of Virginia Press, 1996), 99–127.

14. Paul E. Willis, *Learning to Labor: How Working Class Kids Get Working Class Jobs* (New York: Columbia University Press, 1977), 161.

15. Brennan (op cit.) addresses victims' resistance to being characterized as such. On imprisonment, see Anelynda Mielke, "Challenging Humanitarian Images the Case of Anti-Trafficking." *International Journal of Social Science and Humanity* 5:12 (December 2015): 1056–1061.

16. Soraya Chemaly, "How Not to Report on Sex Trafficking," *Rewire News* (June 21, 2014), http://rhrealitycheck.org/article/2014/01/21/report-sex-trafficking/.

17. DeBoise, "Human Trafficking and Sex Work," 230.

18. Corban Addison, *A Walk Across the Sun* (London: Quercus Press, 2012); James Lee Burke, *Feast Day of Fools* (New York: Simon & Schuster 2011); Linda Fairstein, *Hell Gate* (New York: Dutton, 2010); M. C. Grant, *Beauty with a Bomb* (Woodbury, MN: Midnight Ink, 2014); Brandon W. Jones, *All Woman and Springtime* (Chapel Hill, NC: Algonquin, 2012); Ed Lin, *Snakes Can't Run* (New York: Minotaur, 2010); Ridley Pearson, *Choke Point* (New York: Putnam's, 2013); Joseph Wambaugh, *Harbor Nocturne* (New York: Grove/Atlantic, 2012).

19. Sister Judith Sheridan, Marist Missionary Sisters in San Diego, CA, asserts that orphans are uniquely vulnerable to trafficking for purposes of prostitution, http://www

.voanews.com/content/nun-human-trafficking-children-criminals-victims-internet-exploit-prostitution/2822272.html.

20. Stephanie Hepburn and Rita J. Simon, *Human Trafficking Around the World: Hidden in Plain Sight* (New York: Columbia University Press, 2013), 1. These statistics are derived from International Labor Organization data, a standard reference on the topic.

21. The turkey experiments conducted by Martin Schein and Edwin Hale actually demonstrated that male turkeys would engage in sexual display even when confronted with a bodiless female turkey head on a stick. "The Head as Stimulus for Orientation and Arousal of Sexual Behavior in Male Turkeys," *Anatomical Record* (1957): 617–618.

22. Richard Dienst makes a similar argument in *The Bonds of Debt: Borrowing Against the Common Good* (London: Verso, 2011).

23. Marilyn Corsianos, *Policing and Gendered Justice: Examining the Possibilities* (Toronto: University of Toronto Press, 2009), 95.

24. Sam Mitrani, *The Rise of the Chicago Police Department, Class and Conflict, 1850–1894* (Champaign-Urbana: University of Illinois Press, 2013), 11.

25. Michael Brogden, *The Police: Autonomy and Consent* (New York: Academic Press, 1982), 32.

26. For more on free labor, see Mitrani and Foner (1970), op cit.

27. Madeline K. MacMurraugh-Kavanagh, "What's All This Then?: The Ideology of Identity in *The Cops*," in *Frames and Fictions on Television*, eds. Bruson Carson and Margaret Llewelyn-Jones (Bristol, UK: Intellect Books, 2000), 40.

28. Zizek on Mankell appears here: http://www.lacan.com/zizekmankell.htm; see also Fredric Jameson, "The Synoptic Chandler," in *Shades of Noir: A Reader*, ed. Joan Copjec (Verso, 1993), 33–56. In *Crime and Fantasy in Scandinavia: Fiction, Film and Social Change*, Andrew K. Nestingen counters Zizek's argument, pointing out discontinuities in the neoliberal order.

29. See Marilyn Corsianos, *Policing and Gendered Justice: Examining the Possibilities* (Toronto: University of Toronto Press, 2009).

30. As Sean McCann explains, the hard-boiled is conventionally a liberal. See *Gumshoe America: Hard-Boiled Crime Fiction and the Rise and Fall of New Deal Liberalism* (Durham, NC: Duke University Press, 2000).

31. Giovanni Arrighi, "Hegemony Unravelling I," *New Left Review* (March/April 2005).

SHARAE DECKARD

"TERMINAL INSOMNIA": SLEEPLESSNESS, LABOR, AND
NEOLIBERAL ECOLOGY IN KAREN RUSSELL'S *SLEEP
DONATION* AND ALEX RIVERA'S *SLEEP DEALER*

JONATHAN CRARY'S INFLUENTIAL *24/7: Late Capitalism and the End of Sleep* argues that "in its profound uselessness and intrinsic passivity" sleep presents a stubborn biological barrier to capitalism's theft of time.[1] However, this barrier has been increasingly eroded in the era of neoliberal capitalism, as personal and social identities are reorganized to model "the uninterrupted operation of markets, information networks, and other systems" within the 24/7 environment.[2] The reinscription of human life as "duration without breaks, defined by a principle of continuous functioning" (8) flexibilizes sleep patterns in order to maximize labor, and spurs military and pharmaceutical research into the elimination of the necessity for sleep. According to Jason W. Moore, the "ecological regime" of neoliberalism has been insistent on the financialization of nature and the appropriation of new ecological and labor surpluses through accumulation by dispossession and technics of enclosure: "capitalism's arrogance is to assign value to life-activity within the commodity system (and an alienating value at that) while de-valuing, and simultaneously drawing its lifeblood from, uncommodified life-activity within reach of capitalist power."[3]

Like universal access to clean drinking water, which has been enclosed through pollution and privatization and monetized as a bottled commodity, the creation of insomniac conditions has enabled the creation of scarcity in relation to sleep. The despoliation of sleep has been inseparable from the neoliberal dismantling of social protections and enclosure of ecological commons, and can be understood as the appropriation of a new frontier of uncommodified life activity, through a biotechnical "fix"—the pharmaceutical sleep aid—which chemically induces unconsciousness, but does not resolve the underlying conditions (social violence, anxiety, physical exhaustion, overwork, precarious employment, austerity), which work in conjunction to create sleeplessness. Sleep, or at least a chemically modified state approximating it, can be purchased from the same pharmaceutical companies researching stimulants to end sleep. Use of non-benzodiazepine hypnotics has soared in proportion to ongoing forms of dispossession and social ruin; in 2010 alone, over 50 million Americans were prescribed zolpidem (Ambien) and eszopiclone (Lunesta).[4] However, this capitalization of sleep is characteristic of the temporal logic of neoliberalism, which privileges short-term profit over forms of investment that would enable long-term accumulation, and as such could be seen as signaling the exhaustion of the "four cheaps" of labor, energy, food, and raw materials that have sustained the neoliberal ecological regime.[5] The pharmaceutical "fix" does not resolve but only accelerates the ecological contradictions of "bioderegulation," Teresa Brennan's term for the "brutal discrepancies between the temporal operation of deregulated markets and the intrinsic physical limitations of the humans required to conform to these demands."[6]

Not only do long-term prescription users find that they have to take higher and higher dosages due to drug resistance, but a recent study in the *British Medical Journal* found that patients dependent on prescription sleep aids were nearly five times as likely as non-users to die in a period of two to three years, though the risk was increased even for those taking fewer than twenty pills a year; researchers also discovered a sharp increase of cancer rates amongst heavy users of prescription sleep aids. This phenomenon could be understood in tandem with what Moore calls the "superweed effect"—the tendency for particular ecological regimes to face "blowback" to their modes of appropriation, from the "revolt of extra-human nature" in forms of resistance such as herbicide-resistant pests and weeds in agro-industrial GMO cash-crops, climate change, or the increase in epidemiological vectors, autoimmune syndromes, and mental health disorders affecting humans, when capitalization exceeds the capacity of the web of life to provide ever-expanding ecological surpluses of unpaid work and energy for appropriation.[7]

For Crary, the twenty-first century epidemic of sleeplessness has a particular affective texture that captures a larger collective experience of the erosion of diurnal temporality and a generalized "condition of worldlessness."[8] However, while compelling in his analysis of post-Fordist society, Crary is less attentive to the unevenness of development between capitalist cores and peripheries and the ways in which differential conditions of labor, exploitation, and technological access might affect the time-space sensorium of sleep and temporality. In this essay, I will contrast representations of insomnia and labor in Karen Russell's novella *Sleep Donation* (2014), published only as an e-book in conjunction with an interactive website, and Alex Rivera's "cybracero" film, *Sleep Dealer* (2008). In both texts, I argue that sleeplessness functions not only as an indictment of the insomniac conditions perpetrated by neoliberalism that erode human subjectivity and the imaginative capacity to historicize time and conceive of futurity, but also allegorizes the crisis of the "ecological regime" of neoliberalism itself, shot through with the anxiety that "terminal insomnia" may correspond to a "terminal crisis" of "unravelling American hegemony," as predicted by Giovanni Arrighi.[9]

I

Karen Russell's *Sleep Donation* is set in an insomnia-plagued America in the near future, where a "Slumber Corps" patrols in Mobi-Vans and FEMA trailers, soliciting sleep donations as transfusions for "orexins," insomniacs with a neuropeptide dysfunction that traps them in a state of "untenable hyperarousal."[10] For these sleepless orexins, traditional hypnotics like zolpidem no longer work; they have become resistant to pharmaceutical remedies, and remain conscious for months or even years, imprisoned in an unrelenting vigilance. As such, they are grotesque parodies of capitalism's fantasy of a productivity fix in the form of unsleeping workers, but far from enabling perpetual productivity, their wakefulness causes progressive debilitation, both physical and mental/emotional. After they enter their "Last Day"—the period during which they never again sleep—they become increasingly less able to function psychically and physically, until finally their organs shut down and they die, unless they receive a transfusion that resets their circadian rhythms. The first person narrator, Trish Edgewater, is a campaigner with a legendary ability to solicit transfusions from reluctant donors by evoking the emotive death of her own sister, Dori, from terminal insomnia. Trish is wracked with guilt over her manipulation of donors, a mining of emotion equivalent to the mining of dreamers, and worries that a transactional logic has subsumed all her interpersonal relations. Her anxiety intensifies after she discovers an infant, Baby A, whose purity of sleep can cure any orexin. The Supreme Court passes new legislation allowing infant "donation" since babies are such "rich, deep wells" of dreams, and the Corps proceeds to draw ever-greater transfusions, until Trish discovers that the local heads of the Slumber Corps, the Storch brothers, a pair of toilet-seat designers turned philanthropists, have been selling units of Baby A's sleep for millions on the black market to a Japanese biotech corporation that promises to synthesize an injectable of "artificial sleep" (982).

The allegory of Russell's speculative scenario is complex and shifting, functioning on multiple levels. The LD (Last Day) of the orexins signifies the collapse of the day/night divide, the terminal crisis of debilitated diurnal time. The Slumber Corps, described on the *Sleep Donation* interactive website as "an independent entity that is organized and exists as a non-profit, tax-exempt, charitable institution." works in conjunction with the federal government, but does not receive federal funding.[11] As such, it functions as critique of what Arundhati Roy has called the "non-profit industrial complex" of non-governmental organizations (NGOs) that operate in the vacuum created by the evisceration of welfare states by neoliberal austerity. Working with funds which represent a "miniscule fraction" of the cuts in spending on health care and other "public goods," NGOs occupy the vacuum spawned by the shrinking welfare state. They contain political dissent and act as "a profitable graveyard for social movements" by distributing as charity what people ought to receive by right, altering subjectivities to recast people as victims rather than protestors:[12] "NGOs form a sort of buffer between the sarkar and public, between Empire and its subjects. They have become the arbitrators, the interpreters, the facilitators. [...] It's almost as though the greater the devastation caused by neoliberalism, the greater the outbreak of NGOs."[13]

The global boom in funded NGOs correlates to the application of structural adjustment policies throughout the Global South from the 1970s onwards; as peripheral states were eviscerated according to the demands of the IMF, World Bank and -led capital, NGOs funded by the same agencies moved into the very areas abdicated by the state. In *Sleep Donation*, NGO-ization and the boom of the non-profit industrial complex around sleep correlates to the outsourcing of US state functions, particularly those of health care, after the 2008 financial crisis and banking bailout.

As Trish describes, insomnia is only the latest stage of a "public performance of illness" in a nation characterized by rising homelessness and the steady erosion of healthcare: "Death's dress rehearsal is ongoing at any bus stop in America, where sick people beg us not for minutes of sleep but for metallic dollar-flakes [...] Long before the sleep crisis, our downtown was a maze of sidewalk asylums" (191). At the start of the narrative, Trish is resistant to the marketization of sleep, and believes that her NGO presents a moral response to the crisis: "Nobody in our Mobi-Van would suggest that the raw market would do a better or a fairer job of matching insomniacs and donors than the Slumber Corps. None of us can imagine the solution proposed by certain factions, 'the sale of sleep,' leading to an equitable system" (379). However, she increasingly becomes disillusioned with the sense that sleep donation is "all Ponzi" (711), an unsustainable trade based in extraction of "surplus unconsciousness" (loc. 1471) and permeated with a neoliberal transactional logic. She is disturbed by the way in which her constant performance of the "subjunctive calculus" (1471) of extorting donations restructures her subjectivity and comes to permeates the whole of her social relations: "I'm afraid that working for the Crops may be irreversibly perverting the way I evaluate human exchanges. *Now* who is the donor, the donee? I'll wonder, watching a high school couple kiss at the mall. Are they a match? Will their transfusion be a success? What songs are the corporations piping into her body?" (925). The Slumber Corps acts as a forerunner for privatization and financialization, introducing novel relations of banking and exchange that allow a new industry to emerge. On the e-book's interactive website, the parodic corporate commentary puffs, "'artificial sleep' has been a goal of medical researchers since the sleep banks first started operations," and exults that soon "Americans would have a potentially bottomless 'dream well' from which to make withdrawals."[14] Replacing human donor supply with artificial injectables is posed as a potential cure to the epidemic that only corporate biotechnology can supply, when what it actually represents is an intensive new form of enclosure in which synthesis supplants the more crude extractivism of the "sleep draw." Far from granting "a faucet of unconsciousness, an inexhaustible dream well, 'sleep for all'" (1471), or having a kind of trickle-down of insomnia-relief in which the benefits of privatization will "accrue to every living person" (982), it will make sleep a commodity available only to those who can afford it, while swelling the coffers of the disaster capitalists who profit from the crisis.

In the novella, the sleep crisis acts as affective corollary to the hollowing out of social structures under neoliberalism, both in its drive towards the production of sleepless consumers who buy without end, and through the privatization of new spheres of human subjectivity. The narrative's obsession with affect, mirrored in the form of Trish's solipsistic, circular musings, reflects "the individualization of lifestyles and the intensification of emotional life projects; and the economization of social relationships, the pervasiveness of economic models to shape the self and its very emotions."[15] Trish describes Dori as destroyed by wakefulness, trapped in a state of perpetual continuity which allows no release from individuation in which to disengage from constant sensation and metabolize the material of her days:

> I hated watching her go speechless under the conglomerate weight of so much unrelenting looking and thinking and listening and feeling, her mind worn thin by the sound of every cough and the plinking moisture of every raindrop, these noises exploding like grenades through her naked awareness—her mind crushed, in the end, by an avalanche of waking moments. Once sleep stopped melting time for Dori, she could not dig herself out. She was buried under snowflakes, minutes to hours to months. The official cause of death was organ failure. (138)

As Crary notes, the temporality of sleep functions as a kind of interruption that disrupts neoliberal presentism, providing a space for reverie that refuses "the unsparing weight of our global present."[16] As a form of "historical time," sleep "contains a bond to a future, to a possibility for renewal and hence of freedom. It is an interval into which glimpses of an unlived life, of postponed life, can edge faintly into awareness."[17] In a bravura passage, the novella heralds the extinction of sleep as the extinction of time itself (and secondarily, as the extinction of Walt Whitman's heroic imaginary of the United States):

> Sleep has been chased off the globe by our twenty-four-hour news cycle, our polluted skies and crops and waterways, the bald eyeballs of our glowing devices. We Americans are sitting in an electric chair that we engineered. What becomes of our circadian rhythms, the "old, glad harmonies" that leapt through us like the vascular thrust of water through leaves of grass? Bummer news, Walt: that song's done. And the endogenous clock, the suprachiasmatic nucleus, heredity prize of every human, that tiny star cluster of neurons in the hypothalamus which regulates our yawning appetites for hard winter light and spacey blackness, the master clock that syncs us to one another, and to the Earth's rotation, the sun and the moon? [. . .] Bummer news, everyone: the clock stops for humanity. Time itself will soon become an anachronism. Time, as our species has lived it on this planet, will cease to exist. No more dark/light binary. [. . .] No longer is sunshine the coagulant of consciousness, causing us to clot into personalities, to cohere once more on our pillows each morning. (163–4)

If sleep is an escape from the relentless neoliberal logic of individuation and emotional life-work in which the self itself becomes a site of endless work, orexins are denied this escape, and the "solution" to their nightmare of unending attention is deeper commoditization. The sleep transfusions harvest human energy, drilling down to a vertical frontier of appropriation by transforming the immaterial stuff of dreams into a material commodity.

In an aleatory passage, Trish describes the temporal weirdness of the "sleep draw," shot through with "a frightening, exhilarating charge [. . .] an overpowering sense of ambient destiny, fate crushing in on all sides" (431). This sensation is produced by "proximity to enveloping illusions," to "the unhosted ghosts of these dreams in transit . . . to facilities where they will be tested, processed, plated on ice, awaiting transfusion" (431). The dreams glitter with the fetish of their strange congealment into value, a process made especially eerie by the function of dreams as what Russell calls "world-blueprints:" condensations of sleepers' dreamwork, an unalienated labor engaged in the construction of alternative selves, worlds, possibilities, outside of the homogenous present of capitalism, unfettered by commodity relations. In extracting world-blueprints from sleepers—with all their sense of alternate destiny—the Slumber Corps is effectively mining futurity, acting out the legendary impatience of finance capital, with its avoidance of fixed-capital investment and its insistence on short-term appropriation. That it is babies who are the deepest "wells" of extraction suggests the degree to which the bad medicine of neoliberal austerity has relied on the demolition of the prospects of a future generation for its temporary "fix" to financial crisis. According to a "Fresh Air" interview, Russell originally brainstormed the novella's imaginary inventions for the *New Yorker*'s May 2013 "Innovations" issue.[18] Sleep transfusions were not included in the magazine's final catalogue of utopian innovations, perhaps because of the pessimism of their pointed critique of neoliberalism's tendency to invent new ways of commoditizing spheres outside exchange value rather than producing substantial revolutions in productivity.

The transfusion innovation—imagined as a technological "fix" to the failure of pharmaceuticals to resolve the ecological crisis of sleep—is essentially a failure, producing an iatrogenic epidemic of elective secondary insomnia, after the Donor Y infection is spun into Sleep Blend G-17 and the transfusion pool is infected by "nightmare-prions" inducing night terrors so severe that patients grow "nostalgic for their insomnia" and *choose* never to sleep again (648). The narrative's imagination of literally infectious terror and the subsequent proliferation of government apparatuses and algorithmic arrays such as the nightmare index aimed at surveillance and discipline satirizes the whole post/911 discourse on terror, states of exception, and US policing of its Latin American backyard. The FEMA trailers of the Slumbers Corps evoke natural disasters exacerbated by climate vitality and state abandonment such as Hurricane Katrina, which disproportionately affected socio-economically disadvantaged populations. Like the trailers in which Katrina refugees were housed, the Slumber Corps base camp is designed as temporary accommodation for "local teams working at the frontiers of the crisis," rooted in denial that the "insomnia emergency is now a permanent condition" which the first-response measures of the NGO cannot resolve, especially as they continue to ignore the systemic causes of the epidemic, treating only the symptoms (63). Ironically, as Trish remarks, "the cure is worse than the disease," responding not only to the failed technological intervention and NGO-dependency created by the Slumber Corps, but to the neoliberal state's own manipulation of iatrogenic insomnia to justify an intensification of securitization and expansion of its military-industrial complex rather than substantive investment in public health and preventative care (650).

Securitization is another form of enclosure that transforms concepts, assets, and geography into security concerns and, in so doing, legitimates the occupation of previously non-capitalized spaces. As Eli Jelly-Schapiro argues,

The term 'homeland security' signifies a moment defined by its myriad contradictions—between imperial expansion and imperial decline, between the willful performance of state failure (Hurricane Katrina) and spectacular performance of state power (the 'shock and awe' conquest of Iraq), between the labor imperatives of business and anti-immigrant nativism, between the hypermodern weapons of info-war and atavistic methods of (neo)colonial expropriation, between the universal aspirations of capital and the territorial exigencies of the nation-state.[19]

The novella satirizes the homeland security state—what Naomi Klein calls the "homeland security industry"[20]—in its description of the Dream and Nightmare Tracking and Epidemiology Division, a massive surveillance operation that tracks nightmare outbreaks, analyzing the "biomechanics of 'nightmare-prions,'" and enlisting the Slumber Corps in a public-private partnership with state and federal agencies. The division's aims are territorializing, mapping clusters of dreams across geographies, marking particular nations with a discourse of contamination and alterity: the labelling of a Guyanese woman as Patient Zero, thus attributing the etiology of the crisis to the pathological Global South; the speculation that Donor Y "is a new kind of bio-terrorist, who co-opted Gould's technology to stage an attack" (626); the blaming of the black market sleep labs in Vietnam, Haiti, and Cuba for trading tainted sleep and infecting US citizens, as if with the dangerous ideology of affordable healthcare. However, the nightmare index also performs a predictive and disciplinary function, using logistic regression models to detect probable trends and calculate the risk of infection from exposure to sick dreamers (449). Securitization is conducted within what Antoinette Rouvroy describes as a new mode of "algorithmic governmentality," which predicts behavioral patterns through induction based on infra-personal raw data and metadata, rather than the intent or motivation of individual agents:

> [D]ata mining and profiling techniques seduce industries and governmental institutions with promises of real time, automatic, and thus allegedly "objective" detection, sorting and forward looking evaluation of the invisible opportunities and risks carried by individuals. Opening the way to pre-emptive action to secure commercial profit and forestall dangerous or sub-optimal behaviors, the attunement of individuals' (informational or physical) environments and interactions according to their constantly evolving "profiles" is an unprecedented mode of government.[21]

The novella's speculative scenario of sleep-terror satirizes the war on terror's incitement of an affective state of perpetual vigilance, showing how the pre-emptive actions of the security industry produce a paranoiac national structure of feeling rooted in mass hypochondria: "Entire neighborhoods are having allergic reactions to the Donor Y crisis; even people with no history of insomnia or dream transfusion are suddenly frightened to crawl into bed" (638).

However, the novella also gestures beyond the crisis of the imperial nation-state to the global crisis of neoliberal capitalism. The displacement of the sleep crisis through a biotech fix only produces a more severe crisis, respatialized on a global scale, after nightmare-prions spread out of the American hemisphere to Hunan Province in China: "Naively, we now realize, we believed the dysfunction was bounded by our hemisphere, peculiar to American sleepers. But here is proof that nobody is quarantined by geography—that anybody, anywhere, might become an orexin" (1425). This image can be read as the 'contagion' of financial crisis, if interpreted in light of China's ownership of US bonds and dependence on the United States as a consumer market for its exports. The fact that the Harkonnens sell sleep to their east Asian competitors in search of a technological fix suggests that the United States is no longer the potential site of a revolution that could solve the "plague" of declining productivity.

Yet, the crisis of terminal insomnia is represented in the novella not only as socio-economic, but as profoundly socio-ecological, signifying the larger exhaustion of the neoliberal ecological regime. Over three decades of neoliberalism, frontiers in cheap food, energy, resources, and labor have encountered peak appropriation, no longer able to secure rising surpluses in conjunction with declining unit costs of extraction. Biotechnology has not produced a sufficiently large revolution in productivity to sustain a new wave of accumulation that will resolve systemic crises of under- and overproduction. For Moore, the capitalist world-ecology is in the throes of a developmental, possibly even epochal crisis, of which the potentially terminal crisis of American unilateral power is only one facet.[22] Correspondingly, *Sleep Donation* is permeated with figurations of the "global desertification of dreams" as interdependent with global environmental crisis.

Exhaustion of cheap oil and cheap water haunts the novella's symbolic regime, shadowing the anxious attempts of the US core to eke out its hegemony by opening new frontiers in extreme energy and extreme water. If extreme oil has been used to describe technologies of fossil fuel extraction, which are more expensive and carbon-intensive than their predecessors, including fracking, deep-sea drilling, and tar sands extraction, the term "extreme water" as I use it can likewise designate intensive technologies of water extraction that follow peak appropriation of freshwater, including aquifer pumping, deep drilling, and mega-dam projects. Extreme energy compounds the environmental toll of extreme water, given the vast amounts of crude water consumed and polluted by fracking, mining, smelting, and electronics-manufacturing. Trish is based in a Pennsylvanian city, which she describes as afflicted with "one of the greatest REM-sleep deficits on the East Coast." Drawing on Pennsylvania's association with intensive fracking, she frames her fears of draining Baby A in the extractivist vocabulary of extreme water:

> 'We will never overdraw your daughter...' I make this promise at a moment when people are plunging their straw into any available centimeter of shale and water, every crude oil and uranium and mineral well on earth, with an indiscriminate and borderless appetite. [...] Some animals we've turned out to be. We have never in our species' history respected Nature's limits, the doomsday speculators announce, smacking their lips, until it seems like some compensatory sucrose must flood into their mouths every time they say the words "mass death." According to their estimates, our species will be extinct in another generation, having exhausted every store of water and fuel on the planet. (1471)

This language of exhaustion is both literal and figurative, overlaid with an imaginary of intensified water and oil extraction, which draws an analogy between the vertical frontiers of resource mining and the biotechnological mining of human subjectivity. Donors are described as "dream wells," Baby A is a "fleshy aquifer," the faces of sleepers are "happy and plump, irrigated by sleep" (214); transfusion relies on the "hydrology of human generosity," (685) the Corps are "hydraulic engineers," redistributing "funds, dreams, to eradicate thirst" (576); even Trish's surname, "Edgewater," is suggestive of hydrological crisis. Sleep trouble in this sense can be seen as the crisis of the forms of extraction that fuel particular kinds of predominantly middle-class consumer subjectivity. Elsewhere, the novella fleetingly alludes to the fact that indigenous peoples are often the most exploited by forms of hydro-extractivism and enclosure, drawing a direct link between a Lakota man in a coma whose family claims that the Wyoming Slumber Corps has been "mining him" for sleep and "all the mining, drilling and *earth-rape* they are *actually* doing in Wyoming" (398).

For the most part, the novella sidesteps the question of what forms of collective resistance could be mobilized in response to enclosure, extractivism, and securitization. However, it does intimate the containment of dissent through its dialectical portrayal of the "Night Worlds" which "form spontaneously, on the margins of cities" comprised of "mazes of tents, nocturnally blooming speakeasies" where orexins and elective insomniacs who are either denied sleep transfusions or who refuse them go to seek solace in their sleeplessness (191). Russell's wider oeuvre of short fiction has been consistently concerned with representation of economic busts and recessions, haunted by the Great Depression and the Dust Bowl of the 1930s, traversing western ghost towns and the spectres of a deindustrialized Deep South. Here, the "Night Worlds" produced by the collapse of sleep allegorize the modern-day recession, recalling the tent cities spreading through the United States after the collapse of the housing bubble in 2008 and the epidemic of house foreclosures. They are eruptions of the disenfranchised that allegorize the social violence of debt by imagining insomnia as a kind of fatal bankruptcy of sleep into which masses of people are thrust, cast out of ordinary society and relegated to the peripheries of ordinary existence. But they also have a weird, phantasmagoric energy that signifies their potential to act as sites of the emergence of new collectivities in the wake of socio-ecological disaster. Their "heterogeneous mix of revenants" and "hallucinatory reef" of fairgrounds, poppy fields, and transgressive performances are reminiscent of the carnivalesque atmosphere occasioned by the Occupy movement's occupation of public spaces and conscious generation of new forms of democratic art, education, and political praxis (1056).

At the same time, however, the subversive potential of the Night Worlds to incubate collective dissent and non-normative praxes is quickly assimilated into a circus of 24/7 consumption where sleepless consumers vainly try to sate their insomnia with a cornucopia of novel commodities, drugs, sleep placebos, and life-style experiences. As Trish wryly observes, "America's great talent, I think, is to generate desires that would never have occurred, natively, to a body like mine, and to make those desires so painfully real that money becomes fiction, an imaginary means to some concrete end" (1340). The round-the-clock customers haunting the night bars are described in monstrous terms, scarecrows shuffling through their perpetual purchases but drained of pleasure, like so many zombie consumers. The Night World is a site of social contradictions, seeded with creative potential, but also a dystopian prospect of a future in which capitalism has reworked the planet into a "non-stop work site or an always open shopping mall of infinite choice, tasks, selections and digressions," where "sleeplessness is the state in which producing, consuming, and discarding occur without pause, hastening the exhaustion of life and the depletion of resources."[23]

Trish's own journey into the camp jolts her out of the recursive cycles of her solipsistic anxiety and leads to a new recognition of collective suffering. In the Night World, she is confronted by a microcosm of social totality, as she encounters sleepless from across the class spectrum, finding it "perversely cheering" to see "rich insomniacs [who] have gotten lonely enough to disable their alarms and leave their marble enclaves, coming down the mountain" (1056) to wander restless alongside the outcast and the homeless. Significantly, it is in the liminal space of the Night World, outside of the normative sphere of daylight life, that Mr. Harkonnen confronts Trish about her ongoing exploitation of his daughter and asks her to agree that she won't sleep again until she stops drawing infusions from Baby A. Rather than the crude transactional logic that haunted her Slumber Corps negotiation, her agreement with Harkonnen is a social contract, born of mutuality and transindividual intimacy, in which Trish finally attends to the deep asymmetries of sleep extraction by experiencing them in terms of her own deprivation. She perceives this contract as liberatory rather than oppressive, opening up prospects of future agency that had seemed foreclosed:

> I don't feel like a slave to contract. I don't feel that Mr. Harkonnen tricked or frightened me into it. Each time I stare down at our handshake, I feel the same vertigo, a dislocation that is much stranger than mere anticipation, as though I'm being catapulted forward in time, rocketed to my death, perhaps, or to some absolute horizon, where I get a glimpse of my own life massing into form, a thrilling feel for all that will happen to me now, all that I cannot know, haven't yet done, haven't spoken, haven't thought, will or won't. Just entering the contract does this. [. . .] The simple algebra of our arrangement feels like a ladder that he is holding out to me. (1401)

Newly empowered with an ethos, she concludes the narrative by directly confronting the Storch brothers and exposing their illegal sale of sleep to Japan. This whistleblower conclusion is rather paltry by way of a political gesture, a narrative resolution rooted in the idea of redemptive individual action through official legal channels by a bourgeois agent and the liberal belief that institutions only need reform, rather than thorough-going systemic transformation through collective action. Russell's novella predominantly concentrates on privatized experiences of bioderegulation and affective sleeplessness corresponding to the 24/7 environment in which post-Fordist bourgeois US consumers are immersed. In contrast, Rivera's film, *Sleep Dealer*, as I will demonstrate, foregrounds collective experiences of labor outsourcing, intensified extraction, and uneven development in post-NAFTA Mexico, focusing not on the individual privation of insomnia, but rather on the social totality of "cybraceros" working in "sleep dealer" factories.

II

If in developmental crises of capitalism, the appearance and growth of fictitious capital, the most virtual, immaterial form of capitalization, and primitive accumulation, the most brutally material, are interlinked, then the emphasis on affect and governmentality in Karen Russell's speculative literary aesthetics could be argued to figure more strongly the abstracted mode of financialization in the core, while Rivera's self-termed "science fiction from below" figures the scarring modes of accumulation in the semi-periphery.[24] Rivera is a US director, son of a Peruvian immigrant, whose socially conscious films invert science fiction genre conventions to explore the hierarchical relations between the United States and the wider American hemisphere. *Sleep Dealer*, his first feature, is a Spanish-language film shot in Mexico. In *Sleep Dealer*, the sleeplessness of protagonist Memo Cruz is not an affective plague, neither a privatization of interiority nor an erasure of the capacity to dream, but rather the physical product of overwork in twelve-hour shifts in virtual reality factories, the eponymous "sleep dealers" in which "cybraceros" use nodes to plug into bots which operate remotely in the United States.

Instead of the reddened corneas of Russell's insomniacs (as depicted in the *Sleep Donation* cover image), Rivera's cybraceros present eerie, whitened irises, a zombified glare reflective of their reduction to dehumanized labor. The workers experience spatio-temporal disorientations, electricity-induced blindness, and hallucinations as a result of having their "nervous system" plugged in too long "to the other system—the global economy."[25] The factories literally "deal" sleep—that is, unconsciousness or even death—to cybraceros "when their nervous systems overload from the electrical input" from working uninterrupted shifts.[26] If Russell's sleepless consumers embody the anxious subjectivity of a contracting American middle class that nonetheless remains the market for the export commodities manufactured by Mexican maquiladoras, Rivera's sleepless workers rematerialize the other side—"*el otro lado*," as Memo hails it—of the axial division of labor across the border.[27] The predominance of dusk and twilight scenes in the urban borderland setting—in contrast to the sun-drenched natural light of the opening scenes on the farm in Oaxaca—emphasize the artificial illumination of the factories, the collapse of diurnal distinctions between night and day as the workers pursue virtual shifts. Even the recreational spaces outside the sleep dealers—the Node bar where exhausted workers consume stimulants or depressants, the studio bedsit where the node journalist jacks in to file her stories—are predominantly absent of natural lighting, the interiors murky with crepuscular purples or garish with digital neon.

Rivera criticizes contemporary science fiction thriller films for conceiving of futurity almost solely in terms of cosmopolitan capitalist core cities, while eliding representation of the exploitation of the rural hinterlands or megalopolises of the Global South.[28] *Sleep Dealer* deliberately opens not in a city, but in Memo's home village in the rural countryside of Oaxaca:

> To think about the future of Oaxaca, you have to think how so-called 'development' has been happening there [. . .] It's not superhighways and skyscrapers.

[...] The buildings look older. Most of the streets still aren't paved. And yet ... instead of an old-fashioned TV, there is a high-definition TV. Instead of a calling booth, like they have today in Mexican villages, where people call their relatives who are far away, in this future there is a video-calling booth. There's the presence of a North American corporation that has privatized the water and that uses technology to control the water supply. There are remote cameras with guns mounted on them and drones that do surveillance over the area. The vision of Oaxaca in the future and of the South in the future is a kind of collage, where there are still elements that look ancient, there is still infrastructure that looks older even than it does today, and yet there are little capillaries of high technology that pulse through the environment.[29]

This vision of futurity is foregrounded in uneven development, highlighting the underdevelopment of basic infrastructure in contrast to the overdevelopment of security infrastructure to protect transnational capital and more effectively enclose new frontiers of ecological surpluses (water). Likewise, when the film follows Memo to the borderland city, the gleaming high-tech factories, security apparatus and information telephony sharply contrast the sprawling shantytowns outside the glittering center, where the "netbacks" huddle over rudimentary wood fires.

The film reworks the cyberpunk genre to rebut technotopian fantasies of biophysical transcendence via hyperconnectivity into a mecanosphere. The node workers' minds are set to operating heavy construction mechs and farming avatars in remote locations across the US border in the North, but their bodies, left jacked into the sleep dealers, are still wholly susceptible to the biological limits of sleep exhaustion, even as they are infused with oxygen to keep them more alert, or as they consume shots of "teki" in the node bar to attempt to counteract exhaustion by overstimulating their metabolisms. Overconnectivity in virtualized cyberspace is not the source of morphological freedom from the constraints of human flesh, as in the myth of liberatory transhumanism, but rather a rupture in biological metabolism that heralds death. Automation does not bring salvation from wage-labor, but rather a new form of exploitation that further alienates workers, dematerializing their bodies and removing their capacity to organize in the sphere of production, thus ironically fulfilling the "American Dream" of virtual outsourcing: "We give the US what they've always wanted. All the work, without the workers."[30] As the voiceover in Rivera's satiric short promotional film *Why Cybraceros?* explains, "cyber-bracero means a worker who poses no threat of becoming a citizen ... providing labor at low financial and social costs to you, the consumer."[31] The fantasy of disembodied productivity reflects the peripheralization of Latin American immigrants in the contemporary US political system and the erasure from political consciousness of the suffering and exploitation endured not only by workers in the borderland cities, but all those displaced from their land by mining, megadams, and agri-business corporations in the interior.

As Rivera explains in an interview, his science fiction from below aesthetic is explicitly concerned with foregrounding the hierarchies of combined and uneven development, emphasizing the way in which the wealth of cores is built on the surpluses extracted from peripheries:

> We use the word 'futuristic' to describe things that are . . . explosions of capital, like skyscrapers or futuristic cities. We do not think of a cornfield as futuristic, even though that has as much to do with the future as does the shimmering skyscraper. [. . .] The ancient cornfields in Oaxaca are the places that replenish the genetic supply of corn that feeds the world. Those fields are the future of the food supply. For every futuristic skyscraper, there's a mine someplace where the ore used to build that structure was taken out of the ground. That mine is just as futuristic as the skyscraper. [. . .] *Sleep Dealer* puts forward this vision of the future that connects the dots, a vision that says that the wealth of the North comes from somewhere. It tries to look at development and futurism from this split point of view—to look at the fact that these fantasies of what the future will be in the North must always be creating a second, nightmare reality somewhere in the South.[32]

Memo's metamorphosis into a sleepless laborer acts as a guide into the nightmare reality instituted by the North American Free Trade Agreement, which unleashed violent rounds of accumulation by dispossession to force indigenous peasants off the land and coerce them into casualized forms of proletarian wage labor. In the 1990s, the Mexican state executed a mass privatization of *ejido* lands previously owned collectively by the peasantry and removed import barriers, thus lowering the price of corn and other staple food commodities so that they could not compete with the cheap food imported by the US agro-industry. Millions of migrants flooded into the northern cities to enter the vast reserve of cheap, flexible labor supplying the three thousand assembly plants springing up alongside the border. Deruralization and maquilaization brutally re-organized socio-ecological relations through the mass enclosure of Mexico's land and water commons, exacerbating the burden on local ecologies already under stress after the elimination of state funding for waste storage and water treatment facilities. Maquila factories in the desert ecosystems of the borderlands contributed to extreme water through aquifer pumping, toxification of watersheds by leaking chemicals and illegal dumping of hazardous waste into waterways such as the Rio Grande, while failing to provide basic water infrastructure, sewage, or waste disposal provision for the workers living in the shantytowns encircling the industrial parks.

Rivera's film shares the hydrological imaginary of Russell's novella, conjoining sleeplessness with water crisis, but its split perspective foregrounds the hydroculture of the semi-periphery and periphery in contrast to that of the core, emphasizing the exhaustion of water in conjunction with food, rather than oil. Memo explicitly connects the draining of his life-force in the sleep dealer with the privatization of water in his village in Oaxaca, after the Del Rio water company, a transnational American corporation headquartered in San Diego, dams the local river and charges villagers by the dollar to irrigate their fields. Staring at his desertified *milpa*, Memo's father describes the neoliberal enclosure of the river commons as inducing a material and existential rupture in temporality: "Is our future a thing of the past? [...] We had a future. You're standing on it. When they dammed up the river, they cut off our future."[33] Images of Memo's exhausted body hooked into nodes are juxtaposed with a shot of the overland water pipeline, as he declaims, "My energy was being drained, sent far away. What happened to the river, was happening to me."[34] Appropriation of nature's unpaid work/energy is thus dialectically linked to the exploitation of Memo's labor, as is the spectre of exhaustion: the exhaustion of the worker's body, and the exhaustion of the water and food needed to sustain social reproduction, proposing limits to the appropriation of labor by virtual means and signaling the maxing out of ecological surpluses.

In Rivera's post-NAFTA film, unlike Russell's story, sleeplessness does not provoke a terror of contagion; rather, dehumanizing conditions of labor and privatization of the ecological sources of daily survival are the sources of chronic fear and anxiety. Sleeplessness is not portrayed primarily as an affective disorder of individual privation, but rather as a generalized condition deriving from structural violence and the hierarchical division of labor. Where Russell's novella can only imagine a limited assertion of individual morality in response to systemic crisis, Rivera's film concludes by imagining the possibility for collective resistance to North American capital and the neoliberal Mexican state's heightened discipline. For Rivera's characters, terminal crisis of US hegemony is devoutly to be wished, rather than anxiously avoided through liberal reform. Unlike *Sleep Donation*, in which class distinctions are mostly invisible, the film carefully plots a series of class differentials: Memo, the disenfranchised *campesino* of the rural interior turned precarious cybracero; Rudy, the Mexican-American drone pilot who remotely polices the corporate dam in Memo's Oaxacan village from his security base in California; Luz, the bourgeois creative who turns her memories into story-commodities for TruNode in order to pay off her student debt to a bio-media university. The latter represents the film's self-reflexive meditation on the hollowing out of artistic autonomy by financialization and the subsumption of cultural production by algorithmic govermentality. Luz's "writing" is actually a recording of her memories and feelings, which are bioauthenticated as "truth" by a data recording algorithm. TruNode represents an extreme form of data-mining that mines memories and dreams themselves, a corollary to the commodification of sleep draws in *Sleep Donation*. However, the film carefully differentiates between Luz's immaterial, affective labor and the sheer physical toll of Memo's exploitation, and reveals her perspective and feelings as problematically bound by her own class experience, as when she turns her romantic relationship with Memo into a commodity for exchange in the memory trade, or when she visits his village and describes it as something alien and exotic for her viewers, romanticizing its underdevelopment and poverty: "Going there felt like time travel, like entering a completely new world."[35]

Likewise, the film shows the induction of media consumers into the affect of the security state by including a parody of National Geographic's *Border Wars* shows called *Drone Wars*, a reality TV program that encourages viewers to celebrate as "high-tech heroes use high-technology to blow the hell out of bad guys" and justifies the exercise of force in the service of water enclosure and resource monopoly: "Dams all around the world are the target of massive resistance by legions of aquaterrorists. So the companies fight back."[36] However, here again it is careful to offer a dialectical perspective, juxtaposing the immaterial affects of virtual fear, terror, and celebration of spectacular state and corporate-sponsored violence enjoyed by domestic US consumers of the program with the real physical experience of securitization across the border in Mexico, showing Memo's family running in terror from drone hits as their village is flattened.

Even more importantly, it portrays the possibility of collective political insurgency against the security apparatus, rather than imagining it as an all-subsuming form of governance that leaves no room for agency. Throughout the film, the protagonists witness television segments and street graffiti referencing the "EMLA" or Mayan Army of Water Liberation, who are demonized by the US and Mexican media as eco-terrorists, but embraced by the people. Wearing balaclavas reminiscent of the Zapatistas and demanding water autonomy, the EMLA correspond to the real-life ELZN, the movement of indigenous peasants who rose up against the enclosure of their lands by the neoliberal Mexican state, and now maintain a precarious autonomy in Chiapas. The drone pilot, Rudy, who kills Memo's father in a drone strike after mistaking him for an eco-terrorist, is depicted as experiencing a slow conscionization of his own role in exercising the monopoly of violence to protect US capital interests. Awakened to Memo's humanity by Luz's story of her encounter with him, Rudy crosses the Mexican border in search of him, where he confronts the full reality of structural inequality. Crary argues that "sleeplessness takes on its historical significance and its particular affective texture in relation to the collective experiences external to it" and Rudy's encounter with Memo rematerializes this social collectivity, making visible the forms of dispossession and social ruin with which sleeplessness is concomitant.[37] His journey through the Tijuana maquilas catalyzes anagnorisis, the recognition of a larger social totality founded in the concerted life situation of the semi-periphery, since as Rivera argues in a video interview for the Latino Film Festival, "The periphery is the center," where the hierarchical labor relations underlying global modernity can be discerned.[38] He goes on to highlight the salience of the Mexican borderland as the only land border between the United States core and the (semi)periphery, where the violence of exploitation is therefore peculiarly visible.

Subsequently, Rudy allies with Luz, the memory-worker journalist, and Memo, to hijack a sleep dealer and blow up the transnational dam in Memo's village. This alliance, in which the Hispanic-American professional aligns with the indigenous peasant-turned-proletarian and the female Mexican middle-class intellectual, imagines a class realignment. The "memory cross" of Memo Cruz's name, thus, might signify not only his crucifixion in the node-machine of the factory, but also redemption through the recuperation of political memory. His character acts as a crossroads or axis of resistance through which alienated fractions can be joined into a new solidarity that enables their re-autonomization. As such, the film offers more than the token individual resistance within the constraints of liberal institutions as imagined in Russell's novella, and inspired by its sympathetic proximity to Zapatista struggle, its political imaginary is much broader, seeking instead to dissolve the material and social structures that underlie the hegemony of neoliberal capitalism. The interdependent mutuality of the characters is reinforced by Memo's memory of *milpas*, in which "the beans wrap around the corn and the two help each to grow," an image drawn from the Mayan ecological imaginary, which rejects the idea of nature as a reified object, a surplus to be rationalized and commoditized, or as a source of perpetual competition, in favor of an understanding of interdependent relations in which human and extra-human nature can act together in symbiosis. Their act of *ecotage* is not depicted as act of terror, but rather as the restoration of life, releasing the "miracle" of the river, the first action of a water war that will restore the "future" of the Mexican peasants. The film concludes with Rudy embarking on a bus south, presumably to EMLA territory, while Luz and Memo remain in Tijuana to contemplate their next action. The final shot is of Memo planting a rooftop *milpa*, whilst proclaiming, "But perhaps there's a future for you here on the edge of everything. A future with a past. If I connect. And fight."³⁹ This reassertion of temporality reclaims the dimensions of historical time and futurity, refusing the endless neoliberal present of sleepless, virtualized labor, in favor of a vision of *la lucha continua*, of the possibility of autonomy and solidarity across time. Thus, I would argue that while both Russell and Rivera's texts offer productively dystopian imaginations of the "end of sleep" in the neoliberal era, they do so from across an axial division of labor, offering a kind of uneven and combined geography of sleeplessness whose differing emphasis on affect and governmentality vs. autonomy, and unequal ability to conceive of social collectivity is situated in the contrast between the concerted life-situations of the North American core hegemon and the Mexican semi-periphery.

Notes

1. Jonathan Crary, 24/7 *Capitalism: The End of Sleep* (London: Verso, 2013), 113.
2. Crary, 24/7 *Capitalism*, 113.
3. Jason W. Moore, *Capitalism in the Web of Life* (London: Verso, 2015), 100.
4. Crary, 24/7 *Capitalism*, 179.
5. Moore, *Capitalism*, 17.
6. Crary, 24/7 *Capitalism*, 180; Teresa Brennan, *Globalization and Its Terrors: Daily Life in the West* (London: Verso, 2013), Kindle, 19–22.
7. Moore, *Capitalism*, 121.
8. Crary, 24/7 *Capitalism*, 203.
9. Giovanni Arrighi, "Hegemony Unravelling—I," *New Left Review* 32 (2005) http://newleftreview.org/II/32/giovanni-arrighi-hegemony-unravelling-1.
10. Karen Russell, *Sleep Donation* (New York: Atavist Books, 2014), Kindle, 106. Hereafter cited in parentheses in the body of the essay.
11. Karen Russell, Sleep Donation.com, interactive website, Accessed March 10, 2014. http://sleepdonation.com.
12. Arundhati Roy, "The NGO-ization of Resistance." *Toward Freedom* (September 8, 2014). Accessed April 28, 2017. http://towardfreedom.com/archives/globalism/arundhati-roy-the-ngo-ization-of-resistance/.
13. Roy, "NGO-ization".
14. Russell, Sleep Donation.com.
15. Eva Illouz, *Why Love Hurts: A Sociological Explanation* (Cambridge: Polity Press, 2012), 9.
16. Crary, 24/7 *Capitalism*, 1459.
17. Crary, 24/7 *Capitalism*, 1459.
18. National Public Radio, "'Sleep Donation': A Dark, Futuristic Lullaby for Insomniacs," *Fresh Air* (March 26, 2014). Accessed April 27, 2017. http://www.npr.org/2014/03/26/294820998/sleep-donation-a-dark-futuristic-lullaby-for-insomniacs.
19. Eli Jelly-Schapiro, "Security: The Long History," *Journal of American Studies* 47.3 (2013): 810–811.

20. Naomi Klein, *The Shock Doctrine* (New York: Metropolitan Books, 2007), 301.

21. Antoinette Rouvroy, "Algorithmic Governmentality: A Passion for the Real and the Exhaustion of the Virtual" (2015), Accessed April 28, 2017. https://www.academia.edu/10481275/Algorithmic_governmentality_a_passion_for_the_real_and_the_exhaustion_of_the_virtual.

22. Moore, *Capitalism*, 27.

23. Crary, 24/7 *Capitalism*, 203.

24. Alex Rivera, "Science Fiction from Below: Interview with Mark Engler," ed. John Feffer (May 13, 2009), Accessed April 28, 2017. http://alexrivera.com/2012/10/21/science-fiction-from-below.

25. Alex Rivera, dir. *Sleep Dealer* (2008).

26. Rivera, *Sleep Dealer*.

27. Rivera, *Sleep Dealer*.

28. Rivera, "Science Fiction."

29. Rivera, "Science Fiction."

30. Rivera, *Sleep Dealer*.

31. Alex Rivera, dir. *Why Cybraceros?* (1997).

32. Rivera, "Science Fiction."

33. Rivera, *Sleep Dealer*.

34. Rivera, *Sleep Dealer*.

35. Rivera, *Sleep Dealer*.

36. Rivera, *Sleep Dealer*.

37. Crary, 24/7 *Capitalism*, 123.

38. Alex Rivera, "Interview with Director Alex Rivera, *Sleep Dealer*," Latino Film Festival at UI Cinema (September 30, 2012), Accessed May 3, 2017. https://www.youtube.com/watch?v=dtbBG48m_Eo&index=1&list=PLf1aigmUv94qyTya8kkesm1mkSj8lWf. Video.

39. Rivera, *Sleep Dealer*.

DAN HASSLER-FOREST

POSTCAPITALISM IN SPACE: KIM STANLEY ROBINSON'S UTOPIAN SCIENCE FICTION

It's a very peculiar moment in history, because the disastrous future, the dystopia, is quite possible, and we're in many ways on course to it: if we continue to do what we're doing now, we're heading that way. On the other hand, the possibility for utopia is also there. We're powerful thinkers on this planet, and we can think our way out of this one by using the technology that's called "language," "rule of law," and "justice." These are the technical solution.[1]

IN THE ERA OF global capitalism, Fredric Jameson's famous quip that it's easier to imagine the end of the world than the end of capitalism has become one of the most notorious clichés of critical theory. From Mark Fisher's "capitalist realism" to Subhabrata Bobby Banerjee's "necrocapitalism," neoliberalism's stifling effects on our ability to imagine alternatives has been widely— one might even say exhaustively—diagnosed. Neoliberalism's global trends of industrial deregulation, post-Fordist "just-in-time" delivery systems, and wave after wave of primitive accumulation in the global South are all aspects of twenty-first-century life that have clearly impeded our ability to articulate any meaningful kind of "utopian imaginary."[2]

As slippery and ambivalent a concept as it may be, utopianism is of vital importance to a culture of political resistance. Not only because it holds out the promise of a brighter, better world, but because it insists on imagining alternatives. Or, as China Miéville has put it in his introduction to a new edition of Thomas More's *Utopia*: "Utopianism isn't hope, still less optimism: it is need, and it is desire. For recognition, like all desire, and/but for the specifics of its reveries and programmes, too; and above all for betterness *tout court*. For alterity, something other than the exhausting social lie. For rest. And when the cracks in history open wide enough, the impulse may even jimmy them a little wider."[3] The cultural articulation of utopian science fiction is so important in the neoliberal age because we seem to lack the tools to force the cracks of history wider on those moments when they do seem to open. For even as our cultural, political, and economic realms seem bereft of long-term programs, there has been no shortage of impulses towards organized resistance.

The question, then, is how to make these momentary bursts sustainable in the long term.

The traditional Left's decades-long abandonment of political resistance, exemplified by the Clinton/Blair pivot towards the technocratic and business-friendly "Third Way" that typifies neoliberal governmentality, has been accompanied in the cultural realm by a related turn towards texts that reflect and in many ways normalize a pervasive atmosphere of dystopian inevitability. This is perhaps most obvious in the twenty-first century's increasingly ubiquitous "quality TV" meta-genre, with its structural emphasis on complex characters and elaborate plots that inevitably portray a crisis-prone world in perpetual decline. It is also visible in the surging popularity over the last decade of zombie franchises like *The Walking Dead*, and their ongoing articulation of a bleak and precarious future completely bereft of hope. And it is equally evident in the science fiction film genre's oft-lamented preponderance for dystopian fictions, constantly immersing us in visions of futurity that depict a wide variety of global ecological, economic, technological, social, and political catastrophes.[4]

In this sense at least, science fiction seems to have lost some of the political potential for which philosophers, critical theorists, and literary critics have so often celebrated the genre. Without making overly precise claims about a notoriously "fuzzy" genre, science fiction emerged as a popular genre in the wake of the Industrial Revolution, and provided a cultural vocabulary of imagery and narratives that resonated above all as American capitalism became the defining force in postwar geopolitics. The slick spaceships, intergalactic odysseys, and daring astronauts embodied thoroughly utopian perspectives on a future of uninterrupted growth and technological progress, as interplanetary exploration came to form a dazzling "final frontier" for literally endless colonial expansion.

But in the neoliberal era of looming ecological disaster, unchecked economic crisis, and the swift erosion of a commonly shared public sphere, science fiction's utopian imaginary seems to have been eclipsed and displaced by an *apocalyptic imaginary*. Even when a utopian future is glimpsed, it can only be conceived as something that must be preceded by an apocalyptic nightmare: "This is not quite a dystopia: it's a third form—apocatopia, utopalypse—and it's all around us. We're surrounded by a culture of ruination, dreams of falling cities, a people-less world where animals explore."[5] Nevertheless, in the domain of science fiction literature, affairs are at least somewhat less bleak. As one of the leading voices in American speculative fiction, Kim Stanley Robinson has largely resisted the widespread urge to embrace various forms of sentimental disaster porn, of which Cormac McCarthy's *The Road* may be the pre-eminent example within the literary field. Instead, he has tirelessly worked towards visions of a future that may be described as utopian—not only in the sense that he continues to express hope for a future that has the potential of "betterness," but also because he engages directly with the key question of how to overcome the challenges posed by global capitalism.

In this chapter, I will approach some of the key texts in Robinson's substantial body of work as productive interventions that question, critique, and challenge neoliberalism's cultural logic. Starting with his widely-read "Mars Trilogy"—*Red Mars* (1992), *Green Mars* (1994), and *Blue Mars* (1995)—I will first demonstrate how Robinson constructs a critical utopia in response to the development of global capitalism, while constantly foregrounding the fundamentally political nature of futuristic world-building. I will then contrast this specific type of critical utopia with his later novels *2312* (2012) and *Aurora* (2015), which struggle to maintain his earlier work's optimism while also engaging more directly with the vanishing horizons of neoliberal capitalism that has become increasingly global and increasingly futureless. Throughout the chapter, I will refer to some of his other speculative work to offer a more complete picture of Robinson's literary project, and how it relates back to the genre's increasingly beleaguered utopian potential. But first, I must sketch out the larger context of neoliberalism, and how specific aspects of this cultural logic inform my own approach to literary science fiction.

A Futureless World: Science Fiction and Neoliberalism's "Indebted Man"

When the end of the Cold War inspired Francis Fukuyama to celebrate the passing of Really Existing Socialism as the "end of history," the term had a utopian resonance that has been notably absent in the actual historical era that followed. In the 1990s, the brief illusion of a global capitalism that would allow for limitless growth and accumulation was soon punctured by a tsunami of crises that revealed the material reality of globalization: a landscape of radically uneven development, growing socio-economic inequality, and a thoroughly unstable and crisis-prone economic system.

But at the same time, this post-historical perspective continues to ring true in neoliberalism's fundamentally futureless sensibility. The combination of an increasingly imperial political and economic structure of "flexible accumulation" and the ongoing imposition of austerity policies has resulted in an intensification of capitalism's fundamental unsustainability.[6] As Marc Augé has reflected in his theoretical intervention *The Future*, "The real problems with democratic life today stem from the fact that technological innovations exploited by financial capitalism have replaced yesterday's myths in the definition of happiness for all, and are promoting an ideology of the present, and ideology of the future *now*, which in turn paralyses all thought about the future."[7] In the context of global capitalism, this paralysis clearly impedes our ability to relate to the future as a horizon for change, hope, or improvement. Augé connects this post-historical structure of feeling to neoliberalism as a system of social relations that isolates the individual from any kind of meaningful sense of collectivity. It is the direct result of the clear-cut ways in which neoliberalism reduces individuals to the level of competitors who are forced to act as "entrepreneurs of the self": constantly having to reinvent, re-educate, and rebrand themselves within a flexible and thoroughly precarious environment, where the future has no promise to offer but that of endlessly diminishing returns.[8]

This evaporating horizon of neoliberalism's cultural, political, and economic logic lies at the heart of Maurizio Lazzarato's figure of "the indebted man" as global capitalism's "existential condition."[9] Neoliberal economy is structured entirely upon the debtor/debtee relationship, as the financialization of post-industrial capitalism has created a system in which the vast majority of profits are the product of speculation rather than labor, and in which debt creation "has been conceived and programmed as the strategic heart of neoliberal politics."[10] Examples abound of the many ways in which the debtor relationship has been used as a powerful tool to discipline individuals, communities, and even entire nations, from the European Union's abject humiliation of Greece to the ways in which hedge fund owners profited from subprime mortgage forfeitures in the 2008 financial crisis.

This figure of the indebted man—or, to put it less phallocentrically, the indebted person—is crucial to understanding neoliberalism's futureless world, because our perpetual present is in a very real and quite literal sense already living in a time that is thoroughly out of joint: the precarious wealth and privilege of the Western world is created not on the basis of labor, but of capital that has been "borrowed" from an increasingly dire-looking future. Little wonder, then, that our ability to conceive of any kind of future outside of an ever-more oppressive form of capitalist realism and universal indebtedness has been so thoroughly compromised. Therefore, in this world without alternatives, we not only have great need of speculative narratives that articulate a utopian future, but we have also developed a suddenly-urgent interest in thought experiments that are emphatically *postcapitalist*.

More than any other literary genre, science fiction has a long and varied tradition of expressing utopian motifs in a variety of constellations. While utopian fiction isn't necessarily science-fictional, the political potential of science fiction as a genre makes it particularly productive as a vessel for utopian speculation. For even if some claims about science fiction's privileged relationship to critical theory are perhaps exaggerated, one can nevertheless clearly recognize in its non-fantastic forms of cognitive estrangement an irreducibly political platform for speculating about the future.[11] Moreover, the very genre traditions that have long disqualified science fiction as a legitimate literary form for the vast majority of scholars and critics enhance this political potential: science fiction literature has tended to favor descriptions of complex political, social, and technological systems over psychologically "realistic" representations of individual characters, and have all too often sprawled across multiple volumes.

Key works in this register can be located in American science fiction from the 1930s "Guernsback Age" of pulp fiction through to the 1960s "Second Wave" of the genre. Authors from Edgar Rice Burroughs and Robert A. Heinlein to Isaac Asimov and Arthur C. Clarke drew heavily on industrial capitalism's utopian imaginary of progress through technology and limitless expansion.[12] It is surely no accident that the most iconic embodiment of this particular variety of science fiction was the TV series (and transmedia franchise) *Star Trek*, which was grounded in the spirit of industrial capitalism and its "faith in rationality and long-term planning ... and, above all, by the very gigantism of organizations."[13] *Star Trek*'s sleek, shiny surfaces and post-scarcity melting-pot society expressed a utopian vision that was firmly interlocked with a triumphalist postwar capitalism, its widely appealing vision of the future based on what Raymond Williams described as science fiction's "civilizing transformation, beyond the terms of a restless, struggling society of classes."[14]

Despite the seemingly obvious colonialist implications and uncomfortable militaristic tendencies of *Star Trek*'s particular brand of science fiction, the franchise did also help popularize the genre in a way that foregrounded its progressive agenda and liberal politics, especially within the lively and diverse fan communities that fostered it and kept it alive for many years.[15] Beyond the rather limited ideological reach of the series, or, indeed, beyond that of the most popular literary science fiction of the twentieth century, the genre in this period helped sustain a vision of futurity that was progressive, if only in a somewhat limited and mechanical sense: even the most politically reactionary science fiction authors (of which there have been many) based much of their work on a concept of the future in which humanity had miraculously survived the long twentieth century, emerging into a wide variety of futures that routinely extended beyond the constraints of capitalist exploitation, colonialist oppression, petty geopolitical conflicts, and material scarcity. And in a great many of the now-canonical works in the science fiction tradition, this utopian future was indeed expressly connected to politically progressive social and cultural values.

Therefore, whatever political objections one might justifiably raise against any individual work of science fiction, or even to how the genre's utopian imaginary has also maintained many social, cultural, and economic hierarchies, science fiction has struggled to express utopian alternatives to global capitalism from the 1990s onward. The post-Cold War order in which any system but capitalism was declared irrelevant has stymied the genre and the important cultural work it has always performed. Even as speculative fiction has been increasingly gentrified, readers and critics have frequently complained about the "dystopian trend" that has so clearly afflicted science fiction in the twenty-first century. In literary fiction, as in other media, fantastic fiction has not only been made more fashionable, but also—critically—more "realistic."

The problem, then, in terms of the social and political meaning-making that goes on around a genre like science fiction is that "realism" has become virtually synonymous with "capitalist"—and therefore if not dystopian, at the very least thoroughly anti-utopian. The neoliberal epidemic that has roughly coincided with the age of global capitalism has instilled in us what Fisher has called a "business ontology," in which it is simply taken for granted that nothing makes sense unless it is part of a market and organized for profit.[16] I have described this increasingly ubiquitous embrace of "post-ideological" capitalist realism elsewhere as a kind of *fantastical capitalism*: "'fantastical' because—superficially at least—they present us with story-worlds totally unlike our own, and 'capitalism' because they incorporate and strengthen capitalism's most basic social and cultural logic, while alternatives are systematically rejected as 'unrealistic.'"[17]

The supreme challenge, then, for speculative genres like science fiction in the neoliberal era is to articulate meaningful alternatives that are neither nostalgic pastiches of Space Age techno-futurism, nor the despairing extensions of neoliberal thinking that typify most current varieties of fantastical capitalism. Or, to put it differently: in order for science fiction to regain at least some of its utopian power, it must find ways to counter neoliberalism's futureless mindset with speculative visions that acknowledge capitalist realism's cul-de-sac without falling prey to its omnivorous spirit. Kim Stanley Robinson's Mars Trilogy provides a good starting point for examining some of the ways in which this important cultural work can be accomplished.

"They Could Do Anything": 1990s Utopianism in the Mars Trilogy

"Get Your Ass to Mars!" Arnold Schwarzenegger said it best when his video image addressed his brainwashed self in Paul Verhoeven's iconic science fiction classic *Total Recall* (1990). This eagerly-quoted line—a favorite among film trivia buffs—expresses more than the Austrian Oak's familiar tendency to interrupt violent action movies with idiosyncratic quips and one-liners: the phrase also plays on the genre's longstanding obsession with the Red Planet as a projected space of radical alternatives to our own reality. From the deadly reverse-colonialist invasion of H.G. Wells's *The War of the Worlds* (1898) and its many adaptations to Edgar Rice Burroughs's thrilling adventureland of Barsoom in his *John Carter of Mars* cycle (1912–1964) to Ray Bradbury's *Martian Chronicles* (1950) to the recent paean to neoliberal austerity politics in *The Martian* (2015), the red planet has occupied a privileged position in the genre's long history. And as the most frequently discussed object of potential planetary colonization, getting one's ass to Mars is by now commonly understood to be the most obvious first step towards a human future that extends beyond planet Earth.[18]

Kim Stanley Robinson's Mars Trilogy gave new life to the planet's prominent position within speculative fiction, and definitively established its author's reputation as the most widely acclaimed and politically engaged working within the genre. The hugely prolific novelist has developed an impressively diverse body of work over the past three decades, publishing a long list of speculative works about theology, alternative history, prehistorical human society, near-future fiction, as well as the more traditional type of "hard sci-fi" about rocket ships, space exploration, interplanetary colonization, artificial intelligence, and other well-known science fiction genre tropes. Additionally, he has been actively involved with scholarly work on science fiction studies and climate change, speaking with some frequency at academic conferences, contributing work (both short fictional works and non-fictional essays) to academic publications,[19] and co-editing the scholarly collection *Green Planets*.

The Mars Trilogy constitutes an ambitious attempt to bring together the adventurous space-exploration epics of classic science fiction with more contemporary debates and fantasies about space exploration and resource management. Across three sprawling volumes and the companion volume *The Martians* (1996), the books detail the incremental colonization and terraforming of the planet across a period of 200 years. Like many other works in the hard sci-fi register, long sections of the books are devoted to elaborate descriptions of technological innovations that make human life on other planets possible. The deployment of enormous floating "sun mirrors" that help warm up the Martian atmosphere offers a good example of the books' consistent focus on explanations of how things work, in a way that is familiar from any number of science fiction precursors.

But while Robinson's obviously passionate interest in technology and "hard science" is in many ways typical of the genre and its audience, his treatment of its role in space exploration differs substantially from the aforementioned *Star Trek* tradition. In Robinson's work, technology never represents the straightforward extension of human abilities. Like any good historical materialist, he regards technological innovation not as the positivistic means through which a liberal-humanist ideal of "progress" is made possible. Instead, the books' many futuristic technologies are consistently treated as contingent upon the shifting organization of human social, economic, and political relations, and often as unpredictable in the long-term effects of what Williams describes as science fiction's "technological transformation" of human societies.[20]

While it is notoriously difficult to articulate this perspective in the literary novel, with its stubborn focus on the individual human psyche, the science fiction genre lends itself unusually well for precisely this kind of framework. The serialized world-building book cycle has a particularly strong potential for such an approach, as it has often privileged the generation-spanning description of evolving *systems* of political, social, and economic relations over the detailed specifics of psychological verisimilitude or formal experimentation.

As a trilogy of formidable novels and an expansive anthology of short fiction, the Mars books vividly illustrate Robinson's grand ambition of constructing utopian fiction in the context of neoliberalism. As Philipp Wegner has pointed out, their appearance in the 1990s places them within a unique historical tension: while the unholy geopolitical alliance between Clinton and Blair marked the virtual annihilation of traditional left-wing politics in the richest countries, the end of the Cold War as an expression of global capitalism's fabled "end of history" also opened up a space for dynamic new anti-globalization movements.[21] In other words, while this era certainly saw the swift rise of a new imperial order united under neoliberal doctrine, it was also a moment of possibility for artists, activists, and, indeed, science fiction novelists to explore alternative possibilities. In this sense at least, we can appreciate the Mars books as an elaborate and sophisticated meditation on the radical alternatives that surface as the immanent result of a complex set of economic, political, and technological transformations.

For the uninitiated: the trilogy roughly charts the colonization and terraforming of the red planet, from the arrival of the first manned expedition (populating the planet with the initial group of settlers popularly dubbed the historic "First Hundred") through an eventful 200 years, culminating in the establishment of Mars as a fully habitable ecosystem teeming with diverse life-forms and a thriving post-capitalist society. The first book, *Red Mars*, narrates the development of the first human settlements, focusing on the one hand on the realistic application of speculative science, and on the other on the complex social and political debates that finally erupt into a full-blown revolution on Mars and a devastating world war back on Earth. The second volume, *Green Mars*, introduces the first generation of Mars-born humans, whose radically different life experience yields new social, cultural, and political practices that are reflected metaphorically in the ongoing terraforming around them. Finally, the third book, *Blue Mars*, builds towards a second, more successful political revolution, as the now-habitable Mars establishes its independence from Earth, while also opening itself up further to immigration from humanity's increasingly impoverished and inhospitable home planet.

Throughout the 200 years of future history these books map out across a good 2,200 pages, over two dozen main characters emerge, and countless conflicts, debates, disasters, experiments, innovations, and setbacks constitute an obviously crowded narrative that it would be pointless to summarize in further detail. As a triptych made up of three consecutive novels, the Mars trilogy offers remarkable narrative and thematic coherence due in part to Robinson's most pragmatic *novum*[22]: the introduction of a "longevity treatment" that radically extends the human lifespan, thereby allowing several of the first book's main characters to experience the trilogy's entire chronological span.

In terms of the work's formal qualities as a work of literature, this particular novum facilitates the reader's emotional investment in Mars's future history, as this technological intervention simplifies the seemingly inevitable onslaught of new and unfamiliar characters in most multi-generational epics. Without the structural and emotional continuity provided by a recurring set of characters, such series all too easily descend into the kind of techno-determinism of Isaac Asimov's influential *Foundation* cycle, articulating strangely mechanical utopian trajectories made artificial and unattractive by projecting a weirdly "impoverished form of human life."[23] The Mars trilogy's longevity serum thus kills two birds with one stone by addressing a formal problem in a way that fits elegantly within the books' generic framework. But above all, the way this scientific innovation is developed throughout the cycle offers an ideal illustration of the dialectical role played by technology throughout Robinson's work. What could all too easily become a simplistic way of imagining a posthuman future in which technology provides the easy fulfillment of human needs and desires, is marked here by the messy, unpredictable, and fundamentally political questions that technological advances tend to raise once they start interacting with human communities.

The genre's dominant liberal humanist tradition has largely embraced the Kurzweilian perspective, in which "health, wealth, and immortality—not to mention the coolest computer games and simulations ever—will be available, at no cost, to everyone."[24] But while the promise of a post-scarcity future remains a meaningful ideal for utopian politics, the means by which this is accomplished opens up many ideological pitfalls that play directly into the neoliberal project and its ideological agenda. Or, in other words, approaching science and technology as agents that operate outside of a material, economic, and political context sweeps under the carpet the combined and uneven development of global capitalism. The risk of science fiction's post-Singularity storyworlds is therefore the suggestion of a frictionless utopia that is magically brought about "without incurring the inconvenience of having to question our current social and economic arrangement."[25] If the political function of fantastic and speculative literature is indeed to reflect on possible alternatives to our own social and material conditions, the explicit questioning of political and economic arrangements is therefore obviously a crucial ingredient.

The longevity treatment in the Mars trilogy evades this trap precisely by operating as an *actor* (in the Latourian sense) rather than as the equivalent of a magic bullet. Firstly, the treatments soon prove to be flawed, introducing unexpected side effects that undermine the easy extension of human lifespans. Another complicating factor is the technology's impact on human subjectivity and social relations, as the co-existence of older and younger generations creates a novel and often volatile societal dynamic with—again—unforeseeable and fully immanent consequences. But finally, and most crucially, the longevity treatments are consistently presented as a sign of privilege that is only available to a small elite within an increasingly polarized society. As Martian terraforming takes shape, the distinction between the once-red planet and Earth increasingly resembles the combined and uneven development of contemporary global capitalism, where only the most obscenely wealthy are guaranteed access to advanced technology and life-extending health care.

This move consistently returns the books' focus from the futuristic application of new technologies as straightforward extensions of human abilities to markers of social status and economic privilege. The revolutions, interplanetary conflicts, and civil wars that ultimately pave the way towards a more utopian future—contested and unstable as it may be—revolve primarily around this issue, as the increasingly desperate populations left on Earth constitute a new proletarian class that is understandably anxious to relocate to the flourishing Martian colonies. In other words, Robinson's careful optimism manages to articulate a human future of possibility, struggle, and choice that springs forth from the 1990s' ambivalent "post-historical" moment.

The trilogy's depiction of political struggles like this one makes its utopian energy so meaningful in its specific moment within the larger context of neoliberalism's historical and cultural development. It established Robinson as a distinctly utopian voice within the larger field of contemporary science fiction. But in his more recent novels that revisited the trilogy's physical and thematic terrain, the author has consistently tempered the grandiose world-building ambitions of his most popular and widely read work. In this chapter's second section, I will therefore draw on the two major science fiction novels Robinson published in what Gerry Canavan has described as his "middle period": *2312* (2012) and *Aurora* (2015).

"The Command to be Free Is a Double Bind": *2312*'s Dialectical Accelerationism

If the 1990s marked the dawn of absolute global capitalist hegemony, it also constituted a clear moment of possibility. But the emergent anti-globalization movement, which peaked in 1999 with its successful disruption of World Trade Organization (WTO) meetings in Seattle, was soon undercut and displaced in the wake of the terrorist attacks of September 11, 2001. Using the tried and tested neoliberal enforcement techniques described by Naomi Klein as "the shock doctrine," the attacks became the political justification for a global shock-and-awe campaign that doubled down on capitalist imperialism.[26] The resulting post-9/11 order identified new enemies to justify its never-ending War on Terror, while the 2008 subprime mortgage crisis ended up showing not so much the vulnerability of finance capital, but the extreme lengths to which the political establishment would go to maintain that very system.

Now, after several decades of global austerity and neoliberalism's "There Is No Alternative" (TINA) mantra, utopian scenarios are in short supply indeed. After decades of privatization and deregulation have effectively ruined the publicly funded resources and facilities that made up the welfare state, economic resentments have formed an unholy alliance with the War on Terror's anti-Muslim rhetoric. As a result, the biggest threat to the neoliberal order is no longer the politically progressive anti-globalization movement, or the radical "folk politics" of the various Occupy campaigns: instead, the emergent "populist" fascism of the reactionary far right has forced even Christine Lagarde, president of the International Monetary Fund (IMF), to concede that the neoliberal rulers underestimated how much damage the brutal imposition of austerity policies would inflict.[27]

Thus, even as neoliberal hegemony seems like it might be on its last legs, the past 15 years of capitalist realism have obviously diminished our ability to articulate meaningful alternative futures. Having followed the Martian cycle with the similarly optimistic near-future "Science in the Capital" trilogy (2004, 2005, 2007),[28] Robinson returned to the realm of interplanetary colonization and world-building with the ambitious novel *2312*. While it isn't presented as an official sequel to the Mars books, *2312* takes place in a storyworld that shares many specific elements with his best-known work, including the mobile city of Terminator on Mercury, the availability (again, only to the most privileged group) of longevity treatments, space elevators, and a thriving post-capitalist society on Mars. But while *2312* is stylistically much more ambitious than the Mars Trilogy, its thematic focus is narrower, and its investigation of technology introduces new elements that complicate a straightforward utopian reading of his ongoing future history.

Contrary to the sprawling Mars Trilogy, with its dozens of characters and its 200 years of geo-engineering, revolution, philosophical debate, and civil warfare, *2312* is devoted to a single protagonist and a straightforward narrative arc, which mostly takes the form of a police procedural. The plot revolves around artist and former terrarium designer Swan Er Hong, whose body has not only been transformed by the longevity treatment, but who has also undergone many other forms of elective enhancement and hybridization, including the addition of a penis, a splicing with feline DNA that allows her to purr, and the experimental ingestion of alien microbes, which have taken up residence in Swan's intestines. The book's narrative is set in motion by the death of her step-grandmother, which is followed by a series of mysterious terrorist attacks, one of which brutally destroys the city of Terminator.

As Swan's investigation leads her to unsettling new forms of artificial intelligence, the narrative is repeatedly interrupted by text fragments drawn from computer systems and forms of "mechanical writing" that establish a kind of dialogue with the vocabulary of 1920s American modernists—most notably the fragmentation pioneered by John Dos Passos in his USA trilogy. Like its literary references, *2312* is thoroughly preoccupied with technological acceleration and its utopian implications, but also more emphatically with its alienating and disruptive effects. Thus, in addition to building upon modernism's utopian tendencies, Robinson connects this cultural legacy to twenty-first century anxieties about mechanization, surveillance technology, and posthumanism.

In the context of neoliberalism, labor's perennial "struggle against machinery" has taken on new forms of expression that are fundamental to capitalism's never-ending process of accumulation.[29] In current debates about the necessity to break away from this unsustainable and exploitative cycle, the term *accelerationism* has come to occupy a central position. As Benjamin Noys has explained it, accelerationism has attracted so many theorists of post-capitalism because it suggests a radical embrace of technology rather than the traditional hostility towards mechanization that typifies classical Marxism. And for those of us who worry about the effects of mechanization on wages, unemployment, and global proletarianization, one can certainly understand the attraction of a theoretical framework in which the central premise seems to propose that "the only way out of capitalism is to take it further, to follow its lines of flight or deterritorialization to the absolute end, to speed-up beyond the limits of production and so to rapture the limit of capital itself."[30]

Following the basic logic of what we might call a kind of "banal accelerationism," we can easily identify the obvious correspondence with Kurzweil's techno-fetishism, seeing in technological innovation the easy answers to a post-scarcity future that can come about without sacrificing our ongoing love affair with smartphones, tablets, and corporate-owned social media. In this sense, science fiction in the liberal humanist tradition can all too easily offer a tempting utopian vision that encourages us to double down on our current use of technology without reflecting on it as an active agent within capitalism as a hegemonic system of social relations. In other words, the key tension within the accelerationist debate is the true impasse of neoliberalism, leaving us "neither able to go forward into the 'streamlined' future, nor return to the 'stability' of the Fordist past."[31] Thus, while Robinson's novels clearly present a future that can be described as more "streamlined" in its approach to technology, the key to understanding his politics is precisely the fact that it simultaneously foregrounds technological innovation as a site of struggle.

This ambivalence about technology in a post-capitalist future is much more pronounced in Robinson's middle-period novels like *2312* than it was in the more straightforwardly utopian Mars Trilogy. Always conscientious about showing how technological "progress" rarely occurs without substantial sacrifices, drawbacks, and unforeseen consequences, the 200-year chronology of the Mars books nevertheless reassures us—to misquote Dr. Martin Luther King, Jr.—that the arc of history is long, but still bends towards full communism. In the emphatically post-9/11 *2312*, Robinson expresses a more contradictory (indeed: more properly dialectical) approach to these questions of technological progress and the promises of a notably Janus-faced accelerationism.

These two faces are most clearly articulated in the novel's careful layering of protagonist Swan Er Hong's complex relationship with futuristic technology. Like the best works of science fiction, *2312* works both as an attempt at speculation and extrapolation about the future, and as a metaphorical exaggeration of thoroughly contemporary tensions and anxieties. To illustrate: Swan's quixotic accumulation of physical "enhancements" through technological intervention presents a rationally imaginable future, while at the same time articulating our current tendency to approach these technological hybridizations as consumer choices that are experienced as purely individual forms of liberation and experimentation. The matter-of-fact way in which the book's now-commonplace modification of human bodies has more or less eradicated the traditional gender binary expresses a meaningful (and thoroughly utopian) aspect of current debates about civil rights, gender, and social justice.

By the same token, Swan's physical incorporation of a miniature quantum computer (or "qube") corresponds rather obviously with our growing dependence on mobile technology that we carry on (or even inside) our bodies. Relatable anxieties about such invasive technological enhancement are displaced at least in part, again by using familiar tropes: giving names, voices, and other human-seeming attributes to these new technological agents makes them seem more like pets or servants, and therefore less likely to disturb the traditional binary of power, in which technology is no more than a straightforward extension of human agency. But through the main plot, in which Swan's investigation into the attack on Terminator points her towards Singularity-like developments of exponential AI growth, she becomes more aware of technology's more threatening implications.

We witness this tension firstly through Swan's growing suspicions about her embedded qube, nicknamed Pauline, who she comes to realize is both more alien and less controllable than she had always assumed. After her first encounter with fully artificial human bodies driven by powerful networked qube AI ("Quebes"), Swan discovers that the Terminator attack could only have been carried out by almost immeasurably complex qube calculations, thus raising the question whether quantum computers had been merely complicit in this violent act, or whether it constituted an act of war by this new posthuman intelligence. Therefore, by intensifying the Mars Trilogy's Latourian approach to technology as an active agent within complex social networks, 2312 rejects the positivist Kurzweilian perspective on the Singularity, offering in its place a dialectical conception of this familiar science fiction motif.

This contradiction is emphasized by shifting the Mars Trilogy's ongoing debate about political change from purely human/humanist coordinates to the terrain of radical posthumanism. This, too, builds upon a longstanding genre tradition, the best-known example of which is surely Isaac Asimov's *I, Robot* cycle of short stories. But Robinson inserts this dynamic into a narrative context where the contradictions inherent in accelerationist thought are constantly foregrounded—most obviously in the competing desires between the individual's practical usage for and affective attachment to advanced mobile technology on the one hand, and the larger social, political, and economic threats posed by post-Singularity AI on the other. This double bind would be pushed even further away from the Mars cycle's expansive utopianism in Robinson's next science fiction novel, *Aurora*.

Earth: The Final Frontier—Aurora's *Eternal Return*

Throughout his rapidly expanding literary oeuvre, Robinson has always tempered his utopian optimism with a sustained interest in the material constraints that stubbornly impose themselves on science fiction's flights of fancy. This is evident not only in the dialectical organization of his future histories, but also in his many novels that explore the past, present, and immediate future: the alternative-history *The Years of Rice and Salt*, the Paleolithic coming-of-age narrative *Shaman*, and the near-future "Science in the Capital" trilogy all share an obvious interest in exploring humanity's most basic needs—not only in terms of technologies and material necessities, but also and even especially in creative, social, sexual, emotional, and spiritual well-being. This richness of lived experience gives expression to Robinson's own form of cultural materialism, as he uses the context of speculative fiction to approximate the communist ideal Marx and Engels so famously described as actual freedom: "to hunt in the morning, fish in the afternoon, rear cattle in the evening, criticise after dinner ... without ever becoming hunter, fisherman, herdsman or critic."[32]

If Robinson's work can be described as an ongoing effort to create storyworlds that make this kind of utopianism imaginable if not realizable, the focus in his middle period has shifted to the material constraints that hold back this "communist horizon."[33] As he has repeated throughout his many academic keynotes and public lectures, utopia is not only worth aspiring to, but is credibly realizable through the deployment of existing human technologies such as language, the rule of law, and justice.[34] But at the same time, he has emphasized again and again that this utopia is *not* compatible with a capitalist system. The problem therefore once again becomes how to move beyond the increasingly narrow constraints of austerity policies and neoliberal dogma towards a post-capitalist future that is not merely desirable, but necessary for humanity's survival. It is one thing to joke about refusing to settle for anything less than Fully Automated Gay Space Communism; it's another to comprehend that the alternative seems to be an uninhabitable planet.

Where 2312 illustrated how rapid mechanization and the Singularity trope also introduce new problems that relate back in complex and ambiguous ways to post-9/11 neoliberalism, his more recent novel *Aurora* goes even further in emphasizing the precariousness of human life and our own indebtedness to planet Earth. While both the Mars cycle and 2312 share key components—most notably the longevity treatments—that ground them in similar storyworlds, *Aurora* depicts interplanetary colonization in ways that are simultaneously more ambitious and more constrained. The notable absence of this recurrent Robinsonian trope is in fact key to the novel's narrative organization: it depicts the final stages of a 200-year voyage to one of the nearest habitable planets, aboard a starship on which multiple generations of humans have lived and died over the course of this long journey.

The political issue, then, represents a remarkable inversion of the historical dynamic of the Mars Trilogy: while *Aurora* deals with a similar period and the tantalizing promise of a radically new utopian future, the characters' agency is profoundly limited by their "normal" lifespan. The fact that none of the main characters have experienced life outside of the generation ship even becomes a crucial plot point, as some come to suspect that their revolution may not be the first; in fact, they discover a secret history of failed revolutions pointing towards an undocumented voyage history that has been far more unstable and tumultuous than the strictly linear (and indeed, quite literally teleological) spatial and temporal trajectory they had grown up with.

As with the competing political and ecological visions in the Mars Trilogy, the tension mounts on board between those who insist on seeing the original mission to its end, and those who ultimately decide to turn the ship around and return to Earth. While we never learn the fate of the colonists who persist despite the increasingly dire warning signs, the novel's position is abundantly clear:

> Maybe that's why we've never heard a peep from anywhere. It's not just that the universe is too big. Which it is. That's the main reason. But then also, life is a planetary thing. It begins on a planet and is part of that planet. It's something that water planets do, maybe. But it develops to live where it is. So it can only live there, because it evolved to live there. That's its home. So, you know, Fermi's paradox has its answer, which is this: by the time life gets smart enough to leave its planet, it's too smart to want to go. Because it knows it won't work. So it stays home. It enjoys its home. As why wouldn't you? It doesn't even bother to try to contact anyone else. Why would you? You'll never hear back. So that's my answer to the paradox. (Chapter "In the Wind")

To no one's surprise, many science fiction fans didn't take kindly to what felt to some like a disingenuous dismissal of several of the genre's key narrative tropes, rejecting in one fell swoop both the long-held prospect of first contact with alien life *and* the final frontier of planetary colonization and terraforming. What is more: some have taken this rejection as a turn away from science-fictional utopianism and towards the kind of grim capitalist realism that continues to define the neoliberal era of austerity, precarity, and constantly-diminishing horizons.[35]

But *Aurora*'s politics are more complicated, and indeed far more progressive than such a superficial reading would suggest. For while the ongoing financial crisis continues to build up our debt towards the future with financial derivatives and other forms of speculative finance, the ecological crisis of disastrous climate change is further aggravated by global capitalism's futuristic ambitions. In this sense, proliferating "smart city" initiatives for the wealthy and the rhetorical hyperbole of libertarian "visionaries" like Elon Musk and Peter Thiel resonate uncomfortably with the science fiction genre's tradition of limitless expansion. This kind of techno-futurism all too easily yields bizarre neoliberal fantasies, like the staggeringly obtuse design plans for a skyscraper suspended from an asteroid orbiting Earth, making a "daily pass" over downtown Manhattan.[36]

In this context, *Aurora* grounds sf's utopian imaginary in a return to Earth's biosphere that is as alienating as it is invigorating. The book's rejection of space opera's romantic space-exploration trope leads the characters back to the one biosphere that demands our attention most urgently. It is all the more striking that the book's human protagonist Freya—born in outer space surrounded by technology, and "returning" to a completely unfamiliar home after being cryogenically frozen for over a century—emphatically does not experience it as a sentimental homecoming to a more "natural" environment. In a final scene set among the body-surfers enjoying the rough waves on the beach, *Aurora* uncannily reflects the ending of the film *Gravity* (2014), moving back from space into an elemental world of water and air that poses a radically new kind of challenge. If science fiction's most basic logic of cognitive estrangement is about staging strange encounters that cause us to see familiar surroundings with new eyes, then *Aurora*'s provocative return to Earth's gravity well clearly performs this same task. Or, as Hilary Ashton Strang has argued, "It's very hard to picture what it means to belong on a planet, to live on, in, and through a world as we do. Yet it's urgent, and Robinson suggests that we try to do so."[37]

In this case, the book's emphasis on what it means to belong to a planet gives powerful new meaning to the word "debt," which has played such a defining role in the post-1970s development of global capitalism and neoliberal subjectivity. The settlers' failure to colonize the alien world of Tau Ceti posits a limit point to the kind of speculative expansion that has long informed both space opera and the neoliberal project, in different but mostly complementary ways. As we grow increasingly aware of the devastation wrought upon our biosphere by capitalism's insatiable drive towards limitless expansion, subverting and even reversing this dynamic of indebtedness to the future represents an important critical intervention. The debt being called in is not that of neoliberalism's financialized distortions of temporality, with the sole purpose of "possessing the future in advance by objectivizing it."[38] It is rather the existential debt that humanity owes its own biosphere that is reinforced so strongly in Robinson's mid-period fiction.

While *Aurora* therefore might seem like a turn away from the Mars Trilogy's utopian imaginary, it clearly functions as a specifically neoliberal incarnation of Tom Moylan's "critical utopia": it locates the promise for a better future not in science fiction's expansive and imperialist history, but in the recognition of Earth's own environment as our most basic source of meaning and value. At the same time, *Aurora* refuses to collapse back into the reactionary stance that has too often typified the "Earth First!" movement and many eco-warriors' anti-technological sensibilities. By uniting the primacy of Earth's biosphere with a narrative framework that emphasizes and endorses radical posthumanism, Robinson expresses a utopian vision that is both politically progressive and profoundly anti-capitalist. He proposes that the most important first step for moving beyond capitalist realism lies in the rejection of proto-colonialist frameworks of endless expansion and accumulation. Instead, the far more pressing debt is the one we owe our planet, to which Robinson insists we have no recourse but to return, and return, and return again.

Conclusion

Throughout its long history, science fiction has articulated countless exciting utopian visions of a better future. As a key voice of the genre in the neoliberal age, Kim Stanley Robinson has repurposed some of its most recognizable tropes, and has given them new directions that make them ideologically and politically meaningful in the era of global capitalism. If neoliberalism is indeed defined in many ways by its "futureless" structure of feeling and its apocalyptic sensibility, Robinson has nevertheless found ways of articulating a utopian imaginary that engages directly with global capitalism's defining characteristics.

In the iconic Mars Trilogy, we can recognize the anti-globalization movement's commitment to exploring political and economic alternatives to capitalism in the 1990s. That "interbellum" decade between 1989 and 2001 is now recognized as the period in which neoliberalism became truly hegemonic, as formerly left-wing political parties yielded to global capital's business ontology. But we must also acknowledge that it was at the same time a moment of political struggle and new possibilities, much of which was articulated metaphorically in the Mars books' long road towards an unstable but predominantly utopian post-capitalist future. While the trilogy's sensibility may seem difficult to align with twenty-first-century neoliberalism, the cycle remains insightful in the way it presents its central struggle as an ongoing process with unpredictable outcomes — but nevertheless one in which political alternatives that offer far-reaching improvements to human life are not only debated, but also actively explored.

The author's more recent science fiction novels have clearly emerged from the deeply entrenched neoliberalism of the early twenty-first century: both *2312* and *Aurora* adopt a more mitigated sense of utopian possibility, in which global capitalism's most fundamental threats of proliferating mechanization, climate change, and resource scarcity play ever more prominent roles. Both these novels engage heavily with questions of posthumanism, artificial intelligence, immaterial labor, and environmental crisis, in ways that emphasize different (but complementary) anxieties.

In *2312*, the technological singularity is articulated as a direct threat to humanity's developing utopian future. Cleverly laying bare the economic foundations of the post-9/11 fears about globalization, the novel gives an uncanny reflection of mechanization's profound embeddedness in our daily lives, demonstrating *en passant* how accelerationism offers a tempting fantasy of post-capitalism that all too easily collapses back into neoliberalism's logic of flexible accumulation. Thus, even as it recasts the Mars Trilogy's storyworld from a more critical perspective that mitigates some of the previous books' more teleological utopian tendencies, *2312* also explores the positive effects of a universally embraced progressive identity politics that stands in dialectical counterpoint to fears and anxieties about posthuman forms of intelligence.

Picking up on *2312*'s startlingly utopian final image of thousands of once-threatened animals drifting down from space in balloons to repopulate Earth, *Aurora* offers a more radical depiction that ultimately falls within the recent trend of climate fiction (or "cli-fi"). By his reversal of the traditional "final frontier" logic that has informed decades of science fiction, Robinson turns his ongoing dialogue with contemporary social, economic, and political issues towards questions of scarcity and sustainability.[39] While these more recent works may seem like a retreat from his earlier utopianism, they do stubbornly continue to offer us documents "of hope as much as dread and despair."[40] If these science fictions represent worlds that are broken yet remain hopeful, we find within Robinson's ongoing oeuvre a dedication to utopian alternatives that neither dismiss nor "misunderestimate" the many crises of neoliberalism. To quote China Miéville one last time: "We should utopia as hard as we can." And that is precisely what Kim Stanley Robinson continues to do.

Notes

1. From Kim Stanley Robinson's lecture "Rethinking Our Relationship to the Biosphere," 2015 Bioneers Annual Conference, https://www.youtube.com/watch?v=489IogZlepM.
2. Fredric Jameson, *Archeaologies of the Future: The Desire Called Utopia and Other Science Fictions* (London: Verso, 2005).
3. China Miéville, "Introduction," Thomas More, *Utopia* (London: Verso, 2016).
4. Simon Spiegel, "Some Thoughts on the Utopian Film," *Science Fiction Film and Television* 10:1 (2017): 58–59.
5. Miéville, "Introduction," 21.
6. David Harvey, *The Condition of Postmodernity: An Enquiry into the Origins of Cultural Change* (Oxford: Blackwell, 1990), 147.
7. Marc Augé, *The Future*, trans. John Howe (London: Verso, 2014), 3.
8. Maurizio Lazzarato, *Signs and Machines: Capitalism and the Production of Subjectivity* (Cambridge, MA: MIT Press, 2014), 52.
9. Maurizio, Lazzarato, *The Making of the Indebted Man*, (Los Angeles: Semiotext(e), 2012), 9.
10. Lazzarato, *Indebted Man*, 9.
11. Carl Freedman, *Critical Theory and Science Fiction* (Middleton, CT: Wesleyan University Press, 2000), 30.
12. For a more elaborate discussion of the science fiction genre, see Andrew Milner's excellent historical and theoretical survey *Locating Science Fiction* (Liverpool: Liverpool University Press, 2012).
13. Luc Boltanski and Eve Chiapello, *The New Spirit of Capitalism* (London: Verso, 2006), 18.
14. Raymond Williams, *Culture and Materialism* (London: Verso, 2005), 201. See Hassler-Forest, "*Star Trek*, Global Capitalism and Immaterial Labour," *Science Fiction Film and Television* 9:3 (2016): 371–393.
15. See Henry Jenkins, *Textual Poachers: Textual Poachers: Television Fans and Participatory Culture* (New York: Routledge, 1992).
16. Mark Fisher, *Capitalist Realism: Is There No Alternative?* (Alresford, UK: John Hunt Publishing, 2009), 17.
17. Dan Hassler-Forest, *Science Fiction, Fantasy, and Politics: Transmedia Worldbuilding Beyond Capitalism* (Lanham, MD: Rowman & Littlefield International, 2016), 70.
18. Billionaire entrepreneur Elon Musk has similarly presented ambitious colonization plans as a part of his libertarian and thoroughly neoliberal "vision" for a sustainable human future.
19. See for instance his short story "Mutt and Jeff Push the Button," included in the book-length publication, Fredric Jameson, *An American Utopia* (London: Verso, 2016).
20. Raymond Williams, *Culture and Materialism* (London: Verso, 2006), 199.

21. Philipp Wegner, "Ken MacLeod's Permanent Revolution: Utopian Possible Worlds, History and the *Augenblick* in the *Fall Revolution* Quartet," *Red Planets*, eds. Mark Bould and China Mieville (London: Pluto Press, 2009), 149.

22. Darko Suvin's genre-defining term for the element in a science fiction text that establishes its separation from everyday reality: "SF is distinguished by the narrative dominance of a fictional novelty (novum, innovation) validated both by being continuous with a body of already existing cognitions and by being a 'mental experiment' based on cognitive logic" ("On What is and is not an SF Narration," *Science Fiction Studies* 14:1 (1978)).

23. Gerry Canavan, "Struggle Forever." *Los Angeles Review of Books* (June 14, 2012). Accessed April 4, 2017. https://lareviewofbooks.org/article/struggle-forever/.

24. Steven Shaviro, "The Singularity is Here," *Red Planets*, eds. Mark Bould and China Miéville (London: Pluto Press, 2009), 104.

25. Shaviro, "The Singularity is Here," 106.

26. Naomi Klein, *The Shock Doctrine: The Rise of Disaster Capitalism* (London: Picador, 2008).

27. Nick Srnicek and Alex Williams, *Inventing the Future: Postcapitalism and a World without Work* (London: Verso, 2015), 16.

28. A condensed single-volume edition of the trilogy was later re-published under the title *Green Earth* (New York: Harper Collins, 2015).

29. Karl Marx, *Grundrisse*, translated by Martin Nicolaus (London: Penguin Books, 193), 704.

30. Benjamin Noys, *Malign Velocities: Accelerationism and Capitalism* (Winchester: Zero Books, 2013), x.

31. Noys, *Malign Velocities*, 98.

32. Karl Marx and Friedrich Engels, *The German Ideology*, Marxists.org. Accessed April 4, 2017. https://www.marxists.org/archive/marx/works/1845/german-ideology/cho1a.htm.

33. Jodi Dean, *The Communist Horizon* (London: Verso, 2012).

34. "Kim Stanley Robinson—Rethinking Our Relationship to the Biosphere" Online video clip. YouTube. November 12, 2015. Accessed April 2, 2017. https://www.youtube.com/watch?v=489IogZlepM.

35. See Gregory Benford, "Envisioning Starflight Failing," *Centauri Dreams* (July 31, 2015). Accessed April 4, 2017. https://www.centauri-dreams.org/2015/07/31/envisioning-starflight-failing/.

36. David Freeman, "Firm Floats Plan to Hang Colossal Skyscraper From an Asteroid," *NBC News* (March 28, 2017). Accessed March 29, 2017. https://www.nbcnews.com/storyline/the-big-questions/firm-floats-plan-hang-colossal-skyscraper-asteroid-n739601.

37. Hilary Ashton Strang, "Utopia Here: On Kim Stanley Robinson's Aurora," *The Blackstone Review* (December 2015). Accessed March 25, 2017. https://www.theblackstonereview.com/articles/utopia-here-kim-stanley-robinsons-aurora.

38. Lazzarato, *Indebted Man*, 46.

39. These concerns were addressed even more directly in *Aurora*'s successor *New York 2140* (2017), which hadn't yet been published at the time of writing.

40. Gerry Canavan, "Utopia in the Time of Trump," *Los Angeles Review of Books* (March 11, 2017). Accessed December 14, 2018. https://lareviewofbooks.org/article/utopia-in-the-time-of-trump/.

CONTRIBUTOR BIOGRAPHIES

HAMILTON CARROLL is an associate professor of English at the University of Leeds. He is the author of *Affirmative Reaction: New Formations of White Masculinity* (Duke, 2011).

SHARAE DECKARD is a lecturer in World Literature at University College Dublin. She is author of *Paradise Discourse, Imperialism and Globalization* (Routledge, 2010) and co-author with the Warwick Research Collective of *Combined and Uneven Development: Towards a New Theory of World-Literature* (Liverpool, 2015). Her research centers on world-ecology and world-systems approaches to world literature.

CHRISTIAN P. HAINES is an assistant professor of English at Dartmouth College. His book, *A Desire Called America: Biopolitics, Utopia, and the Literary Commons* (Fordham, 2019) is forthcoming. He is co-editor of a special issue of *Cultural Critique*, "What Comes After the Subject?" (Spring 2017). His work has appeared in journals including *Angelaki*, *boundary 2*, *Criticism*, and *Lit: Literature Interpretation Theory*, as well as in collections such as *The Routledge Companion to Literature and Economics*.

DAN HASSLER-FOREST works as an assistant professor of Media and Cultural Studies at Utrecht University. He has published books and articles on superhero movies, comics, transmedia storytelling, science fiction, critical theory, Tom Cruise, and zombies.

CAREN IRR is a professor of English at Brandeis University. She is the author, most recently, of *Toward the Geopolitical Novel: U.S. Fiction in the 21st Century* (Columbia, 2013).

ELI JELLY-SCHAPIRO is an assistant professor of English at the University of South Carolina. He is the author of *Security and Terror: American Culture and the Long History of Colonial Modernity* (University of California, 2018).

Contributor Biographies

LIAM KENNEDY is a professor of American Studies and Director of the Clinton Institute for American Studies at University College Dublin. He is the author of *Afterimages: Photography and US Foreign Policy* (Chicago, 2016).

DONALD E. PEASE is the Ted and Helen Geisel professor in the Humanities and Founding Director of the Futures Of American Studies Institute at Dartmouth. He is the author or editor of 12 books including *Visionary Compacts: American Renaissance Writings in Cultural Context*, *Cultures of US Imperialism*, *The New American Exceptionalism*, and most recently *American Studies as Transnational Practice: Turning toward the Transpacific*.

STEPHEN SHAPIRO teaches in the Department of English and Comparative Literary Studies at the University of Warwick. His recent publications include *Pentecostal Modernism: Lovecraft, Los Angeles, and World-Systems Culture* (with Philip Barnard, Bloomsbury, 2017) and *Combined and Uneven Development: Towards a New Theory of World-Literature* (co-authored as part of the Warwick Research Collective [WReC], Liverpool, 2015).

MYKA TUCKER-ABRAMSON is an assistant professor of American Literature at the University of Warwick. Her work has appeared in *PMLA*, *Modern Fiction Studies*, and *Edu-Factory*. She is the author of *Novel Shocks: Urban Renewal and the Origins of Neoliberalism* (Fordham, 2018).

INDEX

Tables are indicated with the page number in italics.

accelerationism, 17, 217–21, 225
accumulation by dispossession, 21n28, 29, 116, 148, 155, 187, 201. *See also* primitive accumulation
accumulation by fabrication, 14, 22, 23, 28–32, 35, 37, 39, 42n48
Addison, Corban: *A Walk Across the Sun*, 171, 172, 174
Adenauer, Konrad, 8, 19n13
Agamben, Giorgio, 61, 132, 134n18, 164
Aglietta, Michel, 5, 19n8
AIG, 144
Airbnb, 168
Akademie für Deutsches Recht, 19n13
algorithmic governmentality, 14, 47, 48, 52, 67–68, 194
Allen, Woody, 119
Althusser, Louis, 26, 27, 39, 121
Amazon, 38, 67
Anderson, Benedict, 46
Anker, Elizabeth, 137, 138
anti-racism, 182
anti-trafficking crime fiction, 168–84; depicting the victim, 172–76; investigator's eye, 176–80; kind of labor, 180–84' master narrative, 170–72; police labor, 176–80
Arendt, Hannah, 24
Arrighi, Giovanni, 183–84, 189
art and terror, 112n49
Ascher, Ivan, 134n25
Asimov, Isaac, 211, 215; *I, Robot*, 220
Augé, Marc: *The Future*, 209–10

Austrian School, 40n1
Autonomia, 73, 84, 89n3
autonomy, 19n13, 74, 75, 83, 157, 170, 171, 174, 176, 177, 178, 184, 203, 205
avatar fetishism, 131, 133n15

Back to the Future, 97, 98, 99, 100, 103, 110, 111n13
Banerjee, Subhabrata Bobby, 207
Bastien-Lepage, Jules, 96; *Joan of Arc*, 97, 98, 99–100, 101, 104, 106
Bender, Karen, 116; "Refund," 114–16, 132, 132n1
Benjamin, Walter, 110n2
Bildungsroman, 4, 47, 143, 146
biopolitics, 50, 56, 155; governmentality. *See also* Foucault, Michel: *Biopolitics*, *The Birth of Biopolitics*
bioracism, 120
Blogett, Henry, 144
Böhm, Franz, 19n13
Boltanski, Luc: *The New Spirit of Capitalism*, 27
Bourdieu, Pierre, 66
Bradbury, Ray: *Martian Chronicles*, 213
Brandt, Willy, 11
Brennan, Teresa, 185n15, 188
Bretton Woods Conference, 3
Bretton Woods currency system, 11, 78
Breu, Christopher, 131
Brexit, 47
Brezhnev, Leonid, 11

Brogden, Michael, 177
Brouillette, Sarah, 4
Brown, Wendy, 4, 26–27, 34
Burke, James Lee: *Feast Day of Fools*, 171, 173, 179
Burroughs, Edgar Rice, 211; *John Carter of Mars*, 213
Bush, George H. W., 171
Bush, George W., 141
Butler, Judith, 30

Calvinism, 27
capitalism, 13, 25, 57, 76, 78, 96, 110, 126, 134n25, 152, 153, 158, 161, 187, 189, 192, 195, 197, 198, 204, 218; algorithmic, 67; American, 208; contemporary, 15, 118, 120; development, 57; discipline, 57; fantastical, 212; financialized, 116, 120, 121, 123, 124, 127, 132, 209; free-market, 151; global, 17, 19n8, 73, 74, 77, 88, 95, 157, 207, 209, 210, 212, 214, 216, 223, 224, 225; historical, 19n7, 24, 43–48; industrial, 24, 55, 211; late, 125; liberal, 1; mortality, 28; mutation, 61; necrocapitalism, 207; post-, 219, 225; post-Fordist, 27; post-industrial, 210; postwar, 211; primitive accumulation, 132n2; social reproduction, 117; "spirit," 27
capitalist realism 13, 207, 210, 212, 217–18, 223, 224
Carroll, Hamilton, 15
Challenger, 103–4
Chandler, Raymond, 177, 178
chattel slavery, 24, 170
Cherniavsky, Eva, 95
Chiapello, Eve: *The New Spirit of Capitalism*, 27
Chirbes, Raphael: *On the Edge*, 34–36
Clarke, Arthur C., 211
Clarke, John: *Policing the Crisis*, 30
Clinton, Bill, 12, 208, 214
Cold War, 3, 8, 9, 11, 12, 78, 151, 209, 214; post-, 152, 179, 212
cold war hoodlums, 182, 183

Colloque Walter Lippman, 7
Combahanee River Collective Statement 85
commensurable, 64, 107, 115
Committees for Wages for Housework, 85
"contemporary": definition, 1, 2, 3, 12
Contemporary American literature 2–7, 13–17; Phase I (1929–[1944–1949]–mid-1960s), 7–10; Phase II (mid-1960s to 2008/2010s), 10–13
Cooper, Melina, 133n10
Corsiano, Marilyn, 176
Crary, Jonathan: 24/7, 16, 187, 188, 191–92, 204
crises of accumulation, 29, 34
Critcher, Chas: *Policing the Crisis*, 30
cultural production, 1, 2, 6, 7, 150n21, 151, 203
Cultural Studies, 52
cycle, 3, 12, 58, 111n5, 225; book, 214; business, 44; entrapment, 175; exploitative, 218; Mars, 215, 218, 222

Dalla Costa, Mariarosa, 85; *The Power of Women and the Subversion of the Community*, 84
Dames, Nicholas, 74, 83
Davis, Mike, 153, 166n9
Dean, Jodi, 149n16, 166n12
Debord, Guy, 31
Deckard, Sharae, 16
Deleuze, Gilles, 52, 70n30; "Postscript on Control Societies," 61
Dienst, Richard, 133n11, 186n22
DeLillo, Don, 15, 116, 120, 132; *Zero K*, 118, 119, 128, 129
Deliveroo, 67
democracy, 4, 138, 142; liberal, 16, 165; post-racial multi-cultural, 141; social, 60, 177; transnational, 140
Drone Wars, 203
Dryer, Carl Theodor: *The Passion of Joan of Arc*, 97
Dubey, Madhu, 93
Duhigg, Charles, 64

Index [233]

Duvall, John: "Cricket's Field of Dreams," 149n12

economic cities, 153, 165n6
economy of sacrifice, 118, 119–27, 130, 132
Eggers, Dave: *A Hologram for the King*, 16, 34, 35, 151, 152, 153, 154–55, 156, 158–59, 164, 165
Engels, Friedrich, 221; *The German Ideology*, 46
Enron, 141, 144
Erhard, Ludwig, 8, 11
Esposito, Roberto, 117, 127, 132; *Two*, 134n18
Eucken, Walter, 7, 19n13
expanded reproduction, 14, 22, 23, 25–28, 30, 31, 34, 39, 42n48, 57
expatriate fiction, 137, 138, 148n6, 152, 159, 162

Facebook, 13, 67
Fairstein, Linda, 175; *Hell Gate*, 171, 172
Falangism, 2, 5, 7
Fanon, Frantz: *The Wretched of the Earth*, 31, 32
fantastical capitalism, 212
fascism, 2, 5, 7, 70n20, 217
Federici, Sylvia, 85
feminism: Italian, 85, 91n22; Marxist, 85; militant, 85
financialization, 6, 28, 77, 96, 114, 115, 116, 117, 119, 120, 122, 125, 127, 133n6, 133n10, 133n16, 135n33, 153, 187, 191, 199, 203, 210
Firestone, Shulamith: *The Dialectic of Sex*, 84
Fisher, Mark, 94, 160, 163; *Capitalist Realism*, 106, 207, 212
Flaubert, Gustauve: *A Sentimental Education*, 86
Fleming, Peter, 96, 111
"flexible," 22, 27, 153, 209
Fordism, 2, 5, 7, 28, 54, 61, 76, 77, 82, 217, 219; post-, 19, 27, 34, 38, 61, 75, 188, 198, 207

Foster, Hal: "The Crux of Minimalism," 83
Foucauldian theorization, 5, 121
Foucault, Michel, 14, 19n7, 40n1, 43–68, 163; algorithmic governmentality 61–67; *The Archaeology of Knowledge*, 50; "arts of existence," 128; Berkeley student project, 70n20; biopolitics, 50, 56; *Biopolitics*, 50, 70n33; biopolitics-governmentality, 57; *The Birth of Biopolitics*, 45, 117; Collège de France lectures, 40n1, 48, 49; cultural forms of algorithmic governmentality 67–68; *Discipline and Punish*, 48, 51, 53; "government," 44–45; governmentality, 5, 26, 48–54, 57, 67, 70n20, 70n33; historical epochs and beyond neoliberalism, 62; *History of Sexuality*, 48–49, 50, 70n19; homo oeconomicus, 26; neoliberalism's arrival 54–59; neoliberalism as historical capitalism, 43–48; neoliberal rationality, 26; *On the Government of the Living*, 49; *Society Must Be Defended*, 49; subjectivity, 45, 62, 64; subjectivity and truth, 53; *Subjectivity and Truth*, 49; subject of rights, 45, 57; "transactional reality," 45; *The Use of Pleasure*, 49; veridiction, 43, 45
Franzen, Jonathan: *Freedom*, 34
freedom, 14, 16, 19n13, 27, 32–33, 34, 35, 90n16, 161, 165, 168, 169, 172, 177, 180, 182, 192, 221; consumer, 153, 160; individual, 40n1, 95; ineffective, 179; interplay, 60; market, 169; morphological, 200; movement, 162; political, 153, 160; unfreedom, 32, 33
free labor, 34, 168, 169–70, 171, 174, 175, 176, 177, 184, 186n26
free trade, 4, 25, 34, 47, 95. *See also* North American Free Trade Agreement
Freiburg School, 7, 19n13, 59
French Revolution, 86
Friedman, Milton, 8, 11; *Capitalism and Freedom*, 10
futureless world, 209–12

Gans-Moore, Jordan, 2
General Motors, 10
Ghosh, Amitav: *Sea of Poppies*, 32, 33–34
Google, 13, 67, 72n84, 101, 102, 162
Google+, 13
governmentality, 1, 28, 198, 205, 208; algorithmic, 14, 47, 48, 52, 67–68, 194; biopower, 52, 57; crises, 29, 34; cultural forms, 67–68; dispersion, 65; *The Dog*, 160; Foucault, 5, 26, 48, 52, 53, 54, 57, 67, 70n20, 70n33; liberal regulatory, 68; liberal social 67; post, 52; Rouvroy, 47, 48, 52; situating, 48–54
Gramm-Leach-Bailey Act, 12
Gramsci, Antonio, 38, 52–53, 70n33
Grant, M. C.: *Beauty with a Bomb*, 171, 174
Gray, Richard: "Open Doors, Closed Minds," 136–38
Great American Novel, 46, 138
Great Depression, 2, 7, 77, 197
Greenwald Smith, Rachel, 6; *Affect and American Literature in the Age of Neoliberalism*, 17n2
group modification, 72n84
Grubman, Jack, 144
"Guernsback Age," 211

Haines, Christian P., 15
Hale, Edwin, 186n21
Hall, Stuart, 52; *Policing the Crisis*, 30
hard-boiled, 176, 177, 178, 186n30
Harvey, David, 95; accumulation by fabrication, 28, 29; *Brief History of Neoliberalism*, 21n28, 27; *The Enigma of Capital*, 95–96; "financial coup," 73; *The New Imperialism*, 183–84; *Spaces of Hope*, 21n28; urbanization, 42n48
Hassler-Forest, Dan, 17
Hayek, Friedrich, 8, 40n1, 168, 169; *The Road to Serfdom*, 10, 19n13
HBO: *Oz*, 12
Heinlein, Robert A., 211
Hesford, Wendy, 171

Hilferding, Rudolf, 24
hinge (mid-1960s to mid-1970s), 10–13
Hirohito, 7
historical capitalism, 43
Hitler, Adolf, 7, 19
homeland security, 194
Homeland Security Act, 144
home oeconomicus, 26, 45
Hong, Swan Er, 218, 219–20
Huehls, Mitchum, 6, 94
Hughes, Declan, 138–39
human capital, 15, 60, 64, 65, 114–32, 134n18; economy of sacrifice, 118, 119–27, 130, 132; personhood, 33, 122, 127, 130, 131, 132; final shrine of entitlement, 127–132; financialized personhood, 116–20, 121, 128. See also DeLillo, Don: *Zero K*; Shteyngart, Gary: *Super Sad True Love Story*
Human Rights Watch, 169
Hurricane Irene, 106, 108
Hurricane Sandy, 92–93, 109

indebtedness, 6, 14, 15, 16, 17, 116, 117, 118, 121, 123, 124, 153, 209–12, 222, 224
insecurity, 15, 28, 29, 30, 36, 95, 109, 110
insomnia, 16–17, 187, 190, 191, 196, 197, 198, 199; iatrogenic, 193; terminal, 189, 195
International Labor Organization, 169, 186n20
International Monetary Fund, 126, 217
intimacy, 4, 39, 42n48, 118, 162, 198
Irr, Caren, 16, 148n6; *Toward the Geopolitical Novel*, 152; "Toward the World Novel," 137, 138
Italian feminism, 85, 91n22

James, Marlon: *The Book of Night Women*, 32–33
James, Selma: *The Power of Women and the Subversion of the Community*, 84
Jameson, Fredric, 48, 110, 177, 207
Jefferson, Tony: *Policing the Crisis*, 30
Jelly-Schapiro, Eli, 14, 193–94

Jones, Brandon W.: *All Woman and Springtime*, 171, 172, 175
Jones, Daniel Stedman: *Masters of the Universe*, 27
Joseph, Miranda, 116
Judd, Donald, 96

Kanna, Ahmed, 165n8
Kennedy, Liam, 16
Keynes, John Maynard, 9–10: *General Theory*, 19n13
Keynesianism, 2, 5, 7, 8, 9–10, 11, 12, 40n1, 54, 59, 60, 67, 68, 73, 78; Fordist-, 75, 76, 77
Khrushchev, Nikita, 11
King, Martin Luther, Jr., 219
Koons, Jeff, 96
Kordela, Kiarina, 120, 131, 133n15
Kunkel, Benjamin, 112n43, 151; "Capitalism as Religion," 121; *Indecision*, 34; *Utopia or Bust*, 95, 100
Kushner, Rachel: *The Flamethrowers*, 14–15, 37, 73–89; subsumption, 75, 80

La Berge, Leigh Claire: "Wages Against Artwork," 75
Land Acquisition Act, 25
Lawson, Catherine, 9
Lazzarato, Maurizio, 117–18, 210
Le Blanc, Guillaume, 61–62
Lefebvre, Henri, 31
left neoliberalism, 169–70, 183, 185n7
Lenin, V. I., 24
Lerner, Ben: "Damage Control," 112n43; "The Golden Vanity," 105, 112n31
Lerner, Ben, *10:04*, 15, 92–110, 111n12, 112n22, 112n43; ekphrastic representation, 15, 93, 96–100; fraudulent authority, 100–6; millennial perceptions, 106–10
liberal government, 14, 52, 58, 59, 60, 63, 64
Lin, Ed: *Snakes Can't Run*, 171, 173, 175–76, 181
Locke, John, 23–24

Lockhart, Jeffrey, 128
Lockhart, Ross, 128
Lotta Femminista, 85
Luhnow, Harold, 10, 20n18
Lukács, Georg, 47, 74, 75, 83, 88–89

Magee, John Gillespie: "The Flight," 105–6
Mak, Geoff, 73–74
Mankell, Henning, 177, 186n28
Mansoor, Jaleh, 87
Marclay, Christian: The Clock, 111n13
The Martian, 213
Martin, Randy, 96, 122
Marx, Karl, 19n7, 75; actual freedom, 221; *Capital*, 23–24, 57, 82–83, 132n2; communism, 221; *The German Ideology*, 46; *On the Jewish Question*, 56; primitive accumulation, 29, 31; theological niceties, 127; "turnover time," 78
Marxism, 5; capitalism, 24, 25, 54, 79, 116; classical, 219; feminism, 85; imperialism, 24; Italy, 87; laissez faire, 26; political economy, 115
Matta-Clark, Gordon, 37, 79; "Day's End," 80, 81, 82
McAuliffe, Christa, 103–4, 105
McCann, Sean, 186n30
McCarthy, Cormac: *The Road*, 208
McClanahan, Annie, 119, 121
Michaels, Walter Benn, 185n7
Miéville, China, 207, 226
Miksch, Leonhard, 19n13
Miller, Laura: *Salon*, 73, 74, 84, 87
miracolo italiano, 73
Miriello, Nicholas, 73
Mirowski, Philip, 67, 87–88
Mitrani, Sam, 176
mode of regulation, 5, 19n8
modulations, 61, 70n30
Monk, Daniel Bertrand, 153, 166n9
Mont Perelin Society, 8
Moore, Jason, 90n16, 187, 188, 195
Moraru, Christian, 139
More, Thomas: *Utopia*, 207

Moreau, Frederic, 86
Motherfuckers, 38, 79, 85
Moylan, Tom, 224
Müller-Armack, Alfred, 19n13
Musk, Elon, 223

National Black Feminist Organization, 84
National Geographic: *Border Wars*, 203
Nazism, 5, 7, 8, 20, 40, 59
neoliberal present, 1, 13, 22, 39, 160, 191, 205; late 31
Netflix, 67
New Deal, 2, 5, 7, 9, 10, 12, 54, 67, 68
Nietzsche, Friedrich, 118
9/11, 141, 145, 148n6, 158; post-, 15, 111n12, 136–38, 142, 143, 145, 146, 148, 148n2, 149n7, 149n12, 149n15, 150n20, 150n24, 184, 217, 219, 222, 225; pre-, 144
Noonan, Peggy, 105
normalization, 51, 52, 55, 56, 57, 95
normation, 57
North American Free Trade Agreement, 201
North Atlantic Treaty Organization, 3
Noys, Benjamin, 219

Obama, Barack, 139
Occupy Wall Street, 13, 164
O'Neill, Joseph, 153, 165; *Brooklyn Dream Machine*, 141; *The Dog*, 16, 152, 159–61, 163–64, 167n29; "elective statelessness," 159; *Netherland*, 15, 136–48, 149nn10–11, 149nn15–16, 150n24, 151, 159–61, 164, 173
Operaismo, 73, 89n3
Operation Infinite Justice, 144
Operation Iraqi Freedom, 144
Ordo, 7
ordoliberalism, 7–8, 10, 19n13, 26, 40n1, 59, 60, 72n66
Ostpolitik, 11

Palermo protocol, 170
Parry, Jonathan, 169
Passerini, Luisa, 85

Passos, John Dos, 218
Pearson, Ridley: *Choke Point*, 171, 172, 173
Peasants' War, 54
Pease, Donald E., 15–16
Peck, Jamie, 11
periodization, 3, 11, 22, 45, 111n12
personhood, 33, 122, 127, 130, 131, 132; financial, 116–20, 121, 128
pharmakon, 133n14
physiocrats, 58
Picasso, Pablo, 96
plagiarism, 101, 103, 105
Polanyi, Karl, 26
Polaris Project, 169
primitive accumulation, 14, 22, 23–25, 28, 29, 30, 31, 32, 33, 36, 37, 38, 39, 116, 132n2, 198, 207. *See also* accumulation by dispossession
profanation, 132
Putin, Vladimir, 13
Pynchon, Thomas, 116

Quetelet, Adolphe, 64

racism: anti-racism, 182; bioracism, 120; far right-wing nationalist, 5; nationalist, 56; residual, 181; scientific, 4
Reagan, Ronald, 6, 103–4, 105–6
regime of accumulation, 5, 19n8
relationality 14, 152, 163; inter-, 4
repression, 29, 45, 46, 53
Rivera, Alex: *Sleep Dealer*, 16, 17, 188, 198–202, 204, 205; *Why Cybraceros?*, 200
Robbins, Bruce, 148n6; "The Worlding of the American Novel," 151–52
Roberts, Brian: *Policing the Crisis*, 30
Robinson, Kim Stanley, 207–24; *Aurora*, 209, 217, 221–24, 225, 227n39; *Blue Mars*, 209, 215; *Green Mars*, 209, 215; *Green Planets*, 213; Mars trilogy, 17, 209, 212–17, 219–21; *The Martians*, 213; *Red Mars*, 209, 214–15; *2312*, 209, 217–21, 222, 225; "Science in the

Capital trilogy," 218, 221; *Shaman*, 221; *The Years of Rice and Salt*, 221
Roman Catholic Church, 55
Röpke, Wilhelm, 7, 19n13
Rothberg, Michael, 136, 137, 138
Rouvroy, Antoinette, 69n14; algorithmic governmentality, 47, 48, 52, 54, 61, 63–64, 67, 194; data behaviourism, 63
Russell, Karen, 196–97; *Sleep Donation*, 16–17, 188, 189–90, 192–93, 195, 198, 199, 202–3, 204, 205
Rustow, Alexander, 7; *Ortsbestimmung der Gegenwart*, 19n13

Salvage Art Institute, 112n43
Samuelson, Paul A.: *Economics*, 9–10
Sattelzeit, 3, 11
Scarface, 13
Schein, Martin, 186n21
Schmitt, Carl, 60; *Nomos of the Earth in the International Law of Jus Publicum Europaeum*, 19n13
Schwarzenegger, Arnold, 212–13
"Second Wave," 211
security, 11, 27, 29, 36, 39, 50, 56–57, 58, 81, 142, 157, 193, 194, 200, 203; material, 23. *See also* insecurity
Sennett, Richard, 94
shame, 156, 158, 160, 171, 185n13; sexual, 173, 175
Shapiro, Stephen, 14
Sheridan, Judith, 185n19
Shteyngart, Gary, 15, 116, 120, 124; *Super Sad True Love Story*, 118, 119, 122, 126, 127, 129, 132
"silent compulsion," 22, 24, 25, 30, 34, 35
Simpson, O. J., 104
singularities, 79, 85, 141, 216, 220, 221, 222, 225
slavery, 33, 83, 169, 184; chattel, 24, 170; sexual, 172
sleep, 16–17, 187–205. *See also* River, Alex: *Sleep Dealer*; Russell, Karen: *Sleep Donation*
Slobodian, Quinn, 9, 19n13
Smith, Adam, 2, 3, 4

Smith, Zadie, "Two Paths for the Novel," 139, 149n11, 164
Smithson, Robert, 79, 81, 82; "Spiral Jetty," 80
Snajdr, Edward, 170
social bond, 30, 133n11
Solanas, Valerie, 85; *Manifesto*, 84
Spanish boom, 42n48
Stalinism, 70n20
Standing, Guy, 168
Star Trek, 211, 214
Strang, Hilary Ashton, 223
Strombeck, Andrew, 87, 90n15
subjectivity, 4, 14, 17, 79, 94, 96, 99, 122, 188, 190, 196, 223; Foucault, 45, 53, 62, 64; human, 191, 196, 216; individual, 46; labor-related, 29; liberal, 64; middle-class consumer, 196, 199; millennial, 101, 108; personhood, 117
subsumption, 75, 80, 125, 203
Suvin, Darko, 227n22
symbolic efficiency, 1, 166n12

Target, 64–66
Tarshis, Lorie: *The Elements of Economics*, 9, 10
Tartt, Donna: *The Goldfinch*, 112n49
Telecommunications Act, 12
terminal insomnia 187–205. *See also* Crary, Jonathan: 24/7; Rivera, Alex: *Sleep Dealer*; Russell, Karen: *Sleep Donation*
terrorism, 94, 109. *See also* 9/11
terrorist assemblage, 142, 150n18
Thatcher, Margaret, 6
Total Recall, 213
Trilling, Lionel, 46
Tucker-Abramson, Myka, 15, 16
"turnover time," 78
Twin Towers, 107, 116, 143, 145

Uber, 29, 67, 168
unions 78, 168, 177; anti-union, 41n20
US State Department: Trafficking in Persons, 169
utopianism, 6, 207–26. *See also*

McCarthy, Cormac: *The Road*; More, Thomas: *Utopia*; Robinson, Kim Stanley: *Blue Mars, Green Mars*, Mars trilogy, *Red Mars*

Ventura, Patricia, 6–7
veridiction, 43, 45, 55
Volker Fund, 10
von Mises, Ludwig, 10, 40n1

Wages Against Housework, 84–85, 91n22
Wages for Housework, 84–85
The Walking Dead, 208
Wambaugh, Joseph: *Harbor Nocturne*, 171, 180–81, 182
Warhol, Andy, 85
Wars of Religion, 55
Watt, Ian, 46
Watts riots, 76, 77

welfare state, 7, 22, 30, 70n20, 117, 190, 217
Wells, H. G.: *The War of the Worlds*, 213
Williams, Raymond, 52, 211, 214
Wood, James, 86, 138
workerism, 85, 89n3. *See also* Operaismo
World Com, 144
worlding of American literature, 15–16, 137, 139, 148, 148n2, 150n24, 151–52, 165
world market, 2, 43, 150
World Trade Center, 107, 138, 139, 158
World Trade Organization, 217
World War II, 9, 105, 155; post-, 73, 76

Yom Kippur War, 11

Zemeckis, Robert: *Back to the Future*, 96–97
Zizek, Slavoj, 164, 177, 186n28